The Victory
of Seapower

The Victory of Seapower

Winning the Napoleonic War 1806-1814

Richard Woodman

CHATHAM PUBLISHING

LONDON

In association with
The National Maritime Museum

Contributors

Richard Woodman
All sections, except:

Robert Gardiner
Ships of the Royal Navy: cutters and luggers
Ships of the Royal Navy: the 64-gun ship
Ships of the Royal Navy: the quarterdecked
    ship sloop

Julian Mannering
Notes on Artists

FRONTISPIECE
Oil painting by Nicholas Pocock of the return of the
Bourbon King Louis XVIII to France aboard the British royal
yacht *Royal Sovereign*, 24 April 1814. For many in Britain this
reaffirmation of the principle of legitimacy, and with it the
restoration of the *status quo*, was a victory worth two decades
of war.
NMM ref BHC3612

First published in Great Britain in 1998 by
Chatham Publishing,
1&2 Faulkner's Alley,
Cowcross Street,
London EC1M 6DD

Chatham Publishing is an imprint of
Gerald Duckworth & Co Ltd

British Library Cataloguing in Publication Data
A catalogue record for this book is available from
the British Library

ISBN 1 86176 038 8

Designed and typeset by Tony Hart, Isle of Wight
Printed and bound in Great Britain by
Butler & Tanner Ltd, Frome

CONTENTS

Thematic pages in italic

PREFACE

T HE CHATHAM Pictorial Histories are intended to give the modern reader a impression of how the naval events of previous centuries were seen by those involved, or presented to the public by the visual media of the day – painters, engravers and printsellers. One of our concerns has been to seek out the less familiar, and in some cases the never previously published, so while we do use some finished paintings, we have preferred the artist's own sketchbooks where available; they reveal not only the lengths the painters went to get details correct, but often cover occurrences that are not otherwise represented, or where the art world has lost track of the finished work.

In the search for original and, if possible, eyewitness depictions, we have also dipped into some of the logs, journals and contemporary manuscripts. Naval officers, in particular, were encouraged to observe closely, and part of the training process involved making sketches of everything from coastal features to life on board. To a lesser extent, this was true of army officers, who were often fine mapmakers – especially those in the technical branches like the engineers and the artillery (today most people in Britain are unaware of why the best official mapping of the country is called the Ordnance Survey).

However, the series was specifically inspired by the Prints and Drawings collection of the National Maritime Museum at Greenwich, on the outskirts of London. Reckoned to comprise 66,000 images, it is a surprisingly under-used resource, despite the fact that an ongoing copying programme has made three-quarters of it available on microfilm. While this forms the core of the series, we have also had recourse to the Admiralty Collection of ship draughts – itself running to about 100,000 plans – as well as some reference to the charts collection in the Navigation Department and logs and personal journals kept by the Manuscripts Department. This last is a very substantial holding with no easy mode of access to any illustrations it may contain, so although some

work has been done in this area, it must be said that there is probably far more to discover if only time were available for the task.

The series is intended first and foremost to illustrate the great events of maritime history, and we have made little attempt to pass artistic judgement on any of the images, which were chosen for content rather than style. The pictures are grouped, as far as practical, to show how events were presented at the time. Since this is not primarily a work of art history, for the technical credits we have relied on the Maritime Museum's extant indexing, the product of a massive and long-running documentation programme by many hands with some inevitable inconsistencies, depending on the state of knowledge at the time each item was catalogued. We have reproduced what information there is, only correcting obviously wrong attributions and dates, and quoting the negative number or unique reference number of each illustration for anyone wishing to obtain copies of these from the museum or archive concerned.

Following *The Campaign of Trafalgar* in chronology, *Victory of Seapower* is the fourth of five titles covering the whole of the period of the great French wars from 1793 to 1815. The series follows the order of the original events, except that the War of 1812 fills a single volume of its own, and also includes the few naval events of the 'Hundred Days'; each otherwise covers its period completely. However, the thematic spreads are cumulative in their coverage, because we are keen to illustrate many general aspects of the weapons and warfare of the period which stand outside the chronological structure. Therefore, we devised a single programme of such topics and simply positioned each at an appropriate point in the series. The best example is provided by the many features on individual ship types and their roles, which will add up to a complete analysis of the function of the Navy's order of battle by the end of this five-volume set. This, we believe, avoids predictability and gives every volume variety and additional interest.

Acknowledgements

As with the rest of the 'Pictorial Histories' series, this volume was entirely dependent on the goodwill of the National Maritime Museum, and would have been impossible without the active co-operation of many of its staff. David Spence and latterly Pieter van der Merwe negotiated and set up a workable joint venture; Lindsey Macfarlane provided much information on the prints collection; in researching into logs and journals I received generous and friendly advice from Clive Powell and help above and beyond the call of duty from Alan Giddings; Brian Thynne, as ever, was a fund of knowledge on charts; while the staff of the library did a wonderful job keeping up a normal service during the Museum's massive building works.

However, our greatest thanks must be reserved, as always, for Chris Gray, Head of Picture Research, and his assistant David Taylor, who organised and executed the massive programme of photography that was demanded within our very tight timescale. David has proved particularly dogged and resilient, tracking down 'missing' negatives, sorting out ambiguous references, and cheerfully responding to last-minute changes to our requirements.

For this volume outside Greenwich my debts are less extensive, but I would thank the staff of the Peabody Essex Museum of Salem, Massachusetts and Mystic Seaport, Connecticut, while Mike Stammers and Dawn Littler of the Merseyside Maritime Museum were very helpful in tracking down the Samuel Walters manuscript and arranging the photography of its maps and drawings.

The author would like to acknowledge the assistance of Mr Kai Bech-Nielsen for his translation of Danish material.

Robert Gardiner
London, April 1998

Sources

Archibald Allison, *History of Europe*, Vols 9 to 20, (London 1848)

Edward Baines, *History of the Wars of the French Revolution*, Vol II (London 1818)

Arthur Bryant, *Years of Victory, 1802-1812* (London 1945)

Arthur Bryant, *Age of Elegance* (London 1954)

Sir Thomas Byam Martin, *Letters of Sir Thomas Byam Martin*, Vol 2, Navy Records Society (London 1898)

William Laird Clowes, *The Royal Navy*, a History, Vol V (London 1900, reprinted paperback 1997)

Thomas Cochrane, Earl Dundonald, *The Autobiography of a Seaman*, 2 vols (London 1860-1)

Lord Collingwood, *Selected Correspondence* (London 1828)

H Compton (ed), *A Master Mariner: Being the Life and Adventures of Captain Robert Eastwick* (London 1908)

Patrick Crowhurst, *The French War of Trade: Privateering 1793-1815* (London 1989)

J C Dann (ed), *The Nagle Journal* (New York 1988)

W H Dillon, *A Narrative of my Professional Adventures*, Vol II, Navy Records Society (London 1956)

C S Forester (ed), *The Adventures of John Wetherell* (London 1954)

Edward Giffard, *Deeds of Naval Daring* (London 1910)

J D Grainger (ed), *The Royal Navy in the River Plate, 1806-7*, Navy Records Society (London 1996)

M D Hay (ed), *Landsman Hay, Memoirs of Robert Hay, 1789-1847* (London 1953)

Christopher Hibbert (ed), *Recollections of Rifleman Harris* (London 1970)

William Hutchinson, *A Treatise on Practical on Practical Seamanship* (London 1787, reprinted 1977)

G V Jackson, *The Perilous Adventures and Vicissitudes of a Naval Officer 1801-12* (Edinburgh and London 1927)

William James, *The Naval History of Great Britain*, Vols IV, V & VI (London 1859)

John Keay, *The Honourable Company* (London 1991)

Brian Lavery, *Nelson's Navy* (London 1989)

Basil Lubbock, *The Arctic Whalers* (Glasgow 1937)

David Lyon, *The Sailing Navy List* (London 1993)

Norman Mackenzie, *The Escape from Elba* (Oxford 1982)

Piers Mackesy, *The War in the Mediterranean, 1803-1810* (London 1957)

Sir Frederick Maitland, *The Surrender of Napoleon* (Edinburgh and London 1904)

Geoffrey Marcus, *A Naval History of England*, Vol 2, *The Age of Nelson* (Reprinted Sheffield 1971)

Gilbert Martineau, *Napoleon Surrenders* (London 1971)

H Moyse-Bartlett, *The Pirates of Trucial Oman* (London 1966)

The Naval Miscellany, Vol I, Navy Records Society (London 1902)

The Naval Miscellany, Vol V, Navy Records Society (London 1984)

Carola Oman, *Sir John Moore* (London 1953)

C Northcote Parkinson, *Britannia Rules* (Gloucester 1987)

C Northcote Parkinson (ed), *The Trade Winds* (London 1948)

C Northcote Parkinson, *Trade in the Eastern Seas, 1793-1813* (London 1966)

C Northcote Parkinson, *War in the Eastern Seas* (London 1954)

C Northcote Parkinson (ed), *Samuel Walters, Lieutenant RN* (Liverpool 1949)

Otto von Pivka, *Navies of the Napoleonic Era* (Newton Abbot 1980)

Hugh Popham, *A Damned Cunning Fellow* (Tywardreath 1991)

William Richardson, *A Mariner of England* (Reprinted London 1970)

Lord Russell, *Knight of the Sword* (London 1964)

Owen Rutter, *Red Ensign: A History of Convoy* (London 1942)

A N Ryan (ed), *The Saumarez Papers, Baltic 1808-1812*, Navy Records Society (London 1968)

William Scoresby, *Log Book of the* Resolution, *1806* (Whitby 1981)

Graham Smith, *King's Cutters* (London 1983)

F L Sommer, *A Description of Denmark and a Narrative of the Seige, Bombardment and Capture of Copenhagen* (Colchester 1808)

Jean Sutton, *Lords of the East* (London 1981)

H G Thursfield, *Five Naval Journals, 1789-1817*, Navy Records Society (London 1951)

E G Twitchett, *Life of a Seaman* (London 1931)

Donald Thomas, *Cochrane* (London 1978)

Gomer Williams, *The Liverpool Privateers* (London 1897)

Richard Woodman, *The History of the Ship* (London 1997)

Notes on Artists

E H H Archibald, *Dictionary of Sea Painters* (Woodbridge, England 1980)

E Bénézit, *Dictionnaire critique et documentaire de Peintres, Sculpteurs, Dessinateurs et Graveurs* (Paris 1976)

Maurice Harold Grant, *A Dictionary of British Etchers* (London 1952)

Ian Mackensie, *British Prints: Dictionary and Price Guide* (Woodbridge, England, 1987)

Lister Raymond, *Prints and Printmaking* (London 1984)

Ronald Vere Tooley, *Tooley's Dictionary of Mapmakers* (New York and Amsterdam 1979)

Jane Turner (Ed), *The Dictionary of Art* (London 1996)

Ellis Waterhouse, *The Dictionary of 18th Century Painters in Oils and Crayons* (Woodbridge, England 1980)

Arnold Wilson, *A Dictionary of British Marine Painters* (Leigh-on-Sea, England 1967)

INTRODUCTION 1806 - 1814

WHILE gunfire disturbed his death agonies on the afternoon of 21 October 1805, Vice-Admiral Lord Nelson asked how many prizes the British fleet had taken. He was told fourteen or fifteen, whereupon he gasped 'I bargained for twenty'. In the aftermath he would have been mollified. The van of the Combined Fleet under Dumanoir Le Pelley had escaped to the northward, but on 4 November the French ran into Sir Richard Strachan's squadron off Cape Ortegal. After a hard chase Dumanoir's four ships were taken, completing the reduction of the Combined Fleets of France and Spain to a few battered survivors blockaded in Cadiz. The events of those autumn days not only smashed the only active enemy fleet at sea, they were to establish Great Britain as the greatest seapower known to history. It is, however, a misconception to assume that this fact was known, or indeed was entirely true at the time. Certainly, to have assumed so in the winter of 1805, would have been a grievous folly, but the over-simplifications which come with hindsight, leave the impression that after Trafalgar the Royal Navy rested upon its laurels until given a bloody nose by the upstart United States Navy as a just punishment for its complacency.

This superficial assessment is to some extent bolstered by what one eminent Victorian historian called 'the old-fashioned risky creed' of British superiority which claimed any Briton was the equal of several foreigners. This conceit was gleefully peddled by the gutter-press of the day, making the later successes of American frigates all the more difficult to digest, still less to comprehend. Even *The Times* lamented, 'In the name of God what was done with this immense superiority of force? . . . What hopes will be excited in the breasts of our enemies.' Dramatic though American single-ship victories were, they scarcely affected the war. The exercise of seapower had been assiduously maintained not by a Royal Navy languishing in the shadow of Nelson, but which, during the

decade which followed Trafalgar, fought no more major fleet actions for the simple reason that no major fleet emerged to challenge its command of the sea. This did not mean the Royal Navy had little to do; in fact it increased in size as its commitments and responsibilities grew proportionately. With this expansion came an inevitable dilution in quality, and a degree of high-handedness, a factor precipitating collision with the United States.

But even this is an over-simplification, for the main enemy in Europe was far from inactive. The battle squadrons of the Royal Navy remained blockading those ships the enemy kept as a threat to British seapower, while Napoleon subsumed the fleets of vassal states, and yards within the French sphere of influence continued to turn out warships. Thus the Royal Navy's activities cannot be simply summed up in those magnificent but misleading lines of Captain Mahan whose allusion to those 'storm-battered ships upon which the Grand Army never looked, but stood between it, and mastery of the world' seem to encompass all that now remained for it to do. The economy of Mahan's words inadequately express the immense effort necessary to maintain the presence of those squadrons and to contain the more complex maritime endeavours of the enemy. Mahan enshrines only the policy of close blockade, but the magnitude of the real achievement is far greater.

A further popular misconception about the true nature of Trafalgar itself is that it negated the threat of invasion. The threat gradually withered, though not until 1812, but in October 1805 the *immediate* danger had, in fact, already passed. Two months earlier, after a disastrous exercise at embarking his invasion force from Boulogne, Napoleon abandoned invasion, broke camp and marched the Grand Army east to Ulm and the dramatic victory of Austerlitz on 2 December. Here, on the anniversary of his coronation, Napoleon struck the counterpoising blow to Nelson's,

smashing an Austro-Russian army. The Austrians sued for peace, the Russians withdrew behind their frontiers and the Third Coalition fell apart. Learning of Austerlitz, the British Prime Minister William Pitt presciently ordered the map of Europe rolled up, remarking that it would not be wanted for ten years. He died a few weeks later, on 23 January 1806.

Worse was to follow. After Austerlitz Napoleon's star rose higher. He destroyed the Prussian armies at Jena and Auerstädt on 14 October 1806, and the Russians at Eylau on 7/8 February 1807, and Friedland, 14 June 1807. A few days later he reached a secret accord with Tsar Alexander at Tilsit. Clauses in the subsequent treaty were aimed directly at augmenting the naval armaments available to the new allies by the seizure of the Danish, Swedish and Portuguese fleets. Had they not been frustrated by the pre-emptive action of the British, they might have consolidated Napoleon's hold on Europe, for Britain's fortunes, while they underwent serious setbacks, were not guided by the flawed reason or the fickle whim of one man. The prudent and expert exercise of seapower ensured that at the end of a decade of attrition the advantage lay with the British.

Until after Trafalgar, however, British seapower was very far from being an assured matter. British naval victories had not always been conclusive even though most had been fought with superior forces. Nelson's three great victories at Aboukir, Copenhagen and Trafalgar were remarkable in being won by the inferior force. During the war of the French Revolution (1793-1802) the naval threat to Britain had at best been contained, but not eliminated. In terms of objectives set at the outbreak of the war, nothing had been gained and much lost by the Peace of Amiens in 1802. The French revolutionaries remained in power and in occupation of the Low Countries, while Britain was compelled to surrender many of the overseas gains won by the Royal Navy. In the treaty, King George III relinquished his hereditary, if spurious, claim to the throne of France and the lilies were deleted from his coat-of-arms. This was a small, but highly symbolic point, for the peace marked nothing less than a British defeat. As an indication of the degree to which the British relinquished control of the sea, the Peace of Amiens allowed the French to send a fleet to sea to quell the slave rebellion in Haiti.

In 1802 France was unquestionably the greater power and upon the renewal of the war in May 1803 the situation for Britain had deteriorated even further. The peace was 'necessary to restore a navy . . .' Napoleon wrote, 'to fill our arsenals . . . and . . . because only then [in peace] is the one drill-ground for fleets, the sea, open'. In this, his appreciation was faultless, but he failed to realise that one cannot 'drill' a fleet, one can merely manoeuvre it, and while one might thereby achieve a great deal with acquired expertise, the necessary sea-time was denied to the French fleets by their enemy. When called upon to act with precision, to slot into the Emperor's carefully prepared and integrated plans, the French fleets were quite incapable of doing so. A fleet was not a maritime army corps; even an able admiral was incapable of bending the forces of nature to his will with the ease with which men might be force-marched. Thus, in the months succeeding the renewal of the war, Napoleon and his admirals squandered their advantages. At Trafalgar, notwithstanding Admiral Villeneuve's divination of Nelson's tactics, Nelson capitalised upon this weakness and defeated the Combined Fleet's clumsy line of battle. Thus were the tables turned and the first link forged in the causal chain which would ultimately confirm Trafalgar's importance. At the time, it remained for the Royal Navy to consummate Nelson's victory, to enable the British government to carry out its grand strategy of forming an allied coalition capable of destroying Imperial France.

It was to be an immense task. Domination of the sea meant not merely denying it to any enemy fleet, but defending British merchant shipping. However, it also facilitated raids on the enemy coasts such as wrecked the plans of the two emperors at Tilsit, or which interrupted commercial traffic or helped local aspirations for independence, thereby loosening imperial alliances. Most vulnerable among

these was that with Spain, an alliance which had united the fleets of Gravina and Villeneuve at Trafalgar but was not destined to last. In 1808 the abduction of their Royal Family, and the imposition of Napoleon's elder brother Joseph as their monarch, provoked the Spaniards to rise in armed insurrection. In July 1808, catching Dupont's corps at Baylen, a Spanish force under Castaños, compelled the French to surrender: the invincibility of the Grand Army was proved mythical and the news spread throughout Europe. In London, the British government decided to land an expeditionary force in the peninsula in support of the Spaniards. This was a critical decision and was to affect the outcome of events on the mainland of Europe.

Compared to the Grand Army of Napoleon and his allies, the British army was a puny force, yet its long slogging campaigns of march and counter-march back and forth across the Iberian peninsula, was an important component in maintaining the festering 'Spanish ulcer' in the body of Napoleon's empire. To accomplish this the British army relied heavily upon seapower. Moore's exhausted army retreated to Coruña to be rescued by sea; Wellington's great deception, which fooled Marshall Massena at the lines of Torres Vedras, was only made possible by sea-borne supplies; and when Wellington's battle-hardened battalions made their final, triumphant advance across Spain and into southwestern France, the whole maintenance of an army forbidden to live off the country like the hated and unfortunate French, was achieved in every detail by seapower. Even the customarily overlooked matter of pay was not neglected, and such a policy bore dividends by cementing an alliance with the Spaniards, for what comforts Wellington's Anglo-Portuguese soldiers lacked, they could, when available, purchase from the populace, a circumstance which made them if not welcomed, at least tolerated by the people of the provinces through which they marched.

That the contribution of the British to the land war was made possible by seapower is a fact of such unglamorous importance that it merits scarcely more than a passing mention by military historians, notwithstanding the affirmation of Wellington himself, that 'if anyone wishes to know the history of this war, I will tell them that it is our maritime superiority

[which] gives me the power of maintaining my army while the enemy are unable to do so.' By 'maritime superiority', Wellington alludes to the combination of naval and merchant shipping, the extent of which was formidable.

Other combined operations were a feature of British strategy, made possible by seapower. These limited offensives with defined objectives sometimes achieved astonishing results. The capture of Copenhagen and the destruction of the Danish fleet in 1807 had a profound effect upon the course of the war and the reduction of the Dutch East Indies was an almost extemporised success. On the other hand, the combined operation against Antwerp and the shipbuilding yards on the River Schelde in 1809 turned into a scandalous military disaster.

British ability to exploit this maritime superiority did not go unchallenged at sea, either. There were enterprising French naval officers who evaded the blockade and escaped to raid British trade, and to strike at the widely dispersed and often inferior British cruisers protecting it. Above all, serious damage was inflicted by French privateers. At various times in a world of oscillating alliances, Spanish, Danish, Dutch and Russian ships, both men-of-war and privateers, sought to plunder British merchantmen going about their lawful occasions. The protection of trade remained the chief preoccupation of the British Admiralty, for upon it hung not only the economic life of the country, but also the life of the government and the wealth which filled the war chests of Wellington and his generals and paid the vast expenses necessary to enable the Royal Navy to keep the sea. It also enabled subsidies to be paid to those sovereigns of Europe persuaded to take up arms against Napoleon. The most important of these was Tsar Alexander I of Russia, a vainglorious, weak and vacillating man, who abandoned Great Britain under the blandishments of Napoleon at Tilsit. But Russia relied upon her trade with Britain and Alexander's subjects broke the limitations imposed upon them by the feeble concurrence of their monarch to Napoleon's 'Continental System'. By finally bowing to internal economic pressure, it was Alexander's repudiation of the System which caused the rupture with Napoleon and the Grand Army's fatal invasion of Russia in 1812.

The Continental System was inaugurated

by the victorious Emperor of the French from Berlin on 21 November 1806, following the defeat of Prussia. Napoleon proscribed trade between the French Empire (including the subdued German states) and Great Britain. After Tilsit Russian trade was also forbidden, and the following year the system was extended to Spain and Portugal. The British government promptly responded with Orders in Council, the first of which was issued on 7 January 1807, forbidding neutral ships to trade between French ports, but in November successive Orders declared that a ship with a cargo for a French, or French-held port would be compelled to discharge her cargo in Britain before obtaining an export licence. This provoked further decrees by Napoleon, then in Milan, in November and December 1809. These sanctioned the confiscation of ships and cargoes if they had touched at British ports, and the confiscation of cargoes not certified as originating outside Britain or her colonies. Thereafter, all neutral vessels which had submitted to British naval control (and this meant those that had sailed in convoy) would lose their neutral protection. Regarded as sailing under the enemy's flag, they were thus subject to seizure.

The damaging potential of Napoleon's embargo was immediately obvious. Prussian oak was a fundamental raw material for both naval and mercantile shipbuilding. In the year of Trafalgar 11,841 'loads' were imported, but three years later a mere 27 filtered through, a single shipload. Over the same period Russian mast timbers fell from 12,748 to 459 and while a small supply of oak was smuggled from Dalmatia, timber for merchant ship construction was limited by the government, pushing up the price of commercial tonnage. This British requirement for 'naval stores' – canvas, turpentine, tallow, hemp, iron and timber – was mostly satisfied from Russia. Between 1808 and 1809, naval stores from the Baltic more than doubled. The trade was immense, a convoy of October 1809 amounting to over 1000 merchantmen, with a heavy naval escort including six ships of the line.

Such imports were necessary to Great Britain, but as exports they were to be vital to Russia. Herein lay one reason for the System's failure, but there were others. As an imposition many merchants sought to evade it, for there was as ready a market in Europe for goods from Britain, her empire and the then neutral United States, as there was in Britain for French brandy, Dutch gin and Flemish lace. Moreover, remittance for British exports smuggled or illegally imported into Europe was either goods in kind, or gold, either irresistible not only to European merchants, but even to the Bonapartes themselves. Napoleon was characteristically ambivalent. He had no objection to trading if it drained Britain of gold, or secured him *matériel* he required for military operations. In April 1808 he wrote to his brother Louis Bonaparte, King of Holland, 'If you need to sell your country's gin, the English will buy it . . . make them pay in money, never in commodities'. But Louis was too eager and was forced by Napoleon to abdicate in 1810 for failing to maintain the Continental System. Likewise, Alexander's failure to toe the line arose from his inability to command his domestic economy. The rich wished for British colonial luxuries and their income derived from their estates which grew the mast-timber and flax formerly sold to the British navy. Trade in coffee, silk, tea and sugar trickled continuously through the

The last decisive clash between the battle squadrons of Britain and France was Duckworth's victory off San Domingo on 6 February 1806. Oil painting by Nicholas Pocock, signed and dated 1808.   NMM ref BHC0571

Typical employment for the Royal Navy in the post-Trafalgar era was the capture of enemy colonies, like these operations against the Dutch East Indies island of Banda Neira in August 1810. Coloured aquatint engraved by Thomas Sutherland after an original by Thomas Whitcombe, no date. NMM ref PAD5793

White Sea port of Archangel, except when it was closed by the ice of the arctic winter, and rising prices compelled Alexander to renege on his agreement with Napoleon. On 31 December 1810 he issued a *ukase* repudiating the System. Nor did Spain or Portugal comply, and it was this lack of co-operation that prompted Napoleon's occupation of the Iberian Peninsula, an operation undertaken before turning on the Tsar, whom he still had some hope of influencing. Finally exasperated, Napoleon crossed the Nieman into Russia in June 1812.

The System's secondary objective, a coercive attempt to bully continental manufacturing and agriculture to achieve parity with British methods and therefore reduce the demand for British goods, failed chiefly for lack of raw materials. Various experiments with alternatives were largely unsuccessful, and what was produced was under-cut by illegally imported goods which were cheaper because of the unassailable production technology available to the British. Essentially, a blockade by bureaucratic means was bound to fail, undermined as it was by official exceptions. Smuggling became rife and the Imperial *douaniers* even more unpopular than King George III's revenue officers. Continental demand was so great that it was

only satisfied by more sophisticated solutions than smuggling. Forged documentation proliferated, the corruption of imperial officials was accepted and in March 1809 even the Napoleonic government itself was driven to issue certificates to ease distress in several cities on the shores of the Baltic. Most curious was Napoleon's refusal to take advantage of the disastrous harvest of 1809 in Britain. Such was his tenacious belief that he could ruin Britain by draining her of gold that he permitted 20,000 tons of wheat to be exported from Europe. He was less keen on his marshals emulating him. Sugar, entering Europe via the then Turkish port of Salonika, was carried on mules over the Balkan mountains. Marmont, then Governor-General of Dalmatia, admitted himself powerless to stop this, while the avaricious Massena was fined three million francs from his account at Leghorn for selling licences to trade between Britain and Italy. The punishment neither stopped Massena, nor prevented him making a profit. Everywhere the half-hearted application of the Continental System doomed it, making it a slow burning fuse to the inevitable keg of economic disaster. Despite his partisan relaxations of its strictures, Napoleon perversely persisted. On 18 October 1810 he issued his final decree from Fontainebleau in which he

peremptorily ordered the confiscation and sale by the state of unlicensed goods, the destruction of manufactures and the branding of convicted smugglers. But even this failed to strangle the laws of supply and demand, aided as they were by desire, cunning and venality.

Much forbidden fruit was imported through Hamburg via a British-held island in the German Bight. Helgoland was an important outwork in this economic siege warfare. Over two hundred British merchants established warehouses on the island and formed a Chamber of Commerce to supply the 'free-traders' who used the estuaries of the Elbe, Jade, Weser and Ems to feed European appetites. Intercourse between Helgoland and the city of Hamburg was never properly cut off, though in January 1810 the incorruptible Marshal Davout arrived there to command the Army of Germany and enforce the decrees of his imperial master.

Running concurrently with this economic timebomb, was a political one, for the deprivation of sugar, tea, cocoa, cotton, silk and the coveted luxury goods made in Britain was not only affecting the Russian aristocracy. It inevitably alienated the French *bourgeoisie*, hitherto Napoleon's staunchest supporters, and by depriving all classes of the very means of subsistence in the satellite nations, the emperor's policy fed a rising tide of nationalism, particularly in the German states.

Notwithstanding all this, the Continental System was not a complete failure, for it had a profound effect upon Great Britain and, in combination with the actions of America, might ultimately have succeeded if Napoleon had enforced it with greater strictness, or persisted in implementing it for longer. Despite the early breaking of the System, British exports were steadily reduced by two factors, one of which was a fall in demand. Davout's appearance in Hamburg was just one manifestation of a toughening attitude by the authorities, made possible by the release of troops after the further defeat of Austria at Wagram and the signing of the Peace of Schönbrunn on 14 October 1809. The consequent exclusion of British goods, particularly along the shores of the Baltic had a severe effect; even the carriage of British manufactured goods and colonial produce in neutral ships was virtually strangled. Between 1810 and 1811 British exports dropped dramatically from just over £60 millions, to just under £40 millions. Much of this fall was due to the Non-Importation Act passed against British goods by the United States government of President Jefferson as relations between the two countries steadily deteriorated, but the decline in exports exacerbated a critical socio-economic situation within Britain herself.

Bad harvests in 1808, 1809 and 1810 and the consequent widespread unrest added to the social upheaval inherent in the mechanisation of agriculture and industry then still in progress throughout Great Britain. Dispossession in the country and overcrowding in the new towns led to violent opposition to all things modern. Serious rioting took place in Manchester, while elsewhere turnpike keepers were burned out of their cottages, factory machines were smashed by Luddites and established companies went bankrupt as business failed and inflation depreciated sterling. Boom and bust had long been a feature of the British economy. One French commentator summarised it, asserting that when there was 'peace in Europe there was a crisis in England, and when there was a war in Europe, there was a boom in England'. One ruined victim of the waxing and waning of Anglo-Russian trade, conceiving the government itself to be the author of his misfortunes, petitioned ministers for redress. Receiving no reply, John Bellingham waited quietly in the lobby of the House of Commons on 11 May 1812 and assassinated the Prime Minister and Chancellor of the Exchequer, Spencer Perceval.

During this period of economic crisis, the Peninsular War was also approaching a critical point, with Wellington advancing from Torres Vedras in the wake of Massena's starving soldiers. Gold was necessary to maintain the self-sufficiency of the Anglo-Portuguese army, further straining the British economy. But there were almost no commercial transactions in Rouen, Bordeaux or Lyons either, and the Parisian banks were unsteady following the Tsar's *ukase* of December 1810. By November 1811 a stalemate had been reached and as Napoleon plotted vengeance on Alexander, he unwisely signed licences for the export of wine and the import of sugar and coffee. This was a fatal mistake, for London reciprocated immediately, further weakening the French posi-

tion, issuing licences for European trade from March 1812. In that year, so fateful for Napoleon, British exports rose again to some £50 millions, while the depreciated rouble rose as goods continued to reach Vienna and Paris through Archangel. In short, by relaxing his own rules, Napoleon's action fatally weakened his own policy and by degrees, aided the economies of Britain and Russia.

The fruits of Austerlitz fed Napoleon's self-conceit. Unhampered by the political constraints of parliament, the Emperor's centralised government denied itself the frustrations of seeking advice. As arbiter of the fate of Europe, Napoleon succumbed to the traditions of his Corsican upbringing and to the temptation of the vendetta; he invaded Russia when Alexander broke his promises. It was to be a foolhardy, fateful and fatal enterprise. By committing this blunder at a time when so ambitious a project, even under the most propitious circumstances, put a further strain on his shaky imperial economy, Napoleon dramatically tipped the whole balance of economic power in Britain's favour, for his attack on Russia was not merely militarily foolhardy, it was economically disastrous. The affront of invasion made an implacable enemy of Alexander and the sequence of cause and effect which followed the British victory off Cape Trafalgar was now irreversible. One by one, the Emperor of the French's allies would change sides, augmenting Russia, the only military land-power on earth capable of defeating the Grand Army. In the wake of Napoleon's retreat from Moscow, it was the fickle Tsar's patient, persistent peasant infantry and an electrifying fear of his cossack lancers which caused dread as the allied armies finally overran France, forcing Napoleon's first abdication in 1814. These troops were kept in the field largely by British gold.

Throughout the period, however, Britain's trade remained vulnerable worldwide. In February 1809, *Lloyd's List* was lamenting 'the depredations of the numerous privateers, with which the Channel . . . is now infested'. The problem seemed insuperable, for the British coasting trade alone consisted of 'an endless train of transit.' The *guerre de course* was a form of warfare at which the French excelled. Nor was it only the French who became corsairs. After the assault on Copenhagen in 1807 and the

seizure of their fleet, the Danes were active from the North Cape of Norway to their native shores and enjoyed enormous successes. In the two years after the war resumed in 1803, enemy privateers captured 609 vessels, but these rose to 507 in the year of Trafalgar. In 1806 and 1807 the rise continued, with 519 and 559 captures. Although a drop followed in 1808, with 469 vessels taken, 1809 marked a sharp rise to 571 losses as the crisis of the war approached. In 1810, attacks grew worse, to the tune of 619, most particularly in the Channel where captures were made 'in sight of the farmers of England'. The British suffered most in the Baltic, but badly in the West Indies and worse in the Indian Ocean, where the French base of Île de France provided the resources necessary to support some of France's most successful sea officers. In the economically uncertain year of 1811, with fewer ships at sea only 470 merchantmen were taken, but this decline continued when trade improved. In 1814 only 145 were lost, despite the outbreak of hostilities with United States in 1812, which had added American cruisers and privateers to the gross forces of the enemies ranged against Britain. But by this time the best corsairs had been captured, privateering no longer paid and fewer privateers were fitting out, because the British fleet, in all its manifestations, was immense and truly dominating the oceans, seas and straits of the globe. As the war in Europe drifted to a close, the might of the Royal Navy was swung against the United States, a circumstance which soon terminated hostilities and which is recounted in a separate volume.

It was a Frenchman named Lemierre who wrote 'the trident of Neptune is the sceptre of the world'. It is not too fanciful an image to state that while the trident was in dispute up to 1805, the Battle of Trafalgar wrested it from the grasp of Napoleon. Despite this, it remained a matter of contention for a further decade. To take the metaphor further, Britannia's ultimately successful wielding of the trident was appropriately three-fold. By blockade, striking back and defending her precious trade, she was finally able to decide the matter in her own favour. It was this cumulative, triple-pronged maritime policy that finally deprived Napoleon of his attempt at 'mastery of the world', ensuring the defeat of the greatest military land-power history had so-far seen.

1

The foundations of seapower: trade and finance

THE collective strength of the British merchant marine lay in its size and the extreme vigour and progressiveness of its financial management. With no reason to improve the lot of seafarers, the principal impetus for improvements in merchant shipping and its technology was the emerging influence of under-

2

writers and the insurance market which, by the first decade of the nineteenth century, was well established. The Royal Exchange and London Assurance Companies had been chartered in 1720 and the plethora of coffee houses in which the business of securing ships, cargoes and insurance had become an active and lively part of the London scene. But although underwriters still wrote their own policies in a few coffee houses, the Baltic Exchange (which dealt mainly with grain, hemp and tallow) and the Coal Exchange, most business was conducted at Lloyd's, within the Royal Exchange itself – in 1812, the coffee room became known as the Captain's Room where masters would meet (1). Demands on underwriters for losses due to incompetence and poor navigation rose dramatically with the increase in trade generated by the war, and lobbying by influential underwriters for such measures as better charts was one reaction to this fiscal squeeze.

There was also, both in government and commerce, a ready appreciation of the critical necessity of maintaining the stability of underwriting in wartime. As early as 1693, Tourville's destruction of the annual convoy from the Levant had proved disastrous, strengthening the Elizabethan concept of 'losse lightethe rather easilie upon many, that heavily upon few,' and by 1780, when Cordova captured 58 of the 63 ships in the combined East and West India convoy, Lloyd's was just able to bear the heavy loss of £1.5 millions sterling. By the outbreak of war in 1793, greater expertise and judgement, and an increase in both 'names' (those whose wealth backed the insurance market) and the volume of trade, ensured a consequent uplift in the flow of cash. Just as in other fields, the war brought to prominence men of high financial reputation. As a confidant of William Pitt, John Julius Angerstein, known as 'the Father of Lloyd's', was one of a triumvirate of influential men in this vital institution. Sir Francis Baring, 'the first merchant in Europe' and 'Dicky' Thornton who was 'said to be good for three millions' completed this eminent trio and headed the list of underwriting 'names'.

In times of crisis heavy losses could be sustained, while the curious increasingly international nature of the business transacted at Lloyd's which transcended national borders, had caused some anomalous situations during the war when belligerent vessels, underwritten at Lloyd's, were captured or destroyed. In 1810, when Napoleon ordered a savage tightening of the Continental System and numerous British owned ships were caught in the ports of the Baltic, the Select Committee on Marine Insurance enquiring into the loss, concluded the risks had been well covered and individual burdens were small. Angerstein was said to have lost £1000 against gains of £490,000 during twenty-two years of underwriting, one James Barnes lost £300 against £280,000 and a partnership collecting risks totalling £12,000,000, lost £1600!

In 1809, London underwriters covered the then immense sum of £100 millions with specific risks like specie shipped aboard the frigate *Diana* being insured to the tune of £656,000, all but £25,000 of which was borne by Lloyd's. On his own account Thornton once underwrote £250,000 on a shipment of a government subsidy of gold to St Petersburg and a typical valuation of a vessel bound for Tönning, the entry port for much British goods intended to flout the Continental System, was about £40,000. A West Indiaman of 500 tons burthen would attract £69,000; a fur cargo from Quebec some £200,000 and a laden East Indiaman around £250,000, exclusive of the 'trade goods' her officers were allowed on their private account (2). Underwriting was also carried out at Liverpool from 1802 and, largely in respect of the coastal and short-sea trades, had long been a feature of commercial life in Bristol, Glasgow, Hull and Newcastle.

Fluctuations in insurance rates followed the strategic situation and reflected the realities of the protection afforded trade by the Royal Navy. Villeneuve's appearance in the West Indies in the summer of 1805 doubled homeward West India premiums and the activities of American privateers after 1812 pushed up the rates again. As for the Continental System, its introduction showed the apprehensiveness of the market, with rates of 40 per cent on cargoes bound to Baltic ports in French occupation in 1808. However, these fell back to 21.5 per cent on outward and 17.2 per cent on homeward cargoes when the realities of the system were revealed, despite severe losses during 1810, and by 1814, as a reflection of the mastery of the Baltic by the Royal Navy, rates had fallen to no more than 4 per cent.

The curious cross-border nature of trade and the business conducted at Lloyd's during this period contributed in no small measure to the Royal Navy's success. It was in the interest of Lloyd's members to encourage naval officers in the wearisome business of convoy escort and protection. Want of zeal had periodically been remarked upon, while two convoys had been abandoned by their escorts. To discourage this reprehensible tendency, members subscribed to a fund from which disbursements were made to relieve the wounded and the dependants of naval officers killed in action. Specific and manifest encouragement was further granted in 1803 when Lloyd's Patriotic Fund was established, 'to animate our defenders by sea and land'. The Fund made 'pecuniary awards or honourable badges of distinction for successful exertions of valour or merit', the most prestigious of which took the form of inscribed swords.

3

More significant, however, was the passing of intelligence from Lloyd's contacts abroad, masters of merchantmen or snippets gleaned in the ordinary intercourse of business. It was realised by all parties, that commerce and commerce alone provided the sinews of war and enabled power to be gained and held. Commerce necessitated the trafficking of information during the natural process of bargaining and John Bennet, Secretary to Lloyd's from 1803, caused twice weekly editions of *Lloyd's List* to be published, with confidential items available for perusal in the Subscriber's

4

1. 'Front of the Royal Exchange. The Merchant Seamen's Office over the Royal Exchange was used for Committee Meetings by the Marine Society from July 15th 1756 to April 6th 1758', etching by John Green after an original by Samuel Wale, 1761. *NMM ref PAD1379*

2. 'India House. The Sale Room', coloured aquatint engraved by Thomas Rowlandson, Augustus Charles Pugin and Thomas Sutherland after an original by Rowlandson and Pugin, published by Rudolph Ackermann, 1 December 1808. *NMM ref PAD1361*

3. 'Lloyd's Subscription Room', coloured aquatint engraved by Thomas Rowlandson, Augustus Charles Pugin and Thomas Sutherland after an original by Rowlandson and Pugin, published by Rudolph Ackermann, 1 January 1800. *NMM ref PAD1365*

4. 'The Custom House', etching by Watts after an original by Miller, no date. *NMM ref PAD1386*

5. 'Smugglers. A picturesque representation of the Naval, Military and Miscellaneous Costumes of Great Britain 1808', coloured etching by John Augustus Atkinson after his own original, published by William Miller and James Walker, 1 January 1808. *NMM ref PAD7772*

6. 'The Viper Excise Cutter on a wind, passing the Gunfleet Beacon', coloured aquatint after an original by William Wallace, published by Laurie & Whittle, 4 June 1794. *NMM ref PAF7982*

5

6

Room (3). Ship-movements, political and military information were thus made known and all was passed to the Admiralty. In return the Admiralty were able to bring the greater influence of Lloyd's to bear upon owners and masters who were deficient in the matter of keeping convoy schedules, of bad station-keeping when in convoy, or who ran from the protection of a convoy as soon as they thought they could press for their destination, only too frequently to fall foul of a predatory privateer.

In 1805, liaison between Lloyd's and the Admiralty had resulted in the establishment of a coast signalling system which used the existing signal stations, set up ten years earlier. Such stations were run by naval personnel, commanded by a lieutenant and could warn ships of the presence of privateers. Further naval control of shipping was accomplished by a new Admiralty shutter telegraph network which, when completed in 1808, enabled messages to be transmitted in clear weather between London and the important naval ports and roadsteads of Portsmouth, Plymouth, Chatham, Sheerness, the Downs and Great Yarmouth. This made the operation of the convoy system more efficient and in 1810, at the height of the privateer scare, coastal convoys were introduced for deep-water vessels making for the assembly anchorage for an ocean convoy.

A ship in distress was all too familiar a sight upon the coast. Towards the end of the first decade of the nineteenth century there was an awakening of interest among shipowners as their profits rose in response to the increase in trade. The Society of Shipowners had been formed in 1802, but was never to achieve the stature and influence of Lloyd's, or to work as closely with the Admiralty in the regulation of shipping during the war. Nevertheless, owners began forming into mutual protection and indemnity groups, and in 1813 the Society of Shipowners unsuccessfuly sought limitation of liability in cases of collision or unseaworthiness.

In a long war in which the nub of policy was to cripple the enemy's finances on the one hand, and to provide oneself with the means to wage war on the other, embargo of the enemy's trade went hand in glove with the sale of manufactured goods to the enemy for cash. Both sides strove for this bloodless but important victory. Napoleon gained an ascendancy when he licensed exports of Dutch and even French grain to a hungry Britain, but he lost it when ambition and foolhardiness led him to invade Russia. For such a project boots manufactured in Northampton were an essential and unfortunate necessity, and in the end, with the expense of the war in France reaching enormous proportions, Napoleon's only means of raising more revenue was by the curious and self-defeating expedient of levying duties upon imports of British goods.

To prevent private speculation encouraging a reciprocal traffic and to defend its own sources of income, the Government Revenue Service (4) waged a ceaseless war against smuggling (5), employing their own cutters (6) against a determined and often desperate minority of 'free-traders' whose cargoes were eagerly received throughout the kingdom, not least by minor figures of the establishment, such as the local justices.

Such were the measures taken to facilitate trade and to achieve a commercial seapower which in turn provided Britain with the means to maintain her naval pre-eminence and thus influence the outcome of the war.

Part I BLOCKADE

LESS than a fortnight after Trafalgar, the First Lord of the Admiralty relaxed the British naval blockade. 'It is to little purpose now,' Barham wrote, 'to wear out our ships in a fruitless blockade during the winter'. Toulon was almost empty of line of battle ships, Cadiz retained the shattered remnants of the Combined Fleet and though Salcedo's squadron lay still at Cartagena, those three ports were invested by the assiduous Collingwood. Brest, the remaining concern, could be watched by light squadrons. If the enemy came out, he could be chased and annihilated, for Barham's trust rested upon the 104 line of battle ships Great Britain maintained in commission. Consequently, the Channel Fleet could ride out the worst of the winter gales in Torbay, leaving the gate of Brest ajar, with a few cruisers to watch the enemy. It was a policy not without flaws.

French naval strategy is hard to discern in the period following Trafalgar. This obscurity arises principally from the central control exercised by the Emperor. Napoleon, it seems, vacillated in his demands on the French navy and of those of his allies, veering from an enthusiasm which required impossibly precise regimentation of naval dispositions, to a despair of his squadrons ever achieving anything. When Linois' flying squadron was out-manoeuvred by Commodore Dance of the Honourable East India Company and the homeward bound China 'fleet' in February 1804, Napoleon replied to the lame excuses of his Minister of Marine Denis Decrès, 'All the enterprises at sea which have been undertaken since I became the head of the government have missed fire because my admirals see double, and have discovered, I know not where, that war can be made without running risks . . . .' This justifiable exasperation serves to explain the Emperor's apparent periodic abandonment of any grand strategy at sea. Nevertheless, it is not to be expected that so energetic a genius as Napoleon's would give up so easily and it is contradicted by his diplomatic initiatives which sought constantly to augment the French fleet by either the navies of his allies, or by subsuming the fleets of indecisive neutrals. In addition to this, the building of men of war went on ceaselessly in all the great naval arsenals within the dominions of the Emperor of the French. It seems likely therefore, that somewhere at the back of his mind, Napoleon nurtured the grand design of a further major naval offensive when the time was right. Such we know him to be capable of, though its accomplishment was, in the event, beyond his abilities.

Notwithstanding this, his subordinate admirals seemed curiously lacking in energy and this attitude infused much of the French naval hierarchy. Occasional groups of French men-of-war took advantage of a slant of wind or bad weather and evaded the watching British. They almost always quit the French Atlantic ports with one primary objective in mind, to succour the distant French overseas possessions, most notably in the West Indies, but also in the Indian Ocean. Thereafter, they were under orders to attack British trade, but even when they had achieved escape from the British blockade, the majority of frigate commanders considered they had done their best if they were back in port after a couple of months, though there were notable exceptions, particularly in the Indian Ocean. During their period of freedom they might have enjoyed considerable success against British merchant shipping, but taken overall, they beg the question of whether they were worth the expenditure to the French exchequer. Such observations are made with hindsight; sufficient bold escapes occurred throughout the period under review to keep both the opposing British blockading squadrons and the more distantly cruising frigates and sloops on their mettle. Like the potential menace of a fleet in being, any flying squadron of the enemy threatened the trade routes, while the expenditure necessary to contain the threat always exceeded the resources necessary to mount it in the first place.

The breakout of the Brest squadrons under Vice-Admiral Leissègues and Rear-Admiral Willaumez in December 1805 (covered in detail later) illustrate the point. The elaborate British dispositions made to meet the crisis had widely different effects. One of these pursuing squadrons, under Warren, ran into an entirely unexpected force, that of Linois who was returning from his eventful but largely unsuccessful East Indies cruise; both *Marengo* and *Belle Poule* were taken. Leissègues was followed to the West Indies and totally annihilated by Duckworth's squadron, but Willaumez was luckier: he enjoyed some success commerce-raiding in the South Atlantic and West Indies, avoiding both the local fleet under Rear-Admiral Cochrane and the hunting squadrons of Warren and Strachan. In August the French squadron was dispersed by a hurricane, as was Strachan's, but by 14 September three of the latter had made the rendezvous off Cape Henry when they sighted the *Impétueux*, 74, running for Chesapeake Bay under jury rig. The 74-gun *Bellona* and *Belleisle* and the 36-gun frigate *Melampus* gave chase and Captain Belair was compelled to run the *Impétueux* ashore, striking his colours; the wreck was then burnt. Willaumez's squadron was almost as broken as that of Leissègues; the *Eole* and *Patriote* found unopposed refuge in the Chesapeake, though only the latter ever returned to France; *Valeureuse* made the Delaware and never served again; *Cassard* returned directly to France, while *Foudroyant*, having been refitted in Havana, re-entered Brest in February 1807.

Another French squadron of one 74-gun ship, two frigates and a brig corvette, which had been at large in the South Atlantic since October 1805 was also dispersed by a hurricane on 20 August 1806. Its purpose was to have been to draw off forces from the Channel fleet, to attack British possessions on the coast of West Africa and then cross the Atlantic and wreak havoc among shipping in the West Indies.

Under the command of Commodore L'Hermitte, the squadron took and destroyed several British slavers and merchant ships, and the British sloop *Favourite*. Most of the ships returned safely to France, but on 27 September, when almost within sight of the Biscay coast of France, *Présidente* fell in with a squadron under Rear-Admiral Sir Thomas Louis in the *Canopus* and after a chase, struck her colours. L'Hermitte's squadron was to have created a serious diversion under the command of Napoleon's younger brother Jerome, but it misfired and was another example of French naval mismanagement. The failure to take an African port, the necessity of refitting and the abortive and short-lived cruise in the Antilles

'Revenge 74 off the Gironde', watercolour by George H Halstead, 1814. The blockade of the French Atlantic ports was maintained, with varying degrees of rigour, right up to the end of the war.   NMM ref PAG9765

hardly made this the predatory cruise it had been planned to be, despite the capture of *Favourite*. It was Captain Labrosse's misfortune to run into Louis: part of the British counter to the main French breakout, Louis was waiting for bigger game.

The escape of the squadrons under Leissègues, Willaumez and L'Hermitte were the most complex in the post-Trafalgar period. Though largely ineffective and ultimately costly to the French, they illustrate the potential danger to British trade from the West Indies, India and China posed by their presence at large in the Atlantic. They illustrate also the paramount necessity for the British to maintain a constant and close blockade, the weakness of convoy escorts and, once an enemy squadron was at sea, the increased burden of sending out additional squadrons to search out and waylay them. The misadventures of Leissègues and Willaumez in particular were to reduce the

Brest fleet to the impotence of the ships trapped in Cadiz, for while L'Hermitte's *Régulus* managed to slip into Brest on 5 October, no ship of the line got out during the remainder of 1806.

Consideration of the naval power of France at the period immediately following Tilsit, when on the continent of Europe Napoleon's power seemed unassailable, somewhat rocks the notion that Trafalgar was a victory of annihilation. The perspective of hindsight reveals that Tilsit was the high-water mark and that an inevitable ebb would ensue, just as it reveals that the long-term effect of Trafalgar was a victory of empowerment. In fact the British Admiralty neither had cause for complacency, nor felt it, for in the spring of 1808 the French fleet had either in commission or building over eighty sail of the line, a score of which were completing in the busy yards of Antwerp, Brest, Lorient, Toulon and subsidiary ports.

Most significant of these was Cherbourg, where extensive construction works were in progress and which it was intended would soon prove capable of supporting a fleet of battleships. Notions that French naval energies were in decline were therefore premature.

The British Mediterranean fleet remained an important command, operating as it did along the southern flank of Napoleon's empire and it remained under Collingwood until his death at sea in 1810. In the spring of 1808, Collingwood's task was blockading the principal ports of France and Spain, where at Toulon five of the line were in commission with a further four on the stocks. La Spezia in Italy was a naval port harbouring some frigates, three 74s were building at Genoa and Venice, the navy of which small state had passed under French control. In addition five French sail of the line along with a single frigate remained in Cadiz. Ashore French arms were successful, finally throwing the British and Neapolitan garrison out of their last Calabrian toeholds at Reggio and Scylla. Everywhere land-power confronted seapower.

In January 1808, however, Rear-Admiral Allemand succeeded in slipping out of his anchorage at Île d'Aix, eluding Sir Richard Strachan's blockading squadron of seven of the line which had left their customary anchorage in the Basque Road to rendezvous with some victualling vessels in late November. Due to a combination of circumstances, Strachan failed to get his provisions or regain his station until the new year, by which time Allemand had gone.

Taking advantage of a fine northeasterly breeze on 17 January 1808, Allemand put to sea in *Majesteux*, 120, with the 74s *Ajax, Lion, Magnanime, Jemmapes* and *Suffren*, with a frigate and a brig corvette, brushing aside the British frigate *Phoenix*, 36, and the 18-gun brig *Raleigh*. When the news reached Strachan, he made for Cape Finisterre in chase of Allemand whom he rightly judged was making for the Mediterranean. However, he shortly afterwards ran into heavy weather and had to send the leaking *Donegal* home, having deprived her of her mainyard to repair his own flagship. Allemand suffered similarly from foul weather and was obliged to detach *Jemappes* to Rochefort, but he passed the British squadrons off Ferrol and Cadiz unobserved and similarly slipped into the Mediterranean, destroying several merchant ships before joining Vice-Admiral Ganteaume at Toulon on 6 February. Strachan followed, running past Gibraltar on the 10th, to finally reinforce Vice-Admiral Thornborough at Palermo on the 21st.

By this time, however, the reinforced Ganteaume was at sea, having sailed from Toulon a fortnight earlier. Two days after Thornborough and Strachan joined forces, the French fleet was off Corfu, landing troops stores and supplies on the island. Despite being spotted on more than one occasion, when Ganteaume's fleet weighed again on 16 March for the return passage to Toulon, it was unobserved. Ganteaume's luck held, and Collingwood and his colleagues were cheated of the sequel to Trafalgar which they so earnestly desired.

Collingwood's failure to catch Ganteaume was due to the same kind of accidents that had allowed Allemand to escape Strachan. Although his frigates had spotted the French off Corfu, the news was delayed in reaching the Commander-in-Chief who, the day before it arrived at Syracuse by the *Standard*, 64, had left for Palermo and his rendezvous with Thornborough. A change of wind now prevented *Standard* from sailing and Collingwood had passed beyond contact from the land. Off the island of Marittimo at the western end of Sicily, Collingwood's four of the line joined forces with Thornborough and Strachan on 2 March and still unaware of the position of the French, made for Palermo and then the Bay of Naples where the Commander-in-Chief finally heard from *Standard*. On 22 March he was off the entrance to the Adriatic, but he was too late, though it was six days before he knew it, whereupon he sailed for the area west of Sicily and southeast of Sardinia, his hopes waning. They were dashed on 28 April when the frigate *Proserpine* arrived from Toulon to say that Ganteaume had resumed his old moorings.

The accounts of this sorry tale tell of a degree of confusion. A failure of the handful of cruisers in the Adriatic to disperse the news in favour of shadowing a large fleet against which they could achieve nothing, only to lose contact two days before it finally departed from Corfu, contributed to Collingwood's frustration. As for Collingwood himself, he entertained an unfortunate and misplaced prejudice that the French had greater designs on Sicily than they had. Having found out the pathetic arrangements the Sicilians had made in their own defence, he understandably felt the burden of defending the island should fall upon the British navy. This would have not been so bad a mistake had he caught Ganteaume off North Africa, but in this his frigates let him down. He was still sanguine of action, however, a month later, but thereafter cheated of it. Collingwood was correct insofar as without Sicily maintenance of the Mediterranean fleet would have been difficult. But two other factors should be taken into consideration before censuring Collingwood too severely: the state of Spain and the state of Collingwood's health. The decline of the latter was irreversible; the admiral had not been on shore since before Trafalgar and was not to land in his lifetime. His poor health was exacerbated by anxieties of which Spain was but one, though the most pressing. The increased power of Napoleon in that kingdom was to overthrow the Spanish monarchy and precipitate the Spanish uprising and although this added much wanted allies to the British cause, co-operating with the Spanish rebels was to mean a deal of work for the Royal Navy and its local Commander-in-Chief.

It was this which was now to preoccupy Collingwood who, leaving Thornborough to watch Toulon, made for the south coast of Spain. The uprising of 2 May had by 4 June become a formal war against France, led by a junta who had declared it in the name of the captive King Ferdinand VII. This isolated the French squadron at Cadiz, which was moved to an outer anchorage beyond the range of the city's guns by their commander, Vice-Admiral Rosilly. Offshore, Rear-Admiral Purvis blockading Rosilly with a powerful squadron, offered to help the Spaniards in destroying the French ships, but the offer was declined since Spain and Britain remained formally at war. A few days later, however, submitting to *force majeure*, Rosilly surrendered his squadron which consisted of the *Neptune*, 80, the 74s *Algésiras, Héros, Argonaut* and *Pluton*, the frigate *Cornélie* and a corvette. A month later, Spanish commissioners having visited Britain, peace was formally declared and British cruisers became active in support of the Spanish patriot party in their long fight to oust the occupying forces of France and her allies.

Duckworth at San Domingo

THE largest breakout of French warships in the post-Trafalgar period occurred a little over two months after the battle and as a direct result of Lord Barham's relaxation of the blockade. The Brest fleet, which had remained in harbour during the critical summer of 1805, now bestirred itself; on 13 December, when Cornwallis's blockading squadron had been driven off station by heavy weather, eleven ships of the line, four frigates, a corvette and two dispatch vessels weighed from the Goulet. This force was divided into two squadrons, Vice-Admiral Leissègues squadron which was to convey 1000 soldiers to reinforce the garrison of San Domingo before cruising off Jamaica or, if the British were too strong in that quarter, to return to France by way of the Grand Banks; Rear-Admiral Willaumez's force was to proceed into the South Atlantic and thereafter to make for Cayenne via Martinique or Guadeloupe, returning to France by way of St Helena. The discretionary nature of both admirals' orders offered them alternative cruising grounds, any of which should have offered rich pickings from British trade. The combined sorties illustrate the best that French naval forces could and ought to have achieved, by striking at the source of British wealth and tying down British battle squadrons. Both French forces were powerful and posed a serious threat, for Leissègues' flagship was the 130-gun *Impérial* and he had besides an 80, three 74s and two 40-gun frigates. Willaumez' detachment was of similar strength, consisting of the *Foudroyant* (flag), 80, five 74-gun ships, and two 40-gun frigates.

West of Ushant, the two French admirals were in the act of parting company on 15 December, when they were sighted by the ships of a convoy of twenty-three merchantmen on their way from Cork to the West Indies under escort of Captain Charles Brisbane in *Arethusa*, 38, with *Boadicea,* 38 and *Wasp*, 18, in company. Brisbane split his convoy, which then escaped, and sent *Wasp* home with the news of the sighting.

On 23 December, between Madeira and the Canaries, Brisbane fell in with a British squadron under Vice-Admiral Sir John Duckworth (1) which had been blockading the defeated remnants of the Combined

3

Fleet in Cadiz. In consequence of news borne by Commander Langford of the *Lark*, 18, that a French squadron (thought to be that from Rochefort under Allemand), had dispersed a convoy bound for Gorée, Duckworth had raised the blockade and gone in search of the marauders. Having seen nothing, Duckworth was returning to his station when he met Brisbane whose news now set in train a curious sequence of events which was to produce the last major squadron action of the war. Having sighted nine sail heading south on

Christmas Day 1805 Duckworth began chasing them, but on the forenoon of the 26th, as the leading British ships drew closer, it was seen that only five or six of the strangers were ships of the line.

Unfortunately, Duckworth's squadron was strung out in a long line extending many miles astern of his flagship, the *Superb*, which under the command of Richard Goodwin Keats, an officer popularly believed to be the finest seaman in the Navy, was well in advance of her consorts. This persuaded Duckworth not to bring the

4

5

enemy to battle and the admiral fell back on the mass of his ships, dispatched the frigate *Amethyst* home with the news and, being short of water, set course west for the Leeward Islands. Duckworth's inexplicable decision to permit Willaumez, for it was not Allemand, to escape without gathering his squadron and continuing the pursuit, was compounded by the choice of the Leewards as his next destination. Duckworth's post at Cadiz came under the Commander-in-Chief, Mediterranean, Lord Collingwood, who was exceedingly displeased that Duckworth had not returned to his station.

Duckworth's decision has been attributed to his desire for glory and the example of Nelson. He sent Captain Dunn of the *Acasta*, 40, ahead to make arrangements to water the squadron at St Kitts, and on 12 January 1806 he anchored at Carlisle Bay, Barbados, where he was joined by the then commander of the Windward Station, Rear-Admiral Alexander Cochrane in *Northumberland*, with *Atlas*, both of 74-guns. Both admirals were ignorant of Leissègues' arrival in the West Indies.

Meanwhile, intelligence of the departures from Brest had only reached the Admiralty in London on Christmas Eve and even then it underestimated the strength of the escaped divisions by five of the line. Nevertheless, in conformity with Barham's policy, two squadrons were immediately prepared, one under Vice-Admiral Warren (in the British *Foudroyant*) to make for Madeira and, if nothing had been learned of the enemy, to reinforce Admirals Dacres and Cochrane in the West Indies (the

effort was not wasted for in March he ran into and captured Linois' squadron – see pages 28-9). The second, under Sir Richard Strachan, now a rear-admiral, was to proceed directly to St Helena and thereafter to join Commodore Sir Home Popham and his force on its way to take Cape Town from the Dutch (see pages 64-5). Neither force was ready before the end of January and matters were left in Duckworth's hands for, on 1 February, the vice-admiral was disturbed to learn from Commander Nathaniel Cochrane of the *Kingfisher* that three French line of battle ships had been seen making for San Domingo, whither Duckworth now headed, picking up the *Epervier*, 14 and the frigate *Magicienne* en route.

Leissègues force had been mauled by the weather after it had met and abandoned the chase of Brisbane's convoy but, having disembarked the troops for San Domingo, the French force had been rejoined by its stragglers and was ready for sea. Seeing a British force in the offing, at 0730 on 6 February, the French slipped their cables and, with the light breeze at north-northwest, sailed out of Occa Bay on a westerly course. The French formed line of battle led by *Alexandre*, 80, followed by Leissègues' flagship, *Impérial*, 130, *Diomède*, *Jupiter* and *Brave*, all of 74-guns, with the 40-gun frigates *Félicté*, *Comète* and the corvette *Diligente* forming a second, parallel line inshore.

Duckworth also formed two lines (2, 3), signalling his intention of cutting off the three leading French vessels. His starboard column consisted of the 74s *Superb*,

Northumberland and *Spencer* with the *Agamemnon*, 64; the port column was led by Rear-Admiral Louis in the *Canopus*, 80, supported by the 74s *Donegal* and *Atlas*. The frigates *Acasta* and *Magicienne*, with the sloops *Kingfisher* and *Epervier* lay to starboard of the line of battleships. By 0800 the British were in reasonable order, the *Canopus* just coming abeam of the *Spencer*, but station-keeping was frustrated by the light wind and weed on some of the hulls. *Agamemnon* fell back as did the whole port line. The starboard column to windward, fared much better as the breeze hauled round to the northeast, gaining on the French squadron as both ran to leeward at about eight knots. Shortening sail at 1010, *Superb*'s guns opened fire on the *Alexandre*, whereupon *Northumberland* engaged *Impérial*. On her leader's starboard quarter, *Spencer* commenced a cannonade of the *Diomède*, her forward guns also hitting the French flagship (4).

Being hard-pressed, Garreau of the *Alexandre* hauled out of line to port, trying to pass across the stern of *Northumberland* and attempting to rake *Spencer* by crossing her bows. Unfortunately Garreau misjudged *Spencer*'s speed and Stopford's ship crossed ahead of his own, raking *Alexandre* in the process, before wearing round onto the port tack. Now parallel with *Alexandre*, *Spencer*'s larboard guns poured their shot into the French ship.

Although Stopford, by his bold manoeuvre, received some shot from *Superb* and *Northumberland* in the smoke and confusion, his turning of the tables delivered *Alexandre* into the hands of Rear-Admiral Louis's port division as they passed across her bow then bore up towards the main cannonade. The effect of this was to dismast her and reduce her to a shambles (5). At about 1100, Stopford's fire had ignited the *Alexandre* and he too swung away to join the main action which had become general, with *Canopus* engaging *Impérial*, *Donegal* the *Brave*, and *Atlas, Jupiter*. Shortly afterwards *Alexandre*'s colours came down and ten minutes later those of the *Brave* followed, Captain Malcolm of the *Donegal* having crossed her stern and subjected her to a tremendous raking fire before swinging his ship round to the west again. *Atlas* had now moved ahead of *Jupiter* in support of *Canopus* and *Donegal* now came up on the French ship's starboard side, over-ran her and having set a course across her bows, caused the *Jupiter* to collide. The instant *Jupiter*'s bowsprit loomed over the *Donegal*'s port quarter, it was secured and, without further resistance, the *Jupiter* was boarded and taken in tow. Captain Malcolm, seeing the main focus of the action moving to the west, ordered the *Acasta* to take possession of the *Brave*.

Duckworth, in *Superb*, supported by *Northumberland*,

6

remained in action with the van of the French fleet and had ordered his own ship to overpower the three-decker and her second. For this reason *Atlas* had left *Jupiter* after firing into her, and had come up with and begun to join the vessels engaging the *Impérial*. At this juncture, with the air filled with dense smoke and the confusing concussions of numerous guns, *Atlas*'s tiller jammed, she received fire from the *Diomède*, fouled *Canopus* and lost her bowsprit. Captain Pym coolly had his sails hauled aback and disengaged from *Canopus*, to fall alongside *Diomède* and empty the broadsides of his starboard guns into her. Leissègues' force was shattered and lay close to the shore, between Punta Nisao and Punta Catalana. The *Impérial* swung inshore to run aground, whereupon her last standing mast fell (6).

Having been pounded by *Atlas* and latterly *Spencer*, with the laggardly *Agamemnon* finally getting into action, *Dioméde* followed the flagship aground a few moments later and thus also lay in the shallows, dismasted. Rear-Admiral Louis disdained to haul round after his Commander-in-Chief, but continued to fire into the *Impérial*, supported by *Spencer* and *Atlas*. When, however, the *Impérial* ceased fire and numbers of her crew were seen flocking on the upper deck, Louis stood offshore and, ignoring the fire continuing from the beached *Diomède*, rejoined Duckworth.

Seeing the fate of their principals, the French frigates *Comète*, *Félicité* and corvette *Diligente* made good their escape, as did most of the crews of the *Impérial* and *Diomède*. Both of these grounded ships had lost their bottoms on the reefs and were sent on fire on the 8th by the *Acasta* and *Magicienne* (7).

Although the British fleet had endured a terrific fire from the French only the *Northumberland* had lost her main mast at the end of the action. Casualties of 74 killed and 264 wounded on the British side were far lighter than the French, who suffered some 1500 men either killed or wounded. Of the prizes, *Brave* foundered on her way to Britain, *Alexandre* was too badly damaged to be of further use, but *Jupiter* was added to the British fleet and named *Maida* in honour of the action just then fought by Sir John Stuart's small force in Calabria. Duckworth's conduct was not considered meritorious enough to warrant further honours, though success justified his desertion of Cadiz. As the outgoing First Lord of the Admiralty, Lord Barham, wrote, the victory 'puts us out of all fear from another predatory war in the West Indies'.

7. 'Sir J. T. Duckworth's Action off St. Domingo, Feby 6th 1806', coloured aquatint engraved by Thomas Sutherland after an original by Thomas Whitcombe, 1 February 1817. *NMM neg 2825*

7

1

French frigate squadrons, 1806

2

ALTHOUGH French battle squadrons escaped the British blockade from time to time, they were rarely able to profit fully from their freedom, being relentlessly hunted and, either brought to battle, or reconfined by their implacable opponents. The escape of cruiser squadrons, however, was another matter, particularly given the exposure of British trade, and in its frigates the French navy invested the best of its commanders and crews. As for the ships themselves, they were almost always larger than their British counterparts, usually 40-gun vessels, capable of acting as store and troop ships reinforcing distant French possessions, before reverting to the traditional role of commerce raider.

Captain La Marre La Meillerie commanded one such squadron which ought to have given a good account of itself. On the evening of 26 February 1806, the four frigates and a brig escaped from Cadiz where they had languished since Trafalgar. Learning of their preparation for sea, Lord Collingwood, the Commander-in-Chief, had withdrawn the blockade to tempt them out, leaving only a light force of the 38-gun frigate *Hydra* and the sloop *Moselle*, 18, as observers. But the plan almost backfired when, on the 23rd, a strong easterly wind got up and slowly drove the British detachment too far to the

west, enabling La Meillerie's flying squadron to escape. However, despite the lateness of the hour and the onset of darkness, they did not get away undetected, and Captain Mundy of the *Hydra* steered a parallel course, with *Moselle* in support. Just before midnight, Mundy ordered Carden of the *Moselle* to search for Collingwood and appraise him of the fact that a French squadron was standing to the westward. Mundy himself then gave vigorous chase and by daylight had come up with the brig *Furet*, aftermost ship of La Meillerie's force. The brig struck her colours after a single broadside from *Hydra*, while the remainder of the squadron abandoned her (1).

The conduct of La Meillerie's four frigates is astonishing, given the weakness of the opposition and their own combined force, which consisted of *Hortense*, 40, *Hermione*, 40, *Thémis*, 36 and *Rhin*, 40. Having visited Senegal, Cayenne and cruised off the West Indies, La Meillerie's frigates were returning to France, bound for Rochefort, when, on 27 July, they were sighted by HMS *Mars*, 74, the lookout ship of the blockading squadron under Captain Richard Goodwin Keats (2) then off the port. Captain Oliver of the *Mars* signalled the nearest British ship, the 64-gun *Africa*, that an enemy was in sight and promptly gave chase. Once again, La Meillerrie's squadron ran. All night the chase went on, until with the coming day, *Mars*

1. 'The Capture of Le Furet of 16 guns from a French Squadron by the Hydra off Cadiz, Febry 26th 1806', lithograph engraved by Paul Gauci after an original by George Chambers, printed by Graf & Soret, no date. *NMM ref PAG7115*

2. 'Sir R G Keats, K.B.', anonymous stipple engraving published by J Stratford, 1 March 1810. *NMM ref PAD3466*

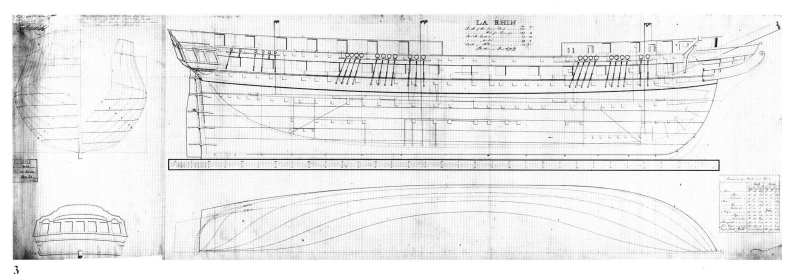

3

began to close the *Rhin*, which had fallen behind her consorts. At this juncture, seeing the British ship alone, La Meillerie finally ordered his ships to fall back in line on the larboard tack to support the *Rhin*, a posture he maintained until the middle of the afternoon when, intimidated by the continuing approach of the *Mars*, his nerve seems to have failed him and he bore away, abandoning the *Rhin* to her fate. Oliver now pressed his quarry and at 1800, as a heavy squall of wind and rain favoured the two-decker, *Mars* ranged up on the *Rhin*'s lee quarter. Oliver fired a shot prior to his full broadside, whereupon Captain Chesneau of the *Rhin*, struck his colours. His frigate was to be purchased into the Royal Navy (3) and was later responsible for the apprehension of several privateers. As for La Meillerie, his conduct seems to have gone uncondemned, but such apparent pusillanimity fed stories of British superiority against all odds and tended to breed a dangerous conceit.

4

By September, Keats had been relieved off Rochefort by Commodore Sir Samuel Hood in the *Centaur*, 74. Hood's squadron consisted of *Windsor Castle*, 98, the 74-gun ships *Achille*, *Monarch*, *Revenge* and *Mars*, with the gun-brig *Atalante* as despatch vessel. At about one o'clock in the morning of the 25th Hood's ships were standing inshore on the larboard tack, the wind being just east of north, heading for Chasseron lighthouse about twenty miles away. The squadron was somewhat dispersed, but the *Monarch* made a signal for an enemy in sight and Hood threw out the night signal to form line in anticipation of the strangers being ships of the line. Shortly afterwards, however, they were identified as frigates which, seeing the approaching British simultaneously, put up their helms, set all possible sail and made off to the south-southwest. Hood immediately ordered a general chase and the squadron responded, with *Monarch* leading and *Revenge* well in the rear.

The enemy comprised four heavy 40-gun frigates, *Gloire*, *Infatigable*, *Minerve* and *Armide*, the 36-gun *Thetis* and the brig corvettes *Lynx* and *Sylphe*. Under Commodore Soleil, they had left Rochefort the previous evening and were bound for the West Indies with stores and troops on board. After four hours of hard chasing in a lively sea and very heavy Biscay swell, *Monarch* was almost up with the rear French frigate, the *Armide*, with *Centaur* still eight miles astern and the remaining British ships lagging behind her. *Armide* now hoisted French colours and *Monarch* engaged with her bow-chasers, *Armide* responding with her stern guns. At about 0600 the *Infatigable* hauled round to the north and made a bid to return to Rochefort, but *Mars* altered course after her. The most southerly and distant of the French ships, the *Thetis*, *Lynx* and *Sylphe* now ran on and escaped, no British ship being capable of catching them, but the *Gloire* and *Minerve* fell back in support of the *Armide*.

Monarch now came under the combined fire of the *Armide* and the *Gloire*, suffering in proportion, for in the

5

3. The lines and profile draught of the *Rhin*, as captured.
NMM neg DR7056

4. 'Sir Samuel Hood's engagement with the French squadron off Rochefort, Septr 25, 1806 . . . the Monarch engaging La Minerve, L'Armide & La Gloire', coloured aquatint engraved by J Clark and J Hamble, publishd by Edward Orme, no date.
NMM ref PAH8049

5. 'Sir Samuel Hood's engagement with the French squadron off Rochefort, Septr 25, 1806, Representing the Monarch with her two prizes in tow La Minerve & L'Armide', coloured aquatint engraved by J Clark and J Hamble, published by Edward Orme, no date.
NMM ref PAH8051

6. 'Hood's action off Rochefort, 25 September 1806: bringing home the prizes', oil painting by Francis Sartorius (c1775-1831), 1807. Although signed and dated, this painting bears little resemblance to the events it purports to depict: not only are the nearest prizes a three-decker and a two-decker instead of frigates, but they are under tow by a 50 and a 64, neither of which type was represented in Hood's squadron.
NMM ref BHC0574

heavy swell the lower deck gun crews of the British ship were frequently unable to open their ports (4). In about twenty minutes, despite a heavy fire from the *Monarch*'s starboard battery, the cannonade of the French ships had reduced the British two-decker to an unmanageable state, and she dropped back, firing into *Minerve*. At this point, however, the *Centaur* arrived on the scene to take on *Gloire* and *Armide*, leaving *Monarch* to batter the *Minerve* alone. Despite the spirited action of the French commanders, the British now gained the ascendant and just before noon, Captain Langlois of the *Armide* struck his colours to the *Centaur* and a few moments later Collet of the *Minerve* struck to the *Monarch* (5). By this time, some distance away, Captain Lukin of the *Mars* had compelled Giradias of the *Infatigable* to surrender and, having taken possession, he made sail to join the flagship. Despite the highly creditable defence put up by the French frigates, Soleil's losses were such that he could entertain no further expectation other than his own destruction and he accordingly swung *Gloire* away to the westwards. Sir Samuel Hood ordered the *Centaur* to chase and, with the undamaged *Mars* now joining the flagship, the two crowded on sail in pursuit. By about 1430 the *Mars* was in a position to open fire on the fleeing *Gloire* and half an hour later she too hauled down her colours.

The British ships were chiefly damaged in their rigging (6), it having been the clear intention of the French to reduce the effectiveness of the enemy and try to escape. Generally casualties aboard the British ships were less than might have been expected from the violence of the enemy's fire, though they were not inconsiderable aboard the *Monarch*. The total on board both *Centaur* and *Monarch* amounted to 9 dead and 29 injured. Among the latter was Hood, whose right arm was amputated after being shattered by a musket ball.

The four French frigates were all fine, comparatively new ships of over 1000 tons each and all were subsequently taken into the Royal Navy – *Minerve* as *Alceste*, *Infatigable* as *Immortalité* and *Armide* and *Gloire* under their original names. It has been conjectured that the quantity of stores and troops they had on board rendered them slower than they might have been, though the conditions clearly favoured the 74-gun ships and the relative expertise and sea-time of the opposing crews needs no undue emphasis.

6

The destruction of Linois

THE brief hiatus in hostilities caused by the Peace of Amiens enabled the French to reinforce their overseas possessions. Chief among the squadrons dispatched in this period was that of Rear-Admiral Linois who sailed from Brest on 6 March 1803. Linois' flag flew in the 74-gun *Marengo* and he had with him two troop transports and several frigates. His orders were to reoccupy Pondicherry, returned to France as part of the settlement of the Peace of Amiens, but the renewal of war prevented this and for some time his ships were loose in the Indian Ocean. Although Linois's force was impressive, it achieved little overall and disgusted its imperial master, particularly by its failure to bag the

homeward East India Company's China ships, valued at some £8 millions sterling, as described in an earlier volume in this series, *The Campaign of Trafalgar*. Linois took isolated British merchantmen and by March 1806, in company with the frigate *Belle Poule*, 40-guns, was making his way home, raiding trade between St Helena and the Canaries. Shortly after midnight on the morning of the 13th, seeing to the eastward several sails which they took for merchant ships in convoy steering to the southeast, Linois ordered a chase.

The force proved to be a squadron under Vice-Admiral Warren, flying his flag in *Foudroyant*, 80, with *London*, 90, the frigate *Amazon* and five other ships to

3

leeward. As pointed out in a previous section, Warren was searching for the squadrons of Willaumez and Leissègues which had recently escaped from Brest. With the wind at west-southwest, Linois ran down towards the 'convoy' but was spotted from the *London*, which was stationed to weather but astern of the flagship on account of her poor sailing qualities. Observing Captain Sir Harry Neale of the *London* making sail, firing blue lights and hauling his wind, Captain William Parker of the *Amazon* followed suit, though he could see nothing of the enemy. As day broke at about 0530, Linois ordered *Belle Poule* to run, and *Marengo* engaged *London* which, after a few broadsides, induced Linois to sheer away (1). Damaged aloft, *London* was in no position to pursue, but the other British ships were now closing. The *Marengo* had herself sustained considerable damage and was unable to escape *London*'s fire to which was briefly added that of *Amazon* as she made after *Belle Poule*.

At about 0830 *Amazon* overtook the French frigate and engaged her in a running fight. Meanwhile the remaining ships of Warren's squadron were closing on *Marengo*, led by *Ramillies*, 74, which opened fire and, with *Repulse*, 74, and *Foudroyant* hard on her heels, compelled the hapless Linois to strike his colours at about 1100 (2). A few miles away at about the same time, Parker's frigate forced Captain Bruilhac to order the *Belle Poule* to surrender.

British losses in the affair were fairly light, but the French suffered heavily, the *Marengo* having 63 men killed and 83 wounded, among whom were Linois and his flag captain, Vrignault. There was not as much difference in the broadside weight of metal fired by the two ships, although *London* had the psychological advantage of being a three-decker, and *Marengo* was badly cut up in the action (3). It cannot be claimed that neither Linois nor

his ships' companies had had sufficient sea-time to meet the enemy on equal terms, the more so since *London* was a poor sailer and *Amazon* inferior to the *Belle Poule*. All in all, the French admiral deserved the obloquy heaped on him by Napoleon after his exchange. Compared with the privateer Robert Surcouf, Linois' extensive cruise cannot be viewed as anything other than a costly exercise in failure and the best that can be said of it was that it had done some material damage, and had a great moral effect. Of his ships, only the frigate *Sémillante* remained at large in the Indian Ocean.

After the action, the ships were overtaken by bad weather and in the strong wind and heavy seas, suffered further. Already battle-damaged aloft, *Ramillies* was worst affected and was almost dismasted, to roll helplessly until the weather moderated and her people could effect jury repairs (4).

All illustrations are from the manuscript journal of Ducros-Legris, NMM ref LOG/F/2. There are seventy-seven full-page illustration; those reproduced and their folio numbers are as follows:

Fol 60. The battle with *London*, 13 March 1806.
NMM neg D9228

Fol 63. The battle with *London*, 13 March 1806.
NMM neg D9229

Fol 64. The badly damaged *Marengo* after the battle.
NMM neg D9227

Fol 66. *Ramillies* dismasted in a storm on the voyage home.
NMM neg D9230

4

The foundations of seapower: seamanship

AT the heart of the Napoleonic conflict lay the vast resources of manpower available in Europe to the leading protagonists, and demands on this reached their apogee in the post-Trafalgar period. On the one hand Imperial France drew on professionals, conscripts from France and her empire and, at varying times, her allies to field the Grand Army; on the other Great Britain, with her small professional army, poured her manpower into her navy. Towards the end, both sides suffered from a dilution of quality, due to the length of the war but, thanks to her immense maritime

base, Great Britain was *just* able to sustain a qualitative advantage sufficient to man and maintain both her warships and her merchant marine. Although some expedient measures were resorted to, such as the employment of Chinese and lascar seamen in Indiamen and the use of American merchant ships to augment British-registered bottoms, nevertheless it was an ascendancy that won the war.

The cost of this was appalling and it relied entirely upon wholesale abduction and virtual enslavement by the state through impressment. Parliament cared nothing for the welfare of seafarers, though it assiduously considered the supply of skilled seamen. In order to provide the Royal Navy with its raw material, Acts had been passed in the reigns of Queen Anne and George III to supplement able seaman with apprentices and maintain these young men free of impressment during the term of their indentures. Moreover, and for no other reason other than to check desertion, merchant seaman had been compelled to sign Articles of Agreement binding them to a ship by an act of 1729. To the general competence of the able seaman to hand, reef and steer, must be added a familiarity with arms. This ability was, of course, what made his nurturing a matter of importance to the state. He and his fellows formed the reservoir from which the highly unpopular Royal Navy drew its so often unpaid prime seamen (1).

The lot of the common sailor, irrespective of ensign, was a grim one and men went to sea largely out of neces-

sity. The only thing that could be said in favour of serving in a merchant ship was that one was paid regularly and the life was relatively more congenial. Threat of the press was ever-present, especially when approaching port, and examples such as the removal of an entire whaler's crew off Spurn Head were not uncommon. Even East Indiamen were not unmolested. In the Downs, homeward bound from Canton, the *Nottingham* was plundered of her entire crew and taken up the Thames by a scratch crew of 'ticket-porters and Greenwich pensioners' drafted for the purpose. While all the officers of an Indiamen were untouchable, only a master, the first mate and the apprentices of an ordinary merchant ship possessed press exemptions. The isolation of the maritime population from the mass of British society prevented any widespread protests being raised. As one officer wrote, 'men-o'-war must be manned', and manned they were, though often below the established complement and with a disproportionate number of landmen and boys, particularly during the post-Trafalgar period when the Royal Navy reached its greatest expansion.

It is impossible to judge the numbers of men at sea across the whole spectrum of Britain's maritime endeavour, but 113,600 seamen and 31,400 marines served the Royal Navy during 1812, the former figure having shown a steady increase from previous years. Although the majority of men on the lower deck were British, men of other European nationalities were not uncommon, as well as Americans and blacks. Nevertheless, ill-used and deprived of the most basic human rights as they were, it was the seamen of the Royal Navy who provided the muscle and blood necessary to work and fight the multitude of ships and vessels in commission.

Within the constitution of a ship's company, a heirarchy existed from the petty officers to the meanest whose duties were the most menial. Great skills resided in certain groups, without which the handling of sailing warships was impossible. In addition to the obvious specialist warrant officers like the carpenter, gunner,

1. 'Mending a sail', watercolour by William Payne, no date. One of a series showing seamen going about their business at Dover about 1815. *NMM ref PAD8641*

2. 'Reefing Topsails', coloured aquatint engraved by Edward Duncan after an original by W J Huggins, published by the artist, January 1832. *NMM ref PAF3760*

3. 'A two-decker furling sails', brown wash by Robert Cantiloe Joy, 1835. *NMM ref PAF6084*

4. 'Stowing the cable', anonymous black & watercolour pen & ink, no date. A large proportion of the crew was involved in handling the huge and cumbersome cable every time the ship up-anchored. *NMM ref PA15027*

5

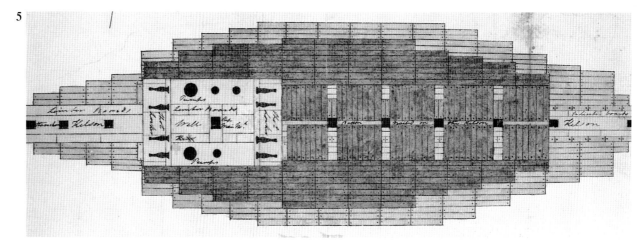

6

sailmaker and so on, the topmen were the cream of the able seamen (2). These men spent much time aloft and in the complex routines of handling sails and spars, their importance cannot be over-stated, for a snarled line, a jammed block or cleat, could mean loss of gear and, not improbably in a tight corner, that of the ship (3). Moreover, a mixture of basic training, example and brutish coercion seems to have capitalised upon a pre-disposition among Britons to become seamen, such that the basic skills were available when required.

Almost nothing today is comparable with the orchestrated teamwork necessary to handle a sailing man-of-war (4). To enumerate its complexities and multiple skills, from carpentry to knotting and splicing, from cool judgement to competent navigation, is a subject in itself. Each officer and man had a station for action and a station for ship-handling and while a watch could handle the ship in a routine manoeuvre in moderate weather, all hands were often required when matters became marginal.

Whilst the Royal Navy acquired an essentially deserved reputation for the brilliance of its ship-handling generally, the manoeuvring of large men-of-war was always a difficult matter, particularly so in confined waters, and most vulnerably, in and out of port. Collisions with other ships were not infrequent in these circumstances, though little real damage was often sustained; while groundings were reprobated, but accepted as part and parcel of the job. Some commanders made a fetish of sail-handling, often neglecting other matters, such as gunnery, but the general standard was competent. It should not be forgotten, however, that much of the technical detail was supervised, not by the captain, but by the master, most of whom had served in merchant ships and knew as much as was then known about stability and stowage (5). Although the training of merchant officers was largely a matter of luck, not regulation, it would be very wrong to imagine them to be useless. The most distinguished navigators of the day rose from a mercantile background and the Royal Navy relied upon an intake of mercantile officers who were given warrants as masters and mates. The sailing master of a man-of-war was not only her chief navigator, but also her chief ship-handler, both in ordinary manoeuvring and in action; he was also the man responsible for her fabric and the loading and stowage of stores and hold, a very important function and one which only training in merchantmen fitted him. While in theory lieutenants were supposed to be able to navigate, the relaxed Georgian attitude to the regulations in respect of age and ability, and the pre-eminence of class and connections, ensured that, even in the period under review when the professional training of young gentlemen was very much improved, great reliance was still placed upon masters. This was recognised in 1805 when a long-standing grievance of these senior warrant officers was addressed by the Admiralty, and they were conferred equal status with commissioned officers.

But even these men were unable to make good the deficiencies of their time. The lack of good charts remained a problem and rendered the knowledge of latitude and longitude less useful when close to danger; much had still to be learned about hydrodynamics and magnetism, while thinking among naval officers tended to be conservative. Problems were resolved by rule of thumb, experience and inspired guesswork. Nevertheless, a ship could feel her way about using the traditional trio of skills, leadline, log and lookout. If she did get in trouble, she often possessed the means of saving herself (6).

A sailing man-of-war, victualled for months and properly stored, was capable of sustaining herself on home or remote stations. Such a vessel was remarkably self-sufficient, possessing in her company and stores, the means to effect repairs or make good wear and tear (7). Knotting and splicing during and after actions broken off for lack of manoeuvrability, often allowed an engagement to be renewed. Storm and battle damage could be repaired at sea, leaks could be stopped and shot holes plugged. If time permitted, basic surveys could be carried out and even meat casks refilled on occasion. Wood and watering parties went ashore when necessary, while arrangements were made to supply certain units of the fleet with comestibles on a regular basis. The blockading squadrons off the Atlantic coasts were supplied with fresh vegetables, meat and water by hoys from Plymouth, while those in the Mediterranean bought bullocks at Tetuan and other North African ports.

All these complex, interrelated skills and influences had, by the first decade of the nineteenth century, produced a navy that was beginning to think of itself in a more cohesive way as 'the Service'. It was imbued by an esprit-de-corps which acted upon the conduct of its commanders as much as the intimidating wording of their commissions, and filtered down throughout the many layers and levels of responsibility in a man-of-war to inspirit the denizens of the lower deck. The crux of the matter was that, despite its deficiencies and shortcomings, the Royal Navy of 1806-1814 was able to man and maintain at sea, some 600 warships, often with little sickness on board. As Napoleon ruefully reflected in exile at St Helena, wherever there was water to float a ship, there you would find a British man-of-war.

5. 'A Plan of the Crescent's Iron Ballast as stowed by the orders of Captain Wm Ge Lobb. Deptford May 1799', pen and ink and watercolour by W H Dillon, 6 May 1799. *NMM ref PAF6016*

6. 'Getting up a kedge anchor', coloured etching by John Augustus Atkinson after his own original, published by William Miller and James Walker, 1 January 1807. Kedge anchors were generally used to move a ship when wind or tide was adverse; the anchor was carried out in a boat for some distance, dropped, and then by hauling in on the capstan the ship was run up and over the anchor, when the process might be repeated. *NMM ref PAD7764*

7. 'Immersion of HMS Samarang in the Sarawak', tinted lithograph engraved by G Hawkins after an original by Richards, published by Reeve, Bentham & Reeve, 1848. A ship could be heaved down by its own crew for 'careening', to clean or repair the bottom. *NMM ref PAD6128*

7

1

Frigates: second line of the blockade

THE global nature of British naval strategy required an immense number of cruisers to be employed and while this generic term covered vessels of disparate size, from heavy frigates to cutters and luggers, it was the Royal Navy's frigates, and to a lesser extent sloops, which provided the most effective force. Such ships were sent 'upon a cruise' to protect trade and intercept contraband cargoes carried in neutral merchantmen, to gather intelligence, harry the enemy's coastal communications and whenever and wherever possible, to bring him to battle. The Royal Navy's cruisers also played their part in fleet strategy, forming the inside line of major blockading forces and often forming the only watch on smaller ports. Many of these cruiser captains achieved great results and it was their daring enterprises that established much of the folklore attaching to the Royal Navy of the day.

Perhaps the most charismatic of such cruiser captains was Lord Cochrane, heir to the Earl of Dundonald, who commanded a series of ships, most of which he made famous, from the tiny brig *Speedy*, whose broadside he claimed he could carry in his pocket, to the *Imperieuse* whose exploits at the Basque Road are featured later. In the spring of 1806, Cochrane was in command of the small fir-built 32-gun frigate *Pallas*, under the orders of Vice-Admiral Thornborough, whose squadron was watching Rochefort. On 14 May, with the wind at north-

east, Cochrane received orders from Thornborough to reconnoitre Allemand's squadron which lay at anchor in the roadstead, covered by batteries on the Île d'Aix. *Pallas* passed the ship sloop *Kingfisher* of 16 guns, whose commander had been given strict orders not to pass within Chassiron lighthouse for fear of taking excessive risks, and stood boldly in towards the French anchorage. Cochrane, who had carried out such a mission before, then anchored just within range of the batteries. Rear-Admiral Allemand immediately ordered the 40-gun frigate *Minerve*, supported by the 16-gun brig corvettes *Lynx*, *Sylphe* and *Palinure* to intercept and destroy the British ship, instructing the *Armide* and *Infatigable* to prepare themselves to assist on signalled instructions.

The wind being in favour of the French, they set all sail including royals and studding sails in an attempt to catch the British frigate before she should escape. Having ascertained Allemand's strength, Cochrane weighed, set his topsails and lay-to in a provocative manner. Holding his fire until the enemy ships were within close range, *Pallas*'s opening fire brought down the main topsail yard of one of the brigs. There followed a brisk action, interrupted by frequent course alterations to avoid grounding on the shoals (1). By about 1300 when under fire from the shore batteries, Cochrane had worked just to windward of the *Minerve*, whereupon *Pallas* fired several broadsides into the larger French frigate and then closed to board.

At this instant, however, *Minerve* struck a shoal and stopped dead, the *Pallas* running into her with such violence that the spars of the two ships tore away (2). *Pallas*'s loaded guns were driven inboard, whereupon they were discharged into *Minerve*'s hull, a broadside which although only comprising 12pdrs was enough to drive the French from their guns. Cochrane's attention was now upon the approach of *Infatigable* and *Armide* and he cut loose from *Minerve*. Fortunately drawing less water, *Pallas* was able to set some sail, though she had lost many of her upper spars, as well as a cathead and bower anchor. Drawing away from the devastated *Minerve*, *Pallas* was taken in tow by Seymour's *Kingfisher*. The two French frigates did not follow and Cochrane, confident that *Minerve* was a wreck, coolly retired.

The determination of the French to strike at sources of British wealth is exemplified by the cruise of Commodore Leduc. Victualled for five months, Leduc left Lorient early on the morning of 28 March 1806 in the 40-gun frigate *Revanche*, in company with the *Guerrière*, 40, *Syrène*, 36 and brig corvette *Néarque*, of 16 guns. Leduc had been master of a Dunkerque whaler and in consequence of his professional knowledge was directed to cruise in the polar regions, off the coasts of Iceland, Greenland and Spitsbergen in order to destroy British and Russian whaling ships. However, he was immediately spotted by the British frigate *Niobe*, which chased and captured the

Néarque, although the rest of the squadron escaped.

The winter was unduly long and ice prevented either the whalers or their pursuers from closing the Spitsbergen shore. In fact the ice-field had shifted south and it was not until the end of May that his ships had reached the ice edge in latitude 72° North. Although they came in sight of Spitsbergen on 12 June, they failed to reach the island and, beset by fogs, *Guerrière* became separated and thereafter proceeded independently. However, the French frigates had by now discovered the whaling fleet (3) and, wearing Swedish colours, had closed and captured several before they could escape in the ice.

Reports of the presence of enemy cruisers in the Arctic had also reached London via Hull by 12 July. Three frigates, *Phoebe*, 36, and *Thames*, 32, and the 38-gun *Blanche* were ordered to rendezvous and operate under the orders of Captain Lavie of the last named. *Phoebe* and *Thames*, learning that one of the French frigates had become detached and was operating alone, did not wait for Lavie but sailed north without delay. Lavie followed on receipt of further news that *Guerrière* alone had taken several ships off the Faeroes. At 1030 on 18 July her lookout spotted a sail heading towards the British frigate from the east-northeast. By now scurvy had broken out among the crew of *Guerrière* and Captain Hubert was in need of water, so was making for the Faeroes. Seemingly unaware that the strange sail was British, Hubert continued to beat to the west, with Lavie approaching from the

2

3

southwest under a light stern-wind. At about 1500 Hubert realised his error, bore up and spread all sail, but he was too late. Under a press of canvas, *Blanche* out-ran him and at 0145 on the 19th poured two broadsides into *Guerrière* before that ship could respond. After a running fight of three quarters of an hour during which the French gunners failed to bring down any of *Blanche's* tophamper while his own mizzen topmast was shot away, Hubert hauled down his colours (4). Already having lost 37 men to scurvy, with many more weakened by the disease, *Blanche* had accounted for a further 50 in killed and wounded.

Meanwhile *Phoebe* and *Thames* failed to find *Revanche* and *Syrène* which had finally taken station off Cape Farewell after watering in Iceland. Leduc hoped to capture the

whalers which had entered the Davis Strait and succeeded in taking several British and Russian trading vessels, letting his prisoners go in one, the *Rose*, whose master reported the sickly state of the two French frigates on his arrival at Hull. A further three British frigates, the *Amethyst*, *Princess Charlotte* and *Diana* were now sent after Leduc, but their quest was unsuccessful. By the time Leduc anchored off Lorient on 22 September, his squadron had destroyed one Russian and 28 British vessels, the majority of which were whalers, but the cost had been half his squadron.

Under the guns of the *Blanche*, *Guerrière* had arrived in Yarmouth Road on 28 July and was purchased into the Royal Navy. In addition to his prize money, Captain Lavie received the honour of knighthood. Leduc's cruise caused consternation in the whaling ports and had far greater a moral than a material effect. It ought to have been more successful, but the ability of the British cruisers to keep the sea and avoid the curse of scurvy was a critical factor in limiting Leduc's depredations. While the British were operating in the nineteenth century, Leduc languished in the eighteenth.

The workings of the blockade often had far-reaching implications. In November 1808, the 40-gun frigate *Thétis*, Captain Pinsum, slipped out of Lorient loaded with reinforcements for Martinique, then suffering under its own British naval blockade. Spotted by the frigate *Amethyst* off Île de Groix on the evening of the 10th, Captain Seymour signalled her escape to the other British ships offshore and made sail in pursuit. At about 2100 the two frigates exchanged fire from their chase guns with *Amethyst* overhauling *Thétis* as both vessels ran before the wind. After about an hour of an intelligently-fought running battle,

4

5

with *Amethyst* drawing ahead, Seymour put his helm up, crossed Pinsum's bow and poured a raking broadside into *Thétis* before turning away and running off before the wind again. In the next few moments the mizzen masts of both vessels fell.

Pinsum now mustered his crew and the troops he had embarked, determined to carry his opponent by boarding but, at the moment of collision, he was met with a furious cannonade, followed by a succession of devastating broadsides which reduced *Thétis* to a shambles, dismounting thirteen guns, beating in her sides and causing terrible losses among her crew. Shortly after midnight,

the British boarded and took *Thétis*, whose two remaining masts fell as the action concluded. An hour later *Triumph*, 74, and *Shannon*, 38, arrived to assist in clearing the prize and transferring prisoners.

By intercepting essential supplies, this action reduced Martinique's chances of resistance, and five months later Seymour and the *Amethyst* were to have a similar effect on another French colony thousands of miles distant. On the night of 5/6 April 1809 the 40-gun *Niemen*, crowded with supplies for Île de France (Mauritius) was chased and brought to action, the superb gunnery of the British frigate reducing her opponent to a wreck (6).

6

1. 'His Majesty's Ship Pallas passing to Windward of La Minerve and between her, and La Lynx, Palinure and Sylph Brigs at one o'clock on the 14th May 1806 under the Batteries of the Isle D'Aix, with a view of the French Squadron', tinted aquatint and etching by Nicholas Pocock after his own original, published by the artist, 15 December 1806.
NMM ref PAH6336

2. 'His Majesty's Ship Pallas, after having run La Minerve on board, with a view of the Rochefort Squadron and the Frigates sent to assist La Minerve and Brigs', tinted aquatint and etching by Nicholas Pocock after his own original, published by the artist, 15 December 1806.
NMM ref PAH6337

3. 'A whaler and other vessels in a light breeze', oil painting by John Askew, 1788.
NMM ref BHC1064

4. 'Capture of La Gueriere by Blanche – July 19th 1806', coloured aquatint engraved by Thomas Sutherland after an original by Thomas Whitcombe, no date.
NMM ref PAD5763

5. 'To Sir Michael Seymour Bart, this View of his first Action when commanding His Majesty's Ship Amethyst capturing the French Frigate Thetis on the 10th Novbr 1808 . . . inscribed by . . . Robert Dodd', aquatint and etching published by Robert Dodd, no date.
NMM ref PAH8067

6. 'To Sir Michael Seymour Bart, his Officers and Seamen, this View of their Action with the Neimen on the 6th of April 1809, being the second French frigate of superior force taken by them, in His Majesty's Ship Amethyst within this space of five months is . . . inscribed by . . . R Dodd', aquatint published by Robert Dodd, no date.
NMM ref PAH8071

1

Post Office packets

2

POSTAL communications overseas were of great importance and were maintained by a small fleet of thirty-seven Post Office packets in 1808. Falmouth (1) was the principal departure and arrival port and the majority of the Falmouth packets were of a standard design by Marmaduke Stalkaart built on private account and chartered for the public service (2). They were of 170 tons burthen, ship rigged and about 61 feet long on the deck. Armed usually with 9-pounder brass cannon which became colloquially known as 'Post Office guns', they were capable of defending themselves (3). Each had a complement of 28 men with accommodation for 6 passengers. There were also four larger packets maintained at Falmouth with crews of 36 men employed on the Brazil service. The vessels were contracted for seven years from master-owners and were regulated by the resident Post Office agent responsible for foreign mails while liability for loss was carried by the Post-Master General's office.

The Packet Service had earned a measure of disrepute, many master-owners sending substitutes to sea while illegal private trading had been common and at the turn of the century reforms were introduced. However, despite being exempt from the press, well-paid and in fast, well-found ships, the relatively cosseted crews struck for increased pay in 1810 and again in 1814. The first strike was dealt with by transferring the service to Portsmouth, the second by manning the packets with men from elsewhere.

Like men-of-war, packets were used for the shipment of specie or bullion. Packet commanders were instructed to run from attack and not engage unless in self-defence. When compelled to submit, they were obliged to ditch the mails. In March 1813 *Express* sailed from Rio de Janeiro carrying mails, dispatches and gold to the value of £20,000. Closing the Cape Verde islands she encountered the American privateer *Anaconda* which chased and overtook her, provoking an hour-long action in which *Express* suffered extensive damage aloft, had several guns dismounted and was badly hulled until she leaked. Seizing the gold, the Americans paroled Captain Quick and his crew, who subsequently brought the mails into Falmouth after an ordeal of some weeks in keeping their ship afloat. Also attacked by an American privateer, Captain Bell of the *Francis Freeling* beat her off three times during a passage from Lisbon to Falmouth, preserving the lives of his passengers and specie worth 130,000 dollars.

Smaller packets were maintained elsewhere. Six 70-ton schooners sailed from Harwich to Helvoetsluis, Hamburg, Helgoland and the Baltic; communications between Weymouth and the Channel Islands were kept open by 50 to 60-ton cutters, more cutters and ship-rigged packets operated between Liverpool and Dublin, or from Holyhead or Milford Haven. Other packet services were run between Whitehaven and Man and Dongahadee. In addition to the Post Office, packets were also run by other government departments like the War Office.

Commanders were expected to sail the moment the mails were on board, irrespective of the weather. This inevitably exposed them to risks and occasional loss, such as occurred to *Lady Hobart* in 1803 when she struck an iceberg off Newfoundland. Others relied on pure seamanship to survive (4).

Postal rates were high: two shillings and two pence to Spain, rising by nine pence to Gibraltar and 'the Squadron off Cadiz'. West India and American services left monthly, Gibraltar and the extended service to Malta introduced in 1806, during the third week in each month. The Lisbon service departed weekly, Gothenburg twice weekly, with the Madeira and South American mails going off once a month. The round trip to Lisbon took a month, to Malta and back 14 weeks, and 'the Brazils' some 18 weeks, mail for Rio de Janeiro costing three shillings and seven pence. The mails contained private and commercial letters, letters of credit, bank-drafts and contracts, important instruments in Britain's overseas trade. Packet commanders were encouraged to report on commercial, political and military developments abroad, and the clerks-in-waiting at the General Post Office in London issued a *General Shipping and Commercial List* conveying some of this information.

In addition to the mails, the packets also bore passengers. Army officers, merchants, government commissaries, diplomats and their families, all made up their passenger lists, for the fares were expensive. Male passengers often joined in the defence if a packet was attacked. When on 15 June 1813, while on passage from Falmouth to Halifax, the packet *Manchester* was attacked by the American privateer *York Town*, her three passengers, an army officer and two civilians, behaved with great courage. Captain Elphinstone of *Manchester* threw his mails overboard and surrendered after a running chase of 40 hours and a close engagement of an hour which had expended his ammunition.

A celebrated action occurred on 1 October 1807 in the West Indies, when a French schooner-corsair caught the packet *Windsor Castle* approaching Barbados. The privateer's crew outnumbered that of the packet; she also carried a heavy armament of six long 6-pounders and an 18-pounder mounted *en barbette* amidships. *Windsor Castle* carried six long 4-pounders and two 9-pounder carronades. In accordance with his standing orders, Acting Commander Rogers attempted to run but the Frenchman closed to board. Of Rogers' 28-man crew, 10 were hit in a fusillade, but Rogers rallied his men repeatedly and, having resisted all attempts of the French to board, Rogers led four men in a counter-attack, carrying the deck of the privateer upon which lay 21 dead and 33 wounded. For his outstanding courage Rogers received a permanent command and a gift of plate from the underwriters of Liverpool, who also subscribed a sum of money to be distributed among the packet's crew. Rogers' losses amounted to 10 severely wounded and 3 killed in an action which lasted almost four hours.

A sad incident of mistaken identity involving a Post Office packet occurred in March 1814. The Falmouth packet *Duke of Marlborough* was off Cape Finisterre on passage to Lisbon when she encountered the 18-gun brig sloop *Primrose* lying with her main topsail to the mast. Both vessels were mutually suspicious and the packet ran with *Primrose* in pursuit. Neither Phillott of the brig, nor Bull of the packet could see the other's ensign and, despite attempts to exchange recognition signals, including those for use at night, *Duke of Marlborough* opened fire on the overhauling brig through her stern ports, cut away some of the *Primrose*'s bowsprit gear and holed her mainsail. An action ensued in which Bull out-manoeuvred Phillott and inflicted casualties, but eventually the

3

4

dreadful mistake was realised. *Duke of Marlborough* had taken two 32-pound carronade balls in the hull and was rapidly filling with water, her masts and rigging were damaged, two passengers, one of whom was an army officer belonging to the 60th Foot, had been killed, and Bull and ten of his men were wounded.

Despite the suspension of the mails between Dover and Calais, communication between Paris and London was kept open, for both the French and British governments maintained formally recognised agents in each others' capitals, chiefly to arrange for the exchange of prisoners. These were periodically carried out in protected vessels known as 'cartels'. Elsewhere, letters might also be sent by the 'ship-letter system' in which mail deposited at coffee houses was picked up by obliging masters of merchant ships.

5

The escape of the Brest fleet, 1809

IN the last weeks of 1808, word of an intended British expedition to the West Indies reached Paris. Orders were sent to Rear-Admiral Willaumez at Brest to sail upon the first relaxation of British vigilance, to raise the blockade at Lorient, release Commodore Troude's three of the line and five frigates, then to proceed to the rendezvous at the Basque Roads. Here he was to pick up a further three of the line, several frigates and the troopship *Calcutta*, which were lying off Rochefort under Commodore Faure. Willaumez was then to reinforce Martinique and, having landed troops and supplies at Port Royal, he was to destroy the British West India trade.

In the middle of February, persistent westerly gales persuaded Admiral Gambier to withdraw his ships from their station off Ushant, whereupon Willaumez slipped his moorings and sailed south, clearing the Raz passage before noon on 21 February 1809. His squadron comprised *Océan*, 120 (flag), *Foudroyant* and *Varsovie*, 80s, *Tourville*, *Tonnere*, *Jean Bart*, *Aquilon* and *Régulus*, 74s; *Indienne* and *Elbe*, 40s with brig corvette *Nisus* and schooner *Magpie*. But they were observed by Captain Paget of the 74-gun *Revenge*, the solitary sentinel, who followed, heading south towards Commodore Beresford who lay off Lorient in *Theseus*, with *Valiant* and *Triumph* in company. The day was already drawing in, but soon after receiving *Revenge*'s intelligence Beresford bravely steered a course to cut off the French squadron (1).

Rear-Admiral Gourdon's division wore in chase, but was soon recalled, for Willaumez knew that now the British had seen him, delay would be fatal to his enterprise. Nevertheless, he tried to fool Beresford by laying to and furling his sails as if to indicate he was anchoring, resetting sail after dark. At daylight when off Île de Groix, Willaumez sent *Magpie* into Lorient to roust out Troude and headed himself for the Pertuis d'Antioche, the passage between the isles of Oleron and Aix where the Rochefort ships were to join him (2).

Willaumez's ruse succeeded, allowing him to get ahead, but Beresford came in sight of him again during the forenoon of the 23rd as both forces sailed southeast, the French inshore of Belle Isle, the British astern to seaward. During the day they lost sight of one another again, but as Willaumez approached the Île de Ré after dark he was closing with another British force, the squadron blockading the twin anchorages of the Basque and Aix Roads which lay behind the Île d'Oleron, guarding the estuary of the Charente and the port of Rochefort. Commanded by Sir Robert Stopford, the squadron consisted of *Caesar*, 80 and the 74-gun ships *Defiance* and *Donegal*, and the frigates *Naiad* and *Emerald* which then lay at anchor off the Chassiron lighthouse on the Île de Oleron. To the north, off the Baleine light on the Île de Ré, lay Stopford's lookout frigate, *Amethyst*. The moment Captain Seymour saw the looming ships of Willaumez' squadrons, he sent up rockets. Stopford immediately weighed and headed north, to catch sight of Willaumez about midnight. Although Stopford altered course to close the French ships, he was too late to pre-

1. 'This Print Representing the Theseus leading the Squadron near the Isle of Grouais, in the face of the Brest Fleet . . . preventing their intended Junction with the Lorient Squadron . . . on the 21 Feby 1809', aquatint and etching by Joseph Constantine Stadler after an original by Nicholas Pocock, published by the artist, 23 September 1809. *NMM ref PAH8069*

2. 'Coast of France from Lorient to the Isle of Re', published by Joyce Gold, 1 May 1813 (Plate 388 from the *Naval Chronicle*, Vol XXIX). *NMM neg D9293*

3. 'The squadron under the command of Rear Adml Stopford engaging three French frigates, 24 Feby 1809', coloured aquatint engraved by Thomas Sutherland after an original by Thomas Whitcombe, no date. *NMM ref PAD5777*

4. 'Combat des Sables D'Olonne . . . 24 Fevrier 1809', coloured lithograph engraved by L Mayer after his own original, published by F Delarue, no date. *NMM ref PAH8070*

1

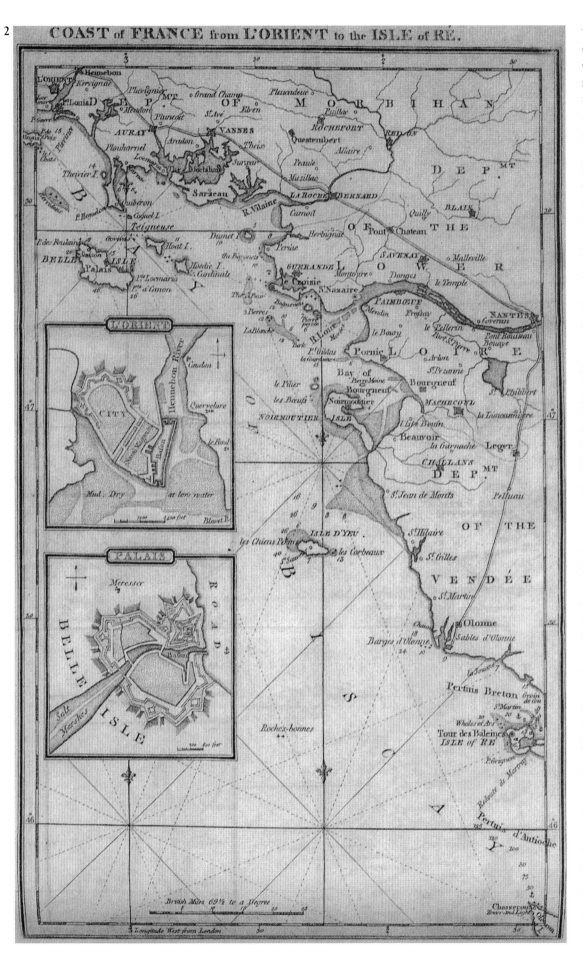

vent them entering the Pertuis d'Antioche at daylight and sent *Naiad* north to inform Gambier. Dundas of *Naiad* shortly afterwards sighted three suspicious sails and still in sight of Stopford, signalled their presence, whereupon Stopford stood to the north, leaving *Emerald* and *Amethyst* to watch Willaumez.

The three strangers were the 40-gun frigates *Calypso, Cybèle* and *Italienne*, under Commodore Jurien, Troude's second, who had sailed from Lorient without Troude, whose deeper ships were unable to get out owing to the state of the tide. They had been chased by the British frigate *Amelia*, 38, and the 18-gun brig *Dotterel*, the lookout ships of Beresford's squadron. Jurien had seen Beresford's main force in the offing but kept away. Captain Irby of *Amelia* and Commander Abdy of *Dotterel* had maintained so close a pursuit of this superior enemy that Jurien had twice been obliged to haul round and protect his rear and these manoeuvres had fatally delayed him. With Irby and Abdy astern, Stopford was now seen coming up from the southward. In the knowledge that a further British squadron lay to the west, Jurien, though in sight of the Baleine lighthouse, was now compromised by a shift of the wind to the southeast by east. The unfortunate commodore was cornered on his own coast and at 0900 bore up for Sables d'Olonne, followed by the tenacious *Amelia* and *Dotterel*. Irby had no intention of letting the enemy escape and for the third time hauled up astern of *Cybèle*, wore under the French frigate's stern and opened fire in passing.

But Jurien could do nothing except stand on and place himself under the heavy shore batteries at Sables d'Olonne, for Stopford's ships were drawing closer. At about 1030 Jurien anchored his ships under the shore gun emplacements and, clapping springs on his cables, awaited events. Stopford's ships formed a line, with *Defiance* in the van and *Amelia* in the rear, closing the coast which was now lined with spectators. Stopford intended to cannonade at a distance but Hotham carried *Defiance* directly at the enemy and at 1100 anchored in seven fathoms about a third of a mile from Jurien's ships, immediately opening fire (3). In the succeeding half an hour all four British ships were exchanging fire with the enemy frigates and the shore batteries.

The gunnery of *Defiance* was lethal, some of her wads reaching the *Italienne* and *Cybèle*, setting them on fire and causing their cables to be cut and the frigates to drift ashore close to high water. Captain Hotham immediately veered cable in order to maintain his fire upon the unfortunate French while *Caesar*, of deeper draught, wore round and edged into deeper water. *Donegal* and *Amelia* kept up the pressure for a little longer before following Stopford. *Calypso*, to clear the fields of fire from her grounded consorts and mitigate the effects of *Defiance*'s guns, also veered cable, but grounded, being

close inshore (4).

With the tide ebbing, Stopford, out of the action to the southward, signalled *Defiance* to disengage and just after noon Hotham cut his cable and withdrew. A final broadside was fired by *Donegal* as she tacked and the British squadron retired to resume its station off the Chassiron light by sunset. The following day, the 25th, Stopford was joined by Beresford. Casualties were light aboard the British ships, though *Defiance* suffered spar damage, while the French had 24 killed and 51 wounded. Their frigates, however, became wrecks.

1

2

Basque Roads, 1809

T HE first part of the French enterprise had failed; now the Basque Road was to prove a dangerous place, for seeking the further shelter of the inner anchorage off Aix, *Jean Bart* touched the Palles shoal off Île Madame and was abandoned as a wreck. The remainder of Willaumez's ships were now in company with Faure's squadron consisting of the 74-gun ships *Cassard, Jemmappes, Patriote,* the 40-gun frigates *Pallas* and *Hortense* and the *Calcutta.* In the week that followed Willaumez sought only his own safety by drawing a heavy boom across the passage into the anchorage.

Though Willaumez was bottled up, it still rankled that he had got out at all. Gambier's fleet joined Stopford off the Île d'Oleron on 7 March, but the Admiralty was anxious; Gambier might be driven off station again and there were pressing political imperatives deriving from the usual anxiety of the West India merchants. Their Lordships concluded that since 'the French fleet might slip out again' they must 'forthwith be destroyed' and as a means of so doing had determined to employ fireships and Congreve rockets. On 19 March Gambier (1) had

been told that twelve transports and five bomb vessels were being prepared, but it would be an extremely hazardous operation and several senior officers, including the ever-pious Gambier had refused to have anything to do with it. Nor could the Admiralty itself face failure; thus, while desiring such an attack to be made, Lord Mulgrave and his Board declined to accept responsibility for making it.

Into this curious situation sailed Captain Lord Cochrane, an officer of high birth and low income who had just arrived at Plymouth in *Imperieuse* after a series of daring raids on the coast of Spain. Scenting a victim, Mulgrave summoned Cochrane and explained the situation with great candour. Cochrane, a Member of Parliament and politically a thorn in the side of Portland's government, knew his failure also meant his ruin, but he was familiar with the waters and considered the plan foolhardy: something more terrible had to be devised. At Mulgrave's insistence, he rapidly drafted a plan, but was reluctant to take command of the attack himself, knowing the jealousy that the arrival of an

3

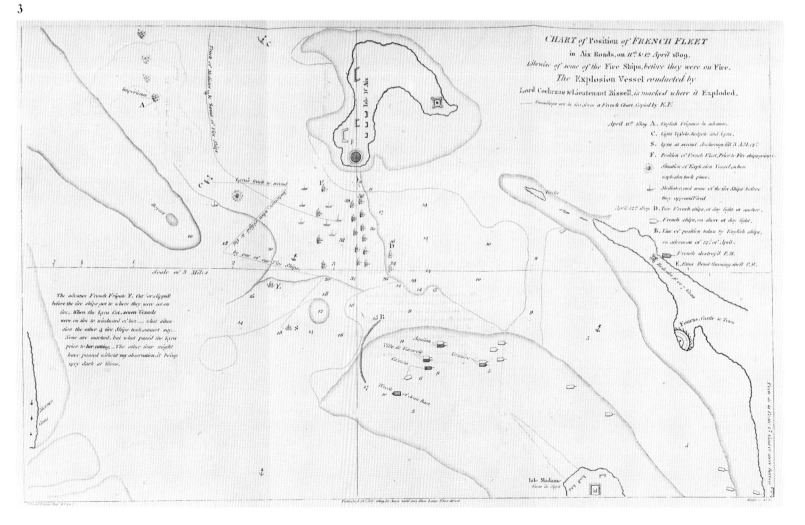

CHART of Position of FRENCH FLEET
in Aix Roads, on 11th & 12 April 1809.
Likewise of some of the Fire Ships, before they were on Fire.
The Explosion Vessel conducted by
Lord Cochrane & Lieutenant Bissell, is marked where it Exploded.

'expert' would arouse in the Channel Fleet. According to Cochrane, it took a direct order from the First Lord to make him accept.

On 3 April 1809 *Imperieuse* joined the fleet now anchored in the Basque Road. Gambier was told that Cochrane was to conduct the attack under his own 'direction' as a means of removing objections by any captains senior to him. Gambier had already decided that an attack by his ships of the line was too risky. He therefore regarded Cochrane's arrival as being as providential as had Mulgrave. Their meeting was marred by Captain Harvey, who demanded that he should command the attack, railing against Gambier's prevarications, his 'methodistical . . . conduct and vindictive disposition'. Harvey was sent home in his flagship, the *Tonnant*, 80, and Cochrane ordered to make his preparations.

Similar feelings were simultaneously stirring in the French fleet. Captain Bergeret of the *Ville de Varsovie* had written to Paris denouncing the misconduct of Willaumez in failing to bring to battle the inferior force of Beresford off Lorient. Bergeret did not share either Willaumez's or Napoleon's belief that ships were safe in Aix Roads. The immediate consequence of his letter to Décres was for his own supercession, the removal of Willaumez (2) and substitution of Allemand.

It was formidable force that now lay in the outer, or Basque Road. Gambier flew his flag in the 120-gun *Caledonia* and with him were two 80-gun ships, eight 74s, the heavy frigate *Indefatigable*, 44, four other frigates, three sloops, seven gunbrigs and three smaller craft. Besides these, *Imperieuse* was preparing eight transports and the former frigate *Mediator* as fireships. Working parties from the fleet were assigned to making powder trains, filling barrels of tar and inflammable materials throughout the ships, festooning strips of tarred canvas everywhere and cutting ports to carry fire upward by way of tar-sodden oakum. Cochrane personally fitted out two transports and a captured French coaster as 'explosion vessels'. These vessels were reinforced to compact the explosive force of 1500 casks of black powder, tamped down with sand. Hundreds of 10-inch shells were spread liberally in the casks and covered with several thousand hand grenadoes, the whole being linked to a fifteen-minute fuse running aft to the stern.

The twelve promised fireships arrived on the 10th, by which time a single bomb vessel, the *Aetna* had also turned up. Cochrane reported to Gambier that he was ready, and after initial hesitation by Gambier on the afternoon of 11 April 1809, *Imperieuse* moved inshore to anchor near the Boyart Shoal. Here at the very entrance to Aix Road Cochrane assembled his force. Anchored with *Imperieuse*, the *Caesar*, 80 and frigates *Aigle, Unicorn* and *Pallas* were to receive the retiring crews of the expendable

4

vessels and to provide their boats for any other service. The small craft *Whiting, King George* and *Nimrod* were all fitted out for firing rockets while *Aetna*, covered by the *Indefatigable* and *Foxhound*, anchored close north of Aix with the object of shelling the fort on the island's southern point and neutralising its guns. *Emerald, Beagle, Dotterel, Conflict* and *Growler* were sent east of Aix to create a diversion, and *Lyra* and *Redpole* were fitted with lights to mark the shoals. The strength of tide and a northwesterly wind curtailed any movement by the remaining ships of the line and they were thus all anchored between six and nine miles from the enemy.

Watching these preparations Allemand had anchored his ships in three lines lying almost north to south, heading north. The inner consisted of *Elbe, Tourville, Aquilon, Jemmappes, Patriote* and *Tonnere*. Lying parallel and just over a cable to the west so that their broadsides covered the intervals, were the *Calcutta, Cassard, Regulus, Océan, Ville de Varsovie* and *Foudroyant*. A shorter line, half a mile further west, consisted of the frigates *Pallas, Hortense* and *Indienne*, beyond which the heavy boom of anchor cables and spars stretched for about two miles, barring the approach. Behind this, on the late afternoon of 11 April, Allemand mustered his boats and alerted the 2000 conscripts garrisoning Aix and the shore batteries. He had also ordered his battleships to strike their vulnerable tophamper, though his frigates were ready to weigh (3).

'The night', wrote Marryat, 'was very dark, and it blew a strong breeze directly in upon . . . the enemy's fleet'. There was also a two-knot tide setting down upon Allemand's lines. At 2030, *Mediator* and her expendable consorts cut their cables, were swung round and headed for the enemy. Cochrane had himself taken post in the

1. 'Lord Gambier', graphite and wash by Sir William Beechey and William Evans, 1809.
NMM ref PAF3549

2. 'Amiral Willaumez: France Maritime', anonymous stipple engraving, no date.
NMM ref PAD3409

3. Detailed folding plan of attack on Aix Roads engraved by Simpkin after an original by Fairfax published by Joyce Gold, 1809 (Plate CCLXXXIX from the *Naval Chronicle*, Vol XII).
NMM neg D9264

4. 'To Admiral Lord Gambier . . . this Plate representing the Attack on the Enemy's Fleet by Fire Ships on the Night of the 11th of April 1809 . . . inscribed by . . . Rob Dodd', coloured aquatint after an original by Robert Dodd, published by the artist, no date.
NMM ref PAH8072

5

leading explosion vessel, Marryat was in the second and their first objective was to destroy the boom. They led the fireships which were followed in turn by the squadrons' boats which had mustered alongside *Caesar*.

At about 2130, having passed the lights of *Redpole* and *Lyra* and approaching what he imagined was the optimum position, Cochrane ordered his men into the boat, lit the fuse and joined them, only to discover that they had left their pet dog aboard. They returned to rescue their mascot, then pulled away. Marryat followed, and a few minutes later the night sky was riven by the first tremendous explosion. Just inside the boom, Allemand's boats were swamped by the wave thrown up and scattered in confusion. Cochrane was saved by the necessity to return for the dog, for he was inside the radius of falling debris, and after the convulsion of the sea, he noted 'nothing but a heavy rolling sea . . . all having again become silence and darkness'. The explosion destroyed the boom and any remnant was further blown away by the explosion of Marryat's vessel.

Mediator and the other fireships swept down through the debris of the boom (4), but the plan now miscarried. Twenty fireships had been prepared, but the commanders of several ignited them when still to seaward of *Imperieuse* and the majority either grounded before penetrating the anchorage, or ran harmlessly up the centre of the channel in the tide. Nevertheless the handful of fireships which drove on and were, for aught the French knew, explosion vessels, caused confusion. The darkness of the night and the bright fires of the burning vessels, *Aetna*'s bombs, the rockets flaring across the sky like low meteorites, the gunfire from every side, all added to the hellish atmosphere (5).

Not all the fireship crews abandoned them prematurely. One drove into the *Régulus*, which got clear only to crash into *Tourville*. *Hortense* cut her cables to drift clear of one fireship, made sail and fired into another, her shot menacing her neighbours. Allemand's *Océan* was obliged to cut and run, but promptly grounded. A few moments later an ably directed fireship crashed into *Océan* as her crew soused their own decks and tried to shove it off. Into this confusion loomed first the *Tonnere* and then the *Patriote*, both of which rammed the *Océan* in their attempts to manoeuvre in the strong tide. Incredibly Allemand's men finally shoved the fireship clear.

By dawn, a disappointed Cochrane was mollified by a sight which seemed one of utter devastation. Only *Foudroyant* and *Cassard* were still afloat, the remainder of the French squadrons were aground, some on soft mud but others bilged on rocks. During the small hours the tide had ebbed and completed what Cochrane had begun. Throughout the morning Cochrane signalled to Gambier in increasing frustration for reinforcement to finish off the stranded enemy, but the C-in-C merely ordered *Aetna*, with *Growler, Conflict* and *Insolent* in support, to add a little to the confusion by throwing shells at the enemy. *Valiant, Bellona, Revenge* and the frigates and sloops were also ordered to move closer and anchor near the Boyart. Seeing what they must have supposed to be the entire fleet under weigh, *Cassard* and *Foudroyant* now cut their cables and made for the Charente, but ran aground. Similarly, as the tide was now approaching high water, *Jemmappes, Patriote, Océan* and *Régulus* refloated, but also ran aground again in the entrance to the Charente.

Without orders Cochrane took *Imperieuse* inshore, aiming to fire into the ships on the Palles shoal and sending further signals in an attempt to force Gambier to send in proper support (6). By 1400, flying a signal requesting immediate assistance on the ground that he was engaged with superior forces, *Imperieuse* had anchored and engaged *Calcutta, Aquilon* and *Ville de Varsovie*. He also ordered *Insolent, Growler* and *Beagle* to move in closer. Compromised, Gambier reluctantly sent some ships in to assist. *Indefatigable* arrived first, just as *Calcutta* struck to Cochrane, and the others took some time to work up against the tide, but by about 1600 the two frigates and sloops already in position were joined by *Valiant, Revenge*, and *Pallas*. The fire of the combined ships compelled both *Aquilon* and *Ville de Varsovie* to surrender just as *Theseus* arrived. Further south the crew of *Tonnere* set her on fire and abandoned her before she exploded, while the burning *Calcutta*'s cargo of ammunition also blew up.

During this unequal engagement, Rear-Admiral Stopford had had three more transports hurriedly converted to fireships and with some boats bearing rockets, stood in under fire from the shore batteries. His flagship,

Caesar, lodged for two hours on the Boyart and the wind drew ahead, frustrating the attack. However, boats from *Valiant* set fire to *Ville de Varsovie* and *Aquilon* which caused a panic aboard *Tourville*.

As soon as the tide served, Cochrane pressed into the Charente with a flotilla of gunbrigs and small craft, firing on *Océan, Régulus* and *Indienne* until the falling tide compelled him to retire. During the afternoon *Redpole, Dotterel* and *Foxhound* all arrived with letters from Gambier ordering Cochrane to withdraw, though Cochrane felt the British capable of yet further destruction. On the 14th *Patriote, Hortense, Elbe* and the French *Pallas* finally worked their way out of danger up the river, and *Tourville* and *Océan* grounded while attempting the same. The following day Cochrane finally withdrew, handing over to Wolfe of *Aigle* and, taking aboard Captain Sir Harry Neale with Gambier's dispatch, *Imperieuse* sailed for England.

6

A final attack was made by *Aetna* and the brigs on the 14th with little effect. *Indienne* was burnt by her crew, leaving only *Régulus*, and on 19 April she was attacked by the newly arrived bomb vessel *Thunder*. Her 13-inch mortar split and with this fiasco matters drew to a conclusion. Admiral Gambier, considering his work done, departed for home.

Courts-martial sat on the conduct of the French commanders, two being imprisoned, while Lafon of *Calcutta* was condemned and shot on 9 September. These unfortunate officers paid the penalty of flawed strategy, scapegoats for Willaumez's timidity in not making boldly for Martinique. Even without Faure's Rochefort squadron, much might have been achieved.

The consequences of the action were almost as unpleasant for the British as for the French navy. Harvey was court-martialled and never afterwards employed. Gambier's dispatch damned Cochrane with faint praise. Despite a Knighthood of the Bath, Cochrane decided to use his membership of Parliament to oppose the formal motion of thanks to Gambier, and tempers became even more frayed when Mulgrave tried first to bully Cochrane and then to bribe him with a plum command. Word spread and the radical press scented a scandal (7); Gambier demanded a court-martial which sat aboard *Gladiator* at Portsmouth between 26 July and 4 August.

The court openly favoured Gambier, being presided over by his friend Sir Roger Curtis, supported by Admiral Young, a jobbing dockyard admiral who disliked Cochrane, and the self-serving Sir John Duckworth.

Cochrane was not allowed into court except to give evidence, was brow-beaten and forbidden to ask questions. The court decided that Gambier's conduct had been tempered by the caution proper to a Commander-in-Chief. Further action, it was implied, was outside the judgement of a mere junior post captain, even though that captain had access to far more accurate French charts which proved the anchorage less dangerous waters than was claimed by the naval establishment. Gambier was 'most honourably acquitted'.

7

STERNHOLD and HOPKINS at SEA or a Slave out of Time.

Ships of the Royal Navy: cutters and luggers

THE smallest regular cruisers in the Navy had much in common, both in terms of their origins and their employment. Neither type was developed by the Navy itself, but came into service through hire, then purchase or capture, and only late in their naval careers by design – in the case of the lugger, only one was ever built expressly for the Navy (*Experiment* of 1793). Both ranked as the smallest cruising warships, operating against minor commerce raiders and defending friendly trade, but both were to acquire fleet roles – principally carrying dispatches, but also undertaking reconnaissance in places where the superior windward performance of their fore-and-aft rigs made them a better bet than the less handy square-riggers.

The deep, V-sectioned single-masted cutter was a product of the English Channel coast, mainly of Kent and Sussex, where they were employed, legally, as fast coastal traders and, illegally, as smugglers, although the distinction was often very subtle (1). The lugger was also a Channel craft and it too was sharp-lined, but somewhat longer and lower, and unlike the cutter carried its canvas on two or three masts. Luggers were very weatherly, but the large lug sails, including lug topsails, required sizable and nimble crews (2). In both cases the Navy adopted the local type in an attempt to counter the undesirable activities of similar craft: it is well known country lore that the best gamekeeper is a reformed poacher. The Navy's first purpose-built cutters were introduced to suppress smuggling in the years after the Seven Years War; the lugger was probably a counter to French coastal privateers using the similar Breton *chasse-marée*, the first in naval service being hired during the American Revolutionary War.

A few very large naval cutters were built in the 1770s, but they proved too difficult to handle – the big cutter's main sail was a huge area of canvas and needed a sub-

1

2

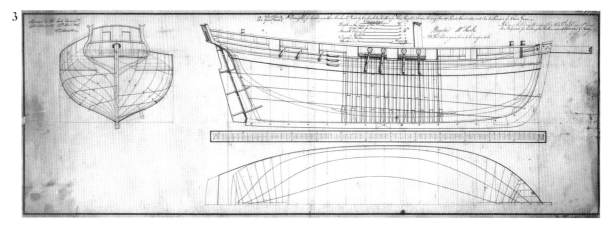

3

stantial crew to manage it; they were replaced by brigs where the principal driving canvas was on two masts not one. Being largely square sails, which could be backed, also gave the brig rig a manoeuvring advantage over the cutter, or indeed the lugger.

Small craft were in demand from the beginning of the war in 1793, but during the 1790s the Navy saw no requirement for purpose-built examples of either type (with the single exception of *Experiment*), relying on hire, purchase and capture. As the Navy's areas of operations expanded so did the need for fast-sailing craft to carry orders to far-flung stations and bring home reports. Cutters and luggers were obvious candidates, but ex-merchant types were often lightly armed and not particularly fast, making them vulnerable to more powerful privateers of traditionally speedy forms like xebecs and luggers. In April 1804, for example, Nelson's dispatches were lost when the 77-ton hired cutter *Swift* was taken by a big privateer xebec; but earlier the cutter *Sprightly* had been lost while carrying important dispatches in 1801.

The Admiralty revived the old concept of an advice boat, a craft intended to carry information (a seventeenth-century meaning of 'advice'), either in the form of dispatches or in the form of intelligence from reconnaissance. Speed was a prime requirement, and the *Express* class of 1800 were extremely long and sharp-lined, but were rigged as schooners. These were not entirely successful, and since the Surveyors were not very highly regarded by the incumbent Admiralty Board of the time, a new schooner design was produced by a commercial builder in Bermuda, 'similar to a Bermudian dispatch boat'. Another Bermudian prototype, the sloop *Lady Hammond*, was then chosen for a new design of twice the tonnage, and some of these were rigged as cutters — court martial records show *Alban*, *Cassandra*, *Claudia* and *Laura* were cutters when lost, and *Alphea*, *Barbara* and *Zenobia* were schooners. The hull form of these Bermudian vessels, with their sharp V-section and deep drag aft were closer to traditional English cutters - hence the alternative rigs. The Navy built small numbers of large cutters in the remaining years of the war (3), but the vast majority of cutters, luggers — and for that matter, schooners and other small craft — were obtained from the enemy or the merchant service.

The cutter served on virtually every station, but there was a tendency to retain luggers in their home waters of the Channel and Biscay coast. In something of a return to their smuggling heritage, luggers were often employed in clandestine operations, landing agents and supplies to support anti-government elements in France. Both types were also useful for close reconnaissance and sometimes served in offensive roles inshore, interrupting local shipping (4).

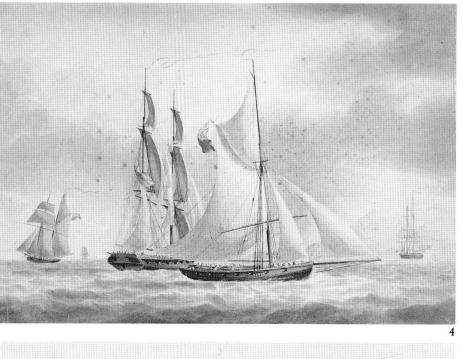

4

5

Less glamorously, cutters and luggers were frequently deployed in the defence of British trade, either cruising against small privateers or even as escort for coastal convoys. In this latter role, the lugger proved surprisingly inept: possibly because tacking the lug rig was not easy, they were dangerously unhandy at close quarters (5). Indeed, a number were run down and sunk by the very ships they were 'escorting' — *Hope*, *Neptune* and *Brave* by merchantmen, and *Spider* by the *Ramillies*, 74. Cutters, on the other hand, were mainly lost from foundering in heavy weather or grounding during the inshore operations that were so often their lot. One odd fate befell the cutter *Constitution*, which was sunk by shellfire during an attack on the Invasion Flotilla in 1804, a direct hit from the mortars of the day being rare indeed.

1. 'The Eagle cutter making West Capel bearing about S.S.E.', black pen and ink by J Robb, 1796. *NMM ref PAH9609*

2. 'A lugger', aquatint and etching by Robert Dodd after his own original, published by the artist, 1807. *NMM ref PAG9426*

3. Lines and partial framing draught for the naval cutters of the *Cheerful* class, 1806. *NMM neg DR6370-65*

4. 'British frigate and cutter and other vessels off a mountainous coast', watercolour by Captain William Moffat, 1807. *NMM ref PAG9738*

5. 'Armed lugger with all sails set', anonymous watercolour, no date. *NMM ref PAG8227*

1

Bonaparte at Boulogne

1. 'Signal Defeat of the French
Squadron of 7 Praams . . . & Fifteen
Brigs off Boulogne, 20th Septr 1811, in
the Presence and Direction of
Bonaparte By H.M.S. Naiad Capt Phil
Carteret, and the Castilian, Renaldo
and Redpole Brigs . . . Capture of Ville
de Lyons', coloured aquatint engraved
by Clark and Duborg after an original
by Lieutenant E Vidal, published by
Edward Orme, 4 June 1812.
NMM neg 8521

2. 'Stationers Almanack 1812. Leap
Year. Plan of the Attack on the
Boulogne Flotilla by the Naiad
Frigate, Captn Carteret, Septr 21, 1811,
in the presence on the Emperor,
Bonaparte, in his barge, when the
Admirals Praam was run ashore and
the Ville de Lyons, Praam, taken',
etching published by I Ryland, no
date.
NMM ref PAF4788

3. 'The Gallant Action off Dieppe,
March 1812. By H.M. Brigs Rosario &
Griffonne, Captns Harvey & Trollope,
Defeating Twelve French Brigs . . . ',
coloured aquatint engraved by Clark
& Duborg after an original by Lt E
Vidal, published by Edward Orme, 4
June 1812.
NMM ref PAF4790

ALTHOUGH after the failure of the main invasion plan of 1805, the French moved the majority of their invasion craft into the Schelde, Boulogne harbour continued to hold a number of prames and small vessels. As a consequence, the port was closely invested by the Royal Navy's smaller cruisers. During the partial hiatus in military operations on the continent in 1811, Napoleon was at Boulogne in September, personally assessing the capability of the French forces there to carry out offensive operations. This had been the venue for earlier humiliations and a brief action had been fought on the 3rd between the 10-gun brigs *Rinaldo* and *Redpole*, and a French prame and brig.

On the 20th, the occasion of the Emperor's visit was made a grand marine review and he was met with the assembled craft decorated *en fête*. Napoleon himself embarked in a decorated barge to carry out his inspection. Anchored just offshore lay the British 38-gun frigate *Naiad*, whose proximity Napoleon found intolerable. He accordingly ordered an attack made by a division of seven 12-gun prames and these pulled seaward under the command of Rear-Admiral Baste. Aboard *Naiad*, Captain Carteret had clapped a spring on his cable and engaged the approaching prames as soon as they emerged, keeping them at a distance for about two hours so that no enemy shot caused the slightest damage to *Naiad*. The French then reinforced Baste with a bomb vessel and ten small 4-gun brigs, but with little more effect,

though *Naiad* weighed to improve her position and repair slight damage to her rigging. As the afternoon drew to a close, however, the ineffective and humiliated flotilla withdrew.

The displeased Emperor ordered the attack resumed next day and the seven prames, supported by fifteen smaller craft again emerged to drive off the British interloper (1). By now, however, *Naiad* had been reinforced by the brigs *Castilian*, 18, *Rinaldo* and *Redpole*, 10, and the smaller, 8-gun *Viper*.

Baste's prame was badly mauled and in coming to her support, the 12-gun *Ville de Lyon* was engaged by the *Rinaldo* and *Redpole* whose gunfire decimated her crew. At this juncture she was boarded by the *Naiad*'s crew and captured under the guns of Boulogne with the Emperor of the French an infuriated witness (2). The vessels drifted inshore and the action was broken off some time later as the British ships came within range of the shore batteries. The chief merit of the action was in its demonstration to Napoleon that he was denied any access to the sea beyond the embrace of his own breakwaters.

Other detachments of invasion craft were ordered to take station in the new harbour of Cherbourg and, in March 1812, some of these were in the process of transferring there from Boulogne. On the 27th, a dozen small brigs and a lugger were spotted off Dieppe on passage to Cherbourg by the British 10-gun brig *Rosario*. An attempt by Commander Harvey to cut off the leewardmost of the

2

brigs was frustrated by her consorts coming to her assistance and *Rosario* drew off, only to come in sight of a second British sloop, the *Griffon* of 16 guns. Signalling for support, Harvey put about and resumed his attack as the enemy closed the approach to Dieppe. After about an hour of fruitless action, Harvey carried *Rosario* into the enemy's heart, forced two brigs to collide, fired into them, engaged and partly dismasted a third, stood after a fourth so that she ran ashore and boarded and captured a fifth (3). *Griffon* now arrived on the scene and immediately drove another brig ashore, boarded a second and then stood offshore as *Rosario* completed her day's work by taking possession of the partially dismasted brig whose crew had abandoned her. For his dash, Harvey was made a post captain.

3

The blockade of Toulon

THE blockade of Toulon was to occupy Collingwood and his successors for the remainder of the war. By early 1809 there were fifteen French ships of the line ready for sea, together with six Russian vessels, Grieg's squadron from the Adriatic. Blockading Toulon was not an easy task, for the mistral from the north made the French coast a weather shore and the Gulf of Lyons is notorious for its gales. The hard usage to which the blockading ships were put, strained them badly and they were easily visible from the land. Whilst the Commander-in-Chief might hold his fleet offshore, every effort was made to keep a few eyes on Toulon Road and at the beginning of 1809, this duty lay with the 32-gun frigate *Proserpine*. Such was her commander's boldness, that it irritated the French and on the bright moonlit night of 27 February, while *Proserpine* lay becalmed to the south of Toulon, Captain Dubourdieu in the 40-gun *Pénélope*, led her consorts *Pomone* and *Pauline* to sea and hugged the high coast in the deep shadow of the moon. The *Pénélope* and *Pauline* made good progress and reached Cape Sicié to the west (1), before standing out to catch *Proserpine*, which was trapped between *Pénélope* on one quarter and *Pauline* on the other, with *Pomone* coming up astern and the 74s *Suffren* and *Ajax* also in pursuit. After an engagement of forty minutes during which *Proserpine*'s rigging was badly shot away and she inflicted little damage to the enemy, Captain Otter was obliged to strike his colours and his frigate was carried triumphantly into Toulon.

1

With a prevailing offshore wind, it was almost impossible to prevent every ship or small squadron escaping from Toulon, and in the spring of 1809 Rear-Admiral Baudin with five sail of the line and some smaller craft, successfully reinforced the French forces under Gouvion St Cyr surrounded in Barcelona. Knowing the French were anxious to repeat the exercise, Collingwood appeared to withdraw his fleet, but when Baudin sailed on 21 October 1809 he was quickly spotted by British frigates and pursued by a division of the fleet. Baudin, his flag in the 80-gun *Robuste*, with the 74-gun *Borée* and *Lion*, the frigates *Pomone* and *Pauline*, was escorting a convoy of transports and storeships again bound for Barcelona. Rear-Admiral Martin in *Canopus*, 80, with seven of the fastest 74-gun ships in the fleet gave chase. The French squadron tried to draw Martin away from the scattering convoy, but the British frigate *Pomone* dashed in amongst the fugitives and took two brigs and some smaller vessels, although the majority of the convoy escaped towards Rosas Bay.

After a two-day chase, mostly close inshore, Martin spotted the French running north on the 25th. Just before noon *Robuste* and *Lion* put up their helms and ran ashore in heavy weather about six miles to the northeast of Cette, into which port *Borée* and *Pauline* ran safely. Seeing this, Martin's frustrated ships stood seawards, in some danger of being cast ashore themselves in the strong wind. *Robuste* and *Lion* were later burnt, the *Borée* and *Pauline* afterwards returned to Toulon.

Baudin's convoy, however, had not entirely escaped; the remains of it had anchored in Rosas Bay, just inside the Spanish frontier, under the guns of powerful batteries (2). Hearing of this, Collingwood sent Captain Hallowell of *Tigre*, 74, with a strong force consisting of a

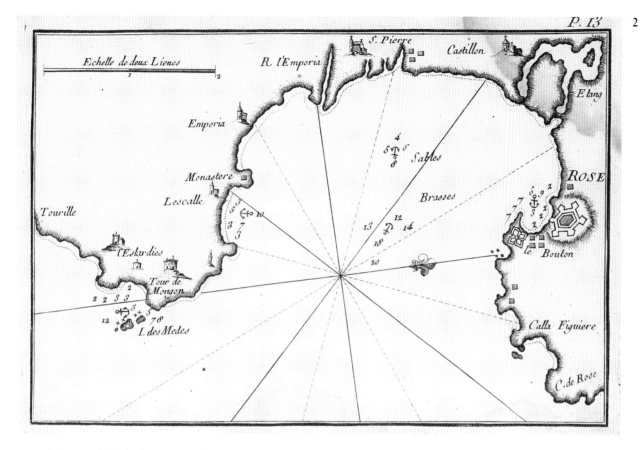

second 74, *Cumberland*, the 38-gun frigates *Apollo*, *Topaze* and *Volontaire*, with the sloops *Philomel*, *Scout* and *Tuscan*. On the night of 31 October, the squadron's boats pulled into the bay where seven transports, the armed storeship *Lamproie*, 16, the armed bombards *Victoire* and *Grondeur* and 10-gun xebec *Normande* lay at anchor. The French were both well prepared and well supported from gunfire and musketry ashore; nevertheless every enemy vessel was either burnt or taken, at a cost of 15 killed and 50 wounded.

More modest in his claims and in a way more remarkable in his achievement was the action of Captain Halliday at the end of August. Three French storeships had been chased under the island of Porquerolles and were being watched by Commander Guion of the 18-gun sloop *Philomel*. One succeeded in reaching Toulon on the 26th, but the other two made another attempt on the 31st. Guion weighed to prevent their passage, while units of the French fleet, commanded by Baudin in *Majestueux*, 120, also weighed and stood seaward. An

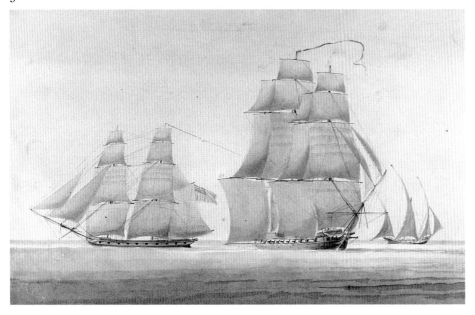

4

1. 'Capture of the Proserpine'
engraved by Baily, published by Joyce
Gold, 30 November 1816 (Plate 473
from the *Naval Chronicle*, Vol XXXVI).
The two views contrast the visibility of
the *Proserpine* (backlit by the moon, No.
1), with the position of the two
French frigates, camouflaged against
the land (No 2).
NMM neg D9277

2. Chart of Rosas Bay 1764 by Joseph
Roux, from *Recueil des principaux plans des
ports et rades de la Méditerranée . . .*
(Marseilles 1764).
NMM neg D9234

5

adverse wind made it impossible to cut off the storeships, but the emerging French, led by two frigates, exchanged shots with the 74-gun *Repulse* lying offshore. Baudin now turned his attention on *Philomel* which had hauled her wind and stood away with the French in pursuit. Seeing the leading French frigates closing *Philomel*, Captain Halliday in *Repulse* crowded on sail and bore up under the *Philomel*'s stern to engage the pursuing *Pomone*, *Pénélope* and *Adrienne*. After fifteen minutes of *Repulse*'s fire they bore away, taking with them the ships of the line, for by now *Warspite* and *Alceste* were coming up from leeward and behind them came the British fleet (3).

A similar game of cat and mouse was played several times, with the French emerging to chase off an inferior force before the superior enemy concentrated against

them. The new French commander, Vice-Admiral Emeriau, missed the opportunity to capture *Temeraire* when she was becalmed near the guns of a battery on Pointe des Mèdes on 13 August 1811, but on 20 November, when only the 38-gun frigates *Perlen* and *Volontaire* lay off the port, Emeriau put to sea with thirteen of the line and a number of frigates. The van division of three battleships and two frigates sighted the two British frigates on the 23rd and got close enough to fire on both ships. Though Emeriau remained at sea for a further three days, with Pellew off Minorca, he had little to fear from carrying out manoeuvres off Cape Sicié. He made a sortie on 9 December with sixteen sail of the line, but did not wish to measure his force against Sir Edward's round dozen when it appeared, and returned to Toulon. The inshore ships were frequently in danger, but relied on their superior seamanship to escape whenever the enemy made a serious move against them (4). In the new year of 1812, Emeriau came out again on 14 January, followed by two large demonstrations in May. The second of these, on the 28th, was intended to cover the return of the frigate *Pauline*, 40, and the 16-gun corvette *Ecureuil* from the Adriatic. These were vigorously pursued by the young Sir Peter Parker in *Menelaus* (5) with such dash that he did not give up until his ship's fore topmast was hit and his rigging and sails were badly cut up.

Notwithstanding the fact that Toulon was one of the most difficult stations to blockade closely and that the fleet there by the end of 1812 consisted of eighteen battleships, five of which were of three decks, the best that can be said of Emeriau's performance is that he exercised his ships to a degree, but that he conspicuously failed to improve either their sea-keeping abilities or their battle experience. This state of affairs is odd when set against the fact that the French fleet in the Mediterranean in particular continued to grow, with building at Toulon, La Spezia, Genoa, Naples and Venice. By the autumn of 1813, there were twenty-one battleships and ten 40-gun frigates ready for sea, with three battleships on the stocks. But all this naval puissance was motionless without men, and the Emperor frequently commandeered seamen for service with the army whence they were drafted, never to return and it was this that formed the chief weakness of the French fleet. Perhaps the greatest battle honours of the squadrons of Allemand, Emeriau and Missiessy were actually the hollow victories of Smolensk and Borodino.

At all events there were to be a couple more ineffective skirmishes off Toulon. The first occurred on 5 November 1813 when Pellew's main body was well offshore to the south, but with an inshore squadron of the 74s *Scipion*, *Mulgrave*, *Pembroke* and *Armada* lying off Cape Sicié. Emeriau's dozen of the line, six frigates and a

6

schooner had emerged briefly, but with the wind turning foul decided to return to Toulon. As Emeriau put about, Rear-Admiral Cosmao-Kerjulien's division (the new 130-gun *Wagram*, five of the line and four heavy frigates) became the leewardmost, and Captain Heathcote of *Scipion* boldly attempted to cut them off as Pellew worked his way up from the south. Just after midday Heathcote was joined by the *Pompée*, 74, and a running engagement began. Then, at 1300, Pellew's flagship *Caledonia*, 120, arrived on the scene with the 112-gun *San Josef* and the 98-gun *Boyne*, cutting across Heathcote's bows and taking up the chase (6). Unfortunately the French escaped and Pellew retired to Minorca, reducing his inshore squadron to a tempting minimum, but the French declined the bait.

In February 1814 the final brush occurred. A new French 74-gun ship built at Genoa was making for Toulon to join the fleet and a squadron consisting of three of the line and three frigates sailed on 12 February 1814 to cover her approach. They were commanded by Cosmao-Kerjulien and having made the rendezvous, were heading south when at daybreak they were sighted by Pellew's lookout frigates. Just before 0800, the French turned to the west to pass inside Les Îles d'Hyeres and secure their passage along the coast to Toulon with a fair wind from the east. Pellew, with an overwhelming force (including nine three-deckers) stormed up from the south, aiming to cut the French off in the very entrance to Toulon. Both fleets were carrying a press of sail and making at least ten knots in the strong easterly wind. In the van of the British fleet *Boyne* managed to overtake the two rearmost French ships, *Adrienne* and *Romulus*, and half an hour after noon opened fire on the *Adrienne* but failed to stop her and concentrated on the last French ship, *Romulus*.

Captain Burlton of the *Boyne* tried to force *Romulus* ashore, but the French ship, possessing local knowledge ran as close as she dared, and when the *Boyne* was signalled to haul away, *Romulus* successfully doubled Cape Brun and cleared for Toulon (7). As Burlton stood past *Caledonia*, the two ships' companies cheered each other, but the entire French squadron escaped with the new ship from Genoa. Burlton's ship was hulled and knocked about aloft, had 2 killed, 40 wounded and two guns disabled. *Adrienne* lost 11 in killed and wounded, *Romulus* 70. This stirring, if ineffectual, incident was the last clash between the fleets of the two great protagonists and was eloquent of the final state of the respective parties. That it was necessary for the French to put to sea with a capital squadron to cover the entrance of single ships into their principal Mediterranean base and that they singularly failed to ever challenge the right of the Royal Navy to camp on its doorstep, is evidence of the victory of seapower.

3. 'Wind E.S.E. Off Toulon 1810. Philomel (2) rescued by Repulse (1) when chased by a French squadron 31 Aug 1810', aquatint engraved by Robert and Daniell Havell after an original by Captain Guions, no date. *NMM ref PAD5796*

4. 'Critical situation of His Majesty's Ship Curacoa off Toulon in the Winter of 1812', watercolour by Captain Pearce, no date. The precise incident is difficult to identify, since the ship was off Toulon in the winter months both at the beginning and end of 1812, and was chased on a number of occasions. The event involved *Curacoa* and *Havannah*, which found themselves the surprise target of four large ships; in attempting to haul off *Curacoa* split some of her canvas, and was lucky to escape. *NMM ref PAH8402*

5. 'HMS Menelaus and Eclair with a settee', grey pen and wash by Lt William Innes Pocock (1783-1863), no date but about 1811. *NMM ref PAF0054*

6. 'Blockade of Toulon, 1810-1814: Pellew's action, 5 November 1813', oil painting by Thomas Luny (1759-1837), 1830. *NMM ref BHC0604*

7. 'Combat du Vaisseau francais le Romulus contre trois Vaisseaux anglais a l'entree de la rade de Toulon, 13 Fevrier 1814. Galerie Historique de Versailles', steel engraving by J Doherty after an original by Gilbert, published by Diagraphe et Pantographe Gavard, no date. *NMM ref PAD5845*

7

1

The unceasing vigil

THE effectiveness of the British blockade ensured that no major actions were to be fought with the battle squadrons of the French in the closing years of the war. This in itself is evidence of the efficacy of British strategy, since in terms of numbers alone the strength of the French line of battle continued to grow relentlessly, and never ceased to pose a threat (1). It was an aggressive, costly business, a major drain on British resources and it required a ceaseless vigilance and the maintenance of a high standard of seamanship and navigation among the officers and men, backed by excellent logistics, repair facilities and the inevitable excesses of the press.

These qualities are exemplified by the conduct of the *Northumberland* in May 1812, which, in the hands of Captain Henry Hotham, and more particularly her master, a Mr Hugh Stewart, the 74 ended the cruise of a small French flying squadron consisting of the 40-gun frigates

Ariane and *Andromaque*, and the brig corvette *Mamelouck* of 16 guns.

The French had sailed from Nantes on 9 January under Commodore Le Foretier, bound for a cruise in the Atlantic, eluding the 40-gun *Endymion* and the 50-gun *Leopard* to take thirty-six merchantmen of British, Spanish, Portuguese and American nationality before serious pursuit was ordered by the Admiralty. On receipt of the Board's orders to the squadron off Ushant, on 19 May Rear-Admiral Neale dispatched *Northumberland* in search of Le Foretier. Hotham was fortunate enough to fall in with the French on the 22nd as they were heading home for Lorient, and in such a position as to have fortuitously interposed his ship between the French squadron and their destination, which he now closed to bar their entrance. In addition, Hotham had fallen in with the gunbrig *Growler* and signalled her to assist.

In a freshening west-northwesterly breeze *Northumberland* closed the coast during the mid-afternoon, drawing fire from the shore batteries and hove-to to await the oncoming French. Then Hotham filled his sails and turned to run parallel with the enemy as they attempted to double Pointe de Pierre-Laye. A spirited action ensued as *Northumberland*'s master showing 'greater familiarity with the charts than the French themselves' held a course so close to Le Graul rock that the *Ariane*, *Andromaque* and *Mamelouck* were compelled to run inside it under full sail, only to ground in succession on the reef between the rock and the mainland (2). Hotham hauled off to repair damage to his rigging and to shift his fore topsail, leaving the stricken French to the effects of the ebb-tide and the torments of *Growler* when she arrived. At about 1700 *Northumberland* came up again, anchored and clapped a spring upon her cable, thereafter bombarding the stranded vessels, beating in their bottoms so that

3

they would fill on the rising tide and sustaining some casualties from the nearest shore battery. *Andromaque* was set on fire and exploded at about 2000 and by midnight *Ariane* was seen to be burning furiously with *Mamelouck* on her beam ends and her bottom riddled with shot holes (3). As *Nothumberland* drew offshore *Ariane* exploded and a few hours later *Mamelouck* also blew up.

The British blockade aspired to exert a total stranglehold on French shipping movements, and under the covering power of the battle squadrons small craft sought to interrupt coastal trade. This was inherently dangerous, and did not always succeed, an example being the boat attack on a small convoy from La Rochelle that had been forced to anchor inside the Île d'Aix in December 1811. Five boats from two frigates and a brig were sent into the roads, where they were met by three gunboats and four launches, and in the fierce little engagement that followed the French drove off the

attack, claiming 118 British killed and taken prisoner (4).

However, the elements were a more potent enemy. The risks which British men-of-war ran on the enemy's coast, which was almost always a lee shore, were consequences of the constant need to carry out the duty of reconnaissance. Often the first indication of the escape of French frigates, was their absence from their previous anchorages and the duties of the sloops and frigates employed off Brest in particular, put them at constant hazard for, notwithstanding the wind, the ferocity of the tides in the locality could make a calm as dangerous as an onshore gale.

Losses were therefore to be occasionally expected, and that of the 38-gun frigate *Blanche* on 4 March 1807 was typical. Caught on a lee shore off Ushant in a gale, she drove aground and was wrecked with the loss of all but 43 of her people, and these unfortunates fell into French hands as prisoners of war (5).

1. 'A View of the Enemy's Fleet in Brest Harbour, reconnoitred by H.M. Ship Rippon on the 12th December 1813', anonymous watercolour, no date.
NMM ref PAH5079

2. 'H.M. Ship Northumberland destroying two French Frigates and a Brig off Lorient after a gallant action in 1812', black & watercolour pen & ink by C M G, no date.
NMM ref PAG9717

3. 'Destruction of the French Frigates Arianne & Andromachee 22nd May 1812', anonymous watercolour of the nineteenth-century British school, after Thomas Whitcombe, no date.
NMM ref PAD8661

4. 'Combat navale en vue de l'Ile d'Aix, 27 December 1811', steel engraving by E Chavane after an original by I Garneray, published by Diagraphe et Pantographe Gavard, *c*1850.
NMM ref PAF4789

5. 'Loss of the Blanche, March 4th 1807. From a plan by Sir T Lavie', coloured aquatint engraved by Thomas Sutherland after an original by Thomas Whitcombe, published by Pyall & Stroud, no date.
NMM ref PAD6062

6. 'This representation of His Majesty's Ship Magnificent, 74 guns . . . Showing (after cutting the Cables in a S.W. Gale) . . . making sail . . . 17th Decr 1812 . . . dedicated . . . John Hayes, Capt', coloured aquatint engraved by C Hunt after an original by Gilbert, published by Ackermann & Co, no date.
NMM ref PAH9217

4

5

6

Occasionally tragedy was averted by seamanship of the highest order, as was accomplished by Captain John Hayes in the 74-gun *Magnificent* on the stormy night of 16 December 1812. Anchored in the entrance of the Basque Roads with his tophamper sent down, Hayes discovered his ship to be dragging and while a second anchor brought her up again, he had a shoal less than 500 yards under his lee with a steadily rising wind, rain, a heavy sea and a tide setting onshore.

Hayes resolved to try and get out of this situation and made his preparations, getting a spring forward onto the small bower cable and swinging his fore and main yards aloft again outside the housed top- and topgallant masts. While this was in progress, the stream anchor cable parted but the bower cable held. Then preparing his sails in stoppings, his yards braced up for the starboard tack, Hayes calmly made his dispositions and called his men to attend his orders with absolute obedience and precision. When the cable was cut, the ship's head failed to fall off to port, but the parting of the spring an instant later made her broach, whereupon Hayes set his fore topsail, squared his main and mizzen topsail yards, leaving the mainyard braced round. As the wind came on the beam, the mizzen topsail was set, and with the wind in that sail and the helm put hard over, *Magnificent* began to turn, at which point the main course and main topsail were set, the crossjack yard hauled and the ship flew round, away from the shoal, now a pistol shot distant. With cool aplomb, Hayes announced to his silent ship's company, 'The ship is safe' and stood offshore (6). This exploit of club-hauling was to earn the captain the soubriquet 'Magnificent' Hayes.

Part II

EXPLOITING SEAPOWER — OVERSEAS

IT was as a global force that the Royal Navy fully exploited its potential to influence events on a world scale. With the largely successful policy of blockade preventing interference from metropolitan France, the far flung squadrons of Great Britain, augmented by the extended power of its cruisers, were able to maintain communications with locations as diverse as India, China, the East and West Indies, Canada and the United States, and 'the Brazils'.

Those French men-of-war which did escape the blockade were ruthlessly hunted down, and while they frequently enjoyed a degree of success, especially in the Indian Ocean, they were nowhere triumphant, for annihilation was their inevitable fate. To French cruisers, must be added their corsairs. These were a plague and it was absolutely imperative for the British to maintain cruisers on many stations, from the Davis to the Sunda Straits, and from Bergen to Basra, to contain them. All these measures were defensive and largely successful; they were intended to protect the global trade required to sustain Britain and to provide it with the wealth that paid for her war effort. They required a tireless expenditure of resources and human energy.

But in addition to this unglamorous task, the Royal Navy was able to take war to the enemy, extirpating privateer nests in the West Indies where it also destroyed the overseas colonies of Spain and France. Such achievements were usually the products of local initiative, as reactions to events on a station; less frequently the direct result of orders from London. Occasionally an expedition was mounted for a specific purpose, such as the force mustered to recover the Cape of Good Hope from the Dutch. Occasionally, as in the River Plate, initiative went too far and disaster followed, but generally British sea officers, whether cruiser captains or admirals, implemented a cohesive, if not a co-ordinated policy. Given the difficulties of overseas communications, this is a remarkable tribute to their gen-

'View of the Harbour of Rio de Janiero', engraved by Bennet after an original by Pocock published by Joyce Gold, 30 June 1808 (Plate CCLIX from the Naval Chronicle, Vol XIX). After the Portuguese Court was evacuated to Brazil, the Royal Navy maintained a squadron based in Rio, with its own storehouse and support facilities, one of the most far-flung of the Navy's commitments.   NMM neg D9263

eral quality and exceptions, such as the Plate, are thrown into their true perspective.

Just as the Dutch lost the East Indies, it was inevitable that in due course the French would lose the Îles de France and Bourbon. Curiously, had Napoleon supported Decaen as he promised, it was not inconceivable that the French might have built up a naval force on the trade route from India and China which would have been of great influence. As it was, the islands gave cause for grave anxiety to Pellew and others, until their reduction was completed.

Most impressive of all the Royal Navy's achievements, however, is its sheer ability to keep the sea, and nowhere is this more certainly evidenced than in the distant fleet in the East Indies. Most severely affected by the manning crisis which influenced the whole of the Navy during the period, short of stores and equipment, bereft of adequate dockyard facilities,

unpaid, driven constantly to improvise and of occasional uncertain temper, its officers and men nevertheless performed prodigies on behalf of a distant and aristocratic Government which scarcely gave them a thought. That a few of its senior officers made fortunes should not obscure the fact that the majority of its personnel failed to come home, and in the case of one frigate the Admiralty were absolved from the necessity of ever having to pay the wage of a single man for her entire commission.

The exploitation of her seapower overseas provided Great Britain with the means to wage her war against Napoleonic land-power. It was the dynamic which defeated the Continental System. Britain was able both to harness the resources open to her to provide for her own industry and thus the demands and desires of her proscribed but eager European markets, and also to substantially make up for those deficiencies which the 'closure' of her former European suppliers denied her. Thus, for instance, some of the shortfall of Russian-supplied 'naval stores' could be offset by supplies from the New World, the Canadian maritime provinces continuing as a source even after the outbreak of war with the United States, while the acquisition of new colonial territories from the French and Dutch, provided more raw materials and consumable commodities. Almost incidentally these gains laid the foundations for the postwar expansion of the British empire.

The consumers of Europe had no such alternative suppliers; Britain was already 'the workshop of the world', her manufactures were cheap, her luxury goods coveted, particularly by the new middle class in France which was growing wealthy on the war. Despite the very considerable effects of the *guerre de course* and the vicissitudes of the British economy, particularly in the matter of grain harvests, advantage lay increasingly with the British because their overall military and economic strategy was integrated. This cohesion was more a product of circumstance than design but, set against the centralisation of the Napoleonic Empire, it proved sensible, sustainable and successful.

Overseas seapower was as much a matter of merchant ships as of purely naval might. British merchant shipping possessed some seri-

One of many dramatic incidents in the ceaseless war against privateers: 'The Rinaldo. Capt J Anderson engaging four privateers 7 Dec 1810. From a sketch by Captn Anderson', coloured aquatint engraved by W Bailey after an original by Captain Anderson and Thomas Whitcombe, no date. NMM ref PAD5798

ous inherent flaws which had arisen from the exclusive protection of the Navigation Acts, but these very acts had provided a huge if disparate and unco-ordinated merchant fleet. The naval control imposed by the Convoy Acts enabled a combination of commercial and naval energies which lay at the very heart of this aspect of British seapower. Even when the demands of the British army in Spain were taking up from trade more and more vessels for military transport and logistics, the British were pragmatic enough to relax the Navigation Acts to the extent of allowing foreign-flag ships, particularly American bottoms until the rupture of 1812, to make up the deficiency. Even after hostilities had opened between the two countries, American merchantmen were not averse to turning to profit a British-generated market in the Peninsula.

Nevertheless, despite her preponderant navy Britain remained vulnerable at sea, for her strength lay entirely upon her trade. It was the Royal Navy's duty to protect the merchant ships which bore her immensity of wealth. By 1806 masters could not obtain their outward clearances until they submitted to convoy. The arrangements for the protection of trade were a matter of absolute necessity, for it was the capture of merchant ships by privateers that seriously weakened Britain's ability to wage war. The demands of convoy escort stretched the Royal Navy to the utmost. In the post-Trafalgar period, cruisers of all classes were commissioned from new tonnage, prizes or bringing out of Ordinary (reserve) ships - and frigates in particular - whose condition was not of the first class. This was an expedient solution; less easy was the means by which to man these

additional warships. The manpower crisis was more significant than the timber shortage, and it impacted upon the Royal Navy's fighting efficiency, not only in the quality of individual ships, but in the overall number of escorts available to protect trade.

But none of these preoccupations perturbed the British cabinet, who threw, in General Napier's phrase, 'the cold shadow of aristocracy' over all. British policy at the highest level remained much as it had developed in the preceding century; a war with the Continental power of France aimed at a restitution of that balance that preserved peace and limited ambition in Europe. This primary objective of the oligarchy was backed by a determined acquisition of wealth and power wherever and whenever opportunity offered. This underlying, opportunist and cynical agenda could be censured by a man like Pellew, or compromised to the point of embarrassed exposure by a man like Popham, but it took advantage of enemy weakness and sought to augment its own, and thus Britain's, power. Its objective was victory and its instrument was the Royal Navy.

Trafalgar stopped the encroachment of French seapower. The epoch following it consolidated that gain, for it was from the rigour of achieving and maintaining seapower overseas that not only the British Empire, but the Pax Britannica consequently arose. Britain did not retain all her conquests at the restoration of peace, for she was arbiter not dictator and the balance of power was still her main objective; nevertheless, she had a far greater say in Vienna than she had had at Amiens and her maritime supremacy was no longer in doubt.

The privateering war

FOR the seafaring communities of St Malo, Dunkirk, Bordeaux, Nantes, La Rochelle and Bayonne, the *guerre de course* provided a means of subsistence during time of war. Before Trafalgar, privateering was sometimes proscribed by the French Government needing seamen for the national battle-fleet; afterwards the tightening British blockade provided ample manpower. *Armateurs* were not slow to seize this opportunity, for the vast volume of British trade made it vulnerable and despite a tortuous process of liquidating prizes, profits could be considerable. The Malouin owners Lemême and Gautier took seven prizes valued at 437,969 francs with the modest 45-ton *Sorcière* before she was taken west of Jersey by the British privateer *Mayflower* in April 1806. In the winter of 1806-7, Gautier's *Confiance*, took prizes worth 25,881 francs. In 1808 the *Confiance* was sent to Martinique on an armed trading voyage, her letter of marque permitting her commander to make war and engage in trade (*en guerre et marchandise*). Such a voyage was intended to enable an owner to take offensive action if a potential prize appeared and the 'armed trading voyage' offered the shipowner a greater return on his investment above mere freight rates, even in times of blockade and consequent scarcity.

The *guerre de course* was soon to provide the British with numerous headaches and not a few humiliations. Off the Needles in a calm on 20 March 1807, the Revenue Cutter *Swan* was quickly captured by the French privateer luggers *Voltigeur* and *Reciprocité* (1). As the French took possession, they found about twenty of the *Swan*'s crew had escaped in her boat. The remaining four, including the commander, Richard Comben, were taken prisoner. Ironically, having lost their press exemption, the escapees were seized upon landing and impressed into the Royal Navy. Comben was not released until October 1814 and at the enquiry it was alleged he had exhibited 'great signs of fear'. The sorry event demonstrates the audacity of French privateers, that they could take a vessel in government service within sight of the Isle of Wight.

Cruising frigates and sloops did excellent work to contain the corsairs and enjoyed some success, but piecemeal destruction was not enough. The *armateurs* were energetic and resourceful and they had a large, idle seafaring community to hand. Before long their small craft swarmed in the Channel, stinging like mosquitoes at the corpus of commerce, causing grave anxiety among the British mercantile community who demanded action.

Occasionally the Royal Navy extirpated refuges used by privateers, such as Désirade and Marie Galante in the

1

West Indies captured in March 1808. Another method of containing the threat was the close investment of the enemy's coast, cruisers of all sizes being ordered to patrol bays and anchorages, expecially those protected by batteries, to smoke out privateers taking shelter under their protection. But the audacious appearance of enemy privateers on the very coasts of England was by far the most alarming aspect of the *guerre de course* because of the enormous value of the coasting trade. In 1810 one French privateer lay for three weeks off the coast, unopposed, and then seized no less than thirty small coasters out of a convoy. The situation, announced a notice posted at Lloyds, 'is beyond precedent'. Prints celebrating events such as the successful defence of the merchantman *Cumberland* against four *chasse-marées* under the very cliffs at Folkestone on 13 January 1811 (2), only served to reinforce the idea that such attacks were all too frequent and a national disgrace.

The lack of a close blockade at the minor ports from which the majority of the smaller French predators emerged was one reason for this humiliation, but little glory attached to the capture of a privateer and many actions with them proved murderous encounters. Neveretheless, there were officers prepared to harry the enemy wherever he was to be found. In January 1810, Commander Arthur of the 10-gun brig *Cherokee* 'dashed into the mouth of Dieppe harbour' to seize and cut out the *Aimable Nelly*, 16, in the face of fire from the batteries. But British attacks were sometimes repulsed, as occurred to the boats of the 36-gun frigate *Fortunée* when they attempted to capture the privateer *Amelie* on February 1810 (3).

1. 'English cutter Swan taken by French privateers La Reciprocite and Le Voltigeur March 1807', black & watercolour pen & ink by Houllets, March 1807.
NMM ref PAH8377

2. 'The Cumberland Merchant Ship engaging 4 French Lugger Privateers off Folkestone, on 13th Jany 1811', coloured aquatint engraved by Merke after an original by G Ballisat, published by the artist, 6 May 1811.
NMM ref PAH8091

3. 'Privateer Amelie beats off an attack by the boats of the Fortunee, 10 February 1810', lithograph engraved by Ferdinand Victor Perrot and Coulon after an original by Perrot, published by Victor Delarue, no date.
NMM ref PAD5799

4. 'Destruction of La Mouche French Privateer of Boulogne . . by H.M. Ship Hermes Septr 14th 1811 off Beachy Head in a Heavy Gale at S.W.', coloured aquatint engraved by I Clark after an original by Captain Philip Brown, no date.
NMM ref PAF4787

5. 'His Majesty's Cutter Entreprenante . . . having engaged . . . the Enemy's Privateers . . . under the protection of Castle Ferro on the 12th December 1810', coloured aquatint after an original by J Pringle, published by George Andrews, August 1812.
NMM ref PAH8090

2

3

During this year a large number of actions marked the approaching climax in the fight against enemy privateers, and by its end the risk of running across a British man-of-war limited success in European waters. It was this fact that induced the successful Malouin corsair Surcouf to return to privateering himself, after having become an *armateur*. He successively fitted out four vessels, but *Dorade* was taken by the sloop *Favourite* after a week at sea, *Auguste* was captured on the Grand Banks by the former French frigate *Rhin*, and while the lugger *Edouard* took a valuable prize worth 63,000 francs, she was herself captured in 1811 by the gunbrig *Derwent*. Finally the cutter *Renard* made two futile cruises between May 1813 and April 1814. Surcouf, meanwhile, had been causing havoc in the Indian Ocean in *Revenant*.

The tactic of lying under capes and headlands made such areas obvious targets for the hunting cruisers. Beachy Head was a favourite privateering ground, but in September 1811 it proved a death trap for *La Mouche* of Boulogne. Caught in a southwesterly gale by the 20-gun ship *Hermes*, the privateer was run down and sunk (4).

After the crisis of 1811, the tide began to turn. Caught

up in this decline was one of the most charismatic of privateer commanders, the Genoese Giuseppe Bavastro who had enjoyed legendary success in the Mediterranean and had been decorated by Napoleon in 1804. At the end of April 1812 he lay with a flotilla of privateers within the mole of Malaga, protected by batteries and a garrison of French infantry. Being advised of this, Captain Ussher of the sloop *Hyacinth*, supported by the brigs *Goshawk* and *Resolute* and gunboat *No 16*, attacked after dark on the 29th. Several prizes were taken but the bright moonlight persuaded Ussher to seize Bavastro's own vessel, the *Intrepido*, and another privateer named the *Napoleone*, and leave the remnant damaged as much as possible. The attack cost the British a third of the force of 149 men engaged in killed and wounded, but the career of Bavastro was over.

In the same waters in December 1810, the cutter *Entreprenante*, 8, lay becalmed between Malaga and Almeria on the morning of the 12th. At about 0800 Lieutenant Williams observed four French lateen-rigged vessels which had been at anchor under the guns of Faro castle, sweeping out towards him. Heavily armed and manned, the largest privateer bore some 75 men with six guns including two 18-pounders. The action was fought 'at pistol-shot', no more than about one hundred yards distance, and by noon the *Entreprenante* had suffered severe damage aloft and had a number of guns dismounted. The enemy twice tried to board, but were driven off, before renewing the attempt for the third time. This was again frustrated, though at the cost of further wounded and more damage (5).

Having failed to carry their enemy, the privateers drew off. The *Entreprenante*'s crew began to cheer and with

4

the two remaining larboard guns, raked the largest, dismasted felucca as she swung away. The double-shotted 4-pounders 'decided the business' and by 1430 the most damaged feluccas were being towed away by their boats. For half an hour, Williams encouraged their retreat, ceasing his fire at about 1500.

Such sharp, vicious actions characterised the attempts of the enemy to destroy British trade and of the varying fortunes attending the boats and small cruisers of the Royal Navy as they strove to oppose them. As a form of economic warfare privateering had posed the British navy with a very real threat which it answered convincingly despite the demands made upon its lighter forces.

5

The Cape of Good Hope, 1806

THE Treaty of Amiens had returned Cape Colony (1) to the Dutch and Pitt ordered an expedition to recover it. By the end of 1805 a military force consisting of some 5000 soldiers under the command of Sir David Baird embarked in sixty transports and four East Indiamen. Commodore Sir Home Riggs Popham, an officer whose career had hitherto been unusual and was afterwards to be controversial, was appointed to command the *Diadem, Raisonable* and *Belliqueux*, all 64s, the old 50-gun *Diomede*, the frigates *Leda*, 38, and *Narcissus*, 32, the brig sloop *Espoir*, 18, and gunbrig *Encounter*, 14. Making a rendezvous off Madeira then stopping at San Salvador on the African coast for provisions, the expedition sighted Table Mountain on 3 January 1806. The following evening the ships anchored to the west of Robben Island in Table Bay, with Popham reconnoitring Blauwberg Bay in anticipation of its suitability for a landing, while *Leda*, together with the transports having on board the 24th Regiment, approached Green Island by way of distracting the Dutch garrison.

The first attempt to land was thwarted by heavy surf, but *Espoir* discovered more favourable conditions at Saldanha Bay and the cavalry, part of the artillery and the 38th Regiment of Foot were ordered to landed there under Brigadier-General Beresford. *Espoir* and *Diomede* were detached to cover this, but the ships concerned had hardly weighed anchor when the westerly wind began to drop. As the surf in Blauwberg Bay immediately dropped, the landing was resumed and during the afternoon the troops again crowded into the ships' boats. Anxious about the untimely arrival of one of the French squadrons then thought to be at sea, Popham directed *Diadem, Leda* and *Encounter* to provide covering gunfire if required, with *Belliqueux* and *Raisonable* providing boats in which were embarked some field guns and two battalions of infantry. At this point the gunbrig *Protector* arrived and was ordered to anchor inshore and join *Encounter* covering the landing beach. Captain Downman of *Diadem* took command of one of the smaller transport brigs which drew only a fathom, running her ashore as a breakwater. Notwithstanding this precaution, the boats approached the beach in an extended line beyond the brig's protection. One, containing highlanders of the 93rd Foot was overset in the surf drowning 35 men. The surf increased as evening approached and operations were suspended for the night.

A small body of Dutch mustered near the head of the bay were engaged next morning by *Leda, Encounter* and *Protector* as they sailed up the bay covering the transports containing the heavy artillery. Their fire dislodged the enemy from a low hill and the landing continued all day. On the morning of the 8th, supported by artillery, the two brigades moved off along the Cape Town road, ascended the Blauwberg and drove off the Dutch light forces stationed there (2). Beyond, Baird's force came upon the main Dutch body of about 5000 men, mostly cavalry with a score of field pieces under Lieutenant-General Janssens. After an exchange of musketry and gunfire, Baird's men cleared the road at the point of the bayonet. Dutch losses were considerable, British casualties were 15 dead, 189 wounded and 8 missing. Janssens fell back to a pass known as Hottentot Holland's Kloof while Baird bivouacked on the Salt River to await the heavy guns from the head of the bay, intending to advance on Cape Town on the 9th. That morning, however, the Dutch made an offer of capitulation under favourable terms. Having occupied Fort Knocke, Baird opened negotiations with Governor Van Prophelow, who ordered the burning of the 68-gun *Bato* in Simon's Bay before surrendering the following morning. On the

1

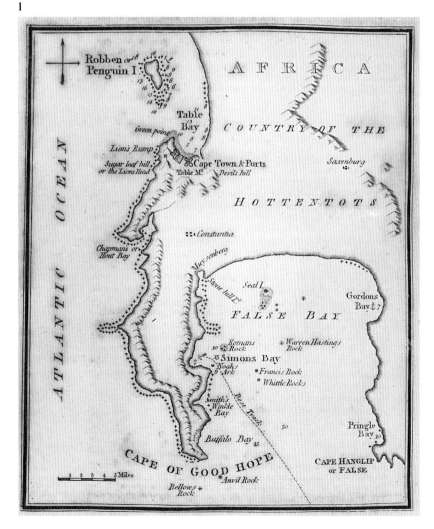

2

12th Baird took possession of Cape Town, whereupon Janssens also submitted. The terms offered the Dutch were designed to make British rule acceptable to the settlers; their troops were embarked for passage to the Netherlands at British expense.

The landing of the heavy artillery at the head of Blauwberg Bay had been accomplished with the assistance of a naval detachment of seamen and marines, brigaded under the overall command of Captain George Byng of the *Belliqueux*. Byng had with him Captain Hardinge and his officers, all of whom were aboard *Belliqueux* on their way out to India to join the new teak-built frigate *Salsette*, 36 guns.

Ironically, on 4 March the French frigate *Volontaire*, 40, which had detached from Willaumez's squadron, sailed into Table Bay, deceived by the Dutch colours flying from one of the forts and the shipping in that roadstead.

The *Diadem* promptly changed her ensign and summoned *Volontaire*'s astonished commander to surrender (3). This he did, revealing that his frigate had on board over 200 British soldiers who had been taken out of troop transports by Willaumez's ships in the Bay of Biscay.

The seizure of the Cape was not merely to protect the India and China trade, but to scotch Napoleon's persistent Oriental ambitions. In the autumn of 1805, the Emperor had declared to his Austrian prisoners, 'I want nothing on the continent. It is ships, colonies and commerce that I want.' False though this was in a European context, it reveals Napoleon's obsession and his need of wealth-generating possessions. Significantly therefore, the recapture of the Cape as a product of both strategic seapower and tactical marine expertise, was the first sign that, stemmed by Trafalgar, French power was no longer inexorable.

3

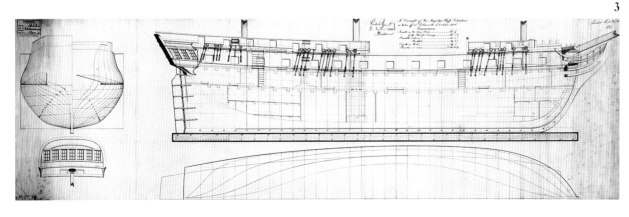

1. 'Cape of Good Hope', published by Joyce Gold, 31 December 1812 (Plate 328 from the *Naval Chronicle*, Vol XXVIII).
NMM neg D9276

2. 'A View of the Cape of Good Hope. This Engraving in Commemoration of the Taking of the Cape of Good Hope, is inscribed to Sir David Baird & Sir Home Popham . . . The Battle previous to the Surrender of the Cape of Good Hope, to Sir Home Popham and Sir David Baird, Jany 8th 1806', coloured aquatint and etching by J Clark and J Hamble, after an original by William Marshall Craig, published by Edward Orme, 4 June 1806.
NMM ref PA16990

3. The lines and profile draught of *Voluntaire*, dated 1817.
NMM neg DR1658

South America, 1806-1808

1

PRIOR to his departure for the Cape of Good Hope, Sir Home Popham had been appointed to the *Diadem*, 64, with a view to her exciting rebellion in the Spanish colonies of South America. General Miranda, the nationalist leader, had been in London and had received some encouragement from Pitt to which Popham had been privy. In the event Miranda was to be disappointed.

Having retaken the Cape, Popham's active mind required diversion. In April the project had been revived, for in conversation with a Captain Waine of the American merchantman *Elizabeth*, he had been assured that the Spanish provinces on the Rio de la Plata were anxious for liberation. This was appealing, for they were rich in beef cattle and flour, of which there was a dearth at the Cape. Moreover, Buenos Aires had links with the trade from the Phillipines. It was a repository of treasure and in its capture the prospect of material gain tempted Popham's cupidity.

Popham had always got on well with army officers, particularly with his colleague at Cape Town, General Baird. Baird unwisely acceded to Popham's request to be loaned 'a few troops for a short time to bring a question

of such importance to an immediate issue'. Popham obtained 700 highlanders of the 71st Foot, along with some dismounted troopers from the 20th Light Dragoons and six field pieces. This minuscule 'army' was put under General Beresford (1). On 9 April 1806, Popham invoked the approaching winter and informed the Admiralty he intended to cruise off the coast of South America in order to intercept any enemy squadrons in the South Atlantic. Four days later he was more specific and told Their Lordships of his intention of conveying troops to the River Plate. Actually they were already embarked in their transports

The next day, the 14th, the squadron, already enjoying expectations of prize money, weighed anchor. In addition to the transports, it consisted of *Diadem*, *Raisonable*, 64s, *Diomede*, 50, *Narcissus*, 32, and the gunbrig *Encounter*. To increase his force still further, Popham diverted the expedition to St Helena, where he 'wheedled' Governor Patten out of some men from the garrison. This reinforcement of two companies, with a 'sea-battalion' of seaman and marines christened by Popham the 'Royal Blues', brought the total force up to 1635 men.

But from Patten Popham learned of the death of Pitt,

2

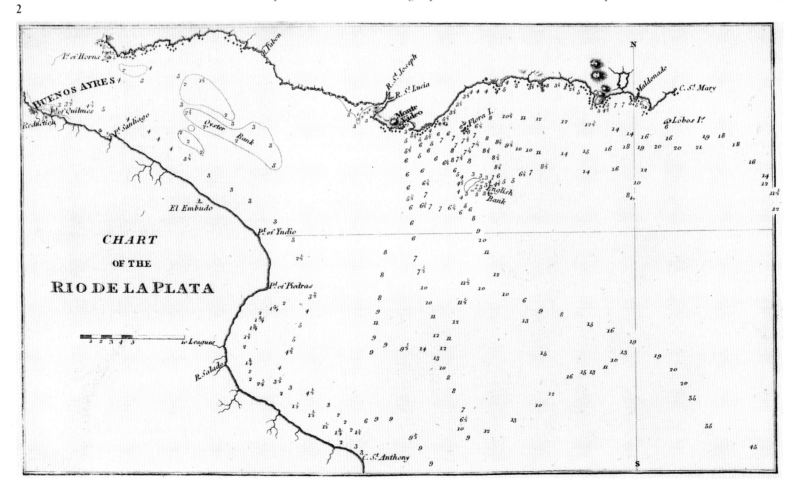

3

the change of government and the loss of his friend Lord Melville at the Admiralty. Popham's unilateral action was thereby dangerously exposed. He wrote to justify himself, pleading the benefit of opening new export markets and improving Miranda's chances of success, whilst claiming the implied approval of the dead Pitt. He also requested immediate reinforcements to consolidate his forthcoming success.

On 2 May the ships left St Helena for the Rio de la Plata. A month later they were in shoal water, dense fog and with bread for only four days, entering the estuary of the Plate (2). *Narcissus* spent a day aground on the Chico Bank, but Popham, embarked in the *Encounter*, sounded his way 130 miles upstream towards Buenos Aires which they had resolved to attack first in the belief that its lack of walls and a proper garrison would make it an easy target. *Raisonable* and *Diomede* had been left cruising off the mouth of the great river, and *Diadem* stood over to the north bank to blockade the regular troops in Montevideo. Meanwhile, *Narcissus* and *Encounter* together with the transports, struggled on towards their objective.

On 25 June 1807, Beresford's soldiers began to wade ashore at Quilmes, twelve miles below Buenos Aires. Brushing aside about 3000 Spaniards that evening, on the 27th the British crossed the Cuello and marched into the city. An article of capitulation was signed by the viceroy, but although private property was respected, the government treasury was ransacked of one million silver dollars with twice as much again being taken from the warehouses in valuable merchandise. The escaping viceroy, the Marquis Sobramente, was captured by a company of highlanders and relieved of 631,684 dollars.

In mid-September when the news reached London, it was greeted with joy, Popham having accompanied his official report with a flamboyant open letter to the merchants of England. Along with the dispatches, at Portsmouth the *Narcissus* landed specie as evidence of triumph. This public approbation ultimately saved Popham, for his report to the Admiralty had a contrary reception: Their Lordships were distinctly displeased, having attempted to scotch the adventure as soon as they knew of it. Elsewhere Popham was being lionised *in absentia*. He and Beresford were made the recipients of gifts from Lloyds' Patriotic Fund while the *Morning Post* of

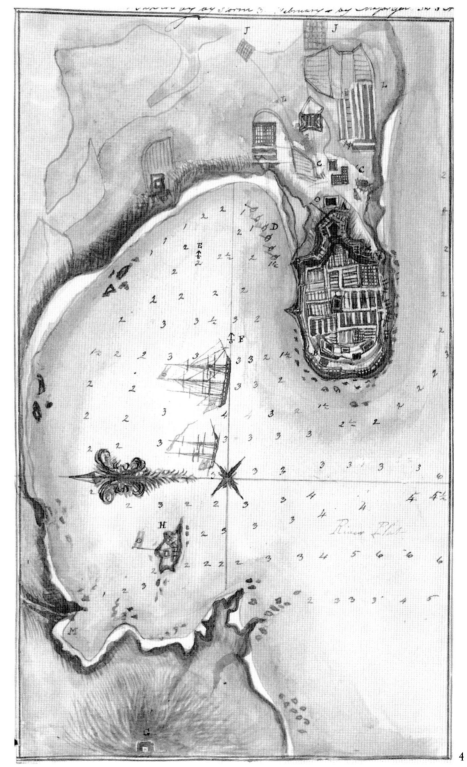

4

1. 'Sir William Beresford', mezzotint engraved and published by Valentine Green after an original by William Beechey, 31 December 1805. *NMM ref PAG6559*

2. 'Chart of the Rio De La Plata', engraving by Arrowsmith after his own original, published by Joyce Gold, 31 October 1806. *NMM ref PAH5910*

3. 'Vue de la Ville de Montevideo, prise de la mer, distance ½ mille, le soir', watercolour attributed to A Roux, 1822. *Peabody Essex Museum, Salem MA ref M3754*

4. 'Sketch of the Town and Harbour of Monte Video Taken by Storm 3rd February, by Major Genl. Sir S Auchmuty . . .', watercolour by Lt Samuel Walters, who was an eyewitness to the attack. Key: A. Citadel. B. St Philip Fort. C. English Batteries. D. Spanish Gun Boats. F. Anchorage, Ships of War. G. Light house on the Mount. H. Rat Island. I. Church in the Centre Town. JJ English Army. LL. Where the breach was made. M. Where the Gun Boats went after the storm. *Merseyside Maritime Museum ref N98.0288*

5. 'Sketch of Maldonado &c', watercolour by Lt Samuel Walters, present in the *Raisonable*. Key: A. Where the Squadron under Sir Home Popham's command anchor'd 30th October . . . in 6 fathoms water. B. Where the *Raisonable* anchoring to cover the retreat; if necessary for our Army to do so, in case of being overpower'd. C. The low land running out which forms the East point. D. The Island of Gorrita, three batteries and some store houses on it. E. Where the *Raisonable* touch'd in trying to arrive from A to B and where the *Raisonable* got aground in attempting to anchor at B, and in consequence was obliged to go round the Island of Gorrita N.W. passage. Near it the *Agamemnon* was lost after in 1809. . . . . Her track round. *Merseyside Maritime Museum ref N98.0285*

6. 'Storming of Monte Video Feby 3rd 1807. Dedicated by Permission to General Sir Samuel Auchmuty . . .' aquatint and etching by Clark and Dubourg after an original by Lieutenant George Robinson RM, printed by Edward Orme, no date. *NMM neg 7065*

7. 'The Ghost of Byng', coloured etching after an original by Isaac Cruikshank, published by S W Fores, 28 March 1808. The cartoon compares Whitelocke's treatment to the fate of Admiral Byng, who was shot in 1757 for 'an error of judgement' which led to the loss of Minorca. *NMM ref PAG8598*

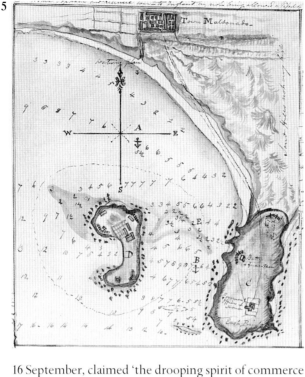

16 September, claimed 'the drooping spirit of commerce is wonderfully revived'. No impropriety was suspected for '. . . it cannot be supposed that an enterprise of such importance would have been undertaken, if the Commanders of it had not . . . received some instructions, probably of a private nature.' The same day, however, *The Courier* reported Popham had been recalled and on the 23rd the *Morning Post* spoke ominously of arrest.

On the Plate things had already worsened; opposition to the British quickly crystallised. A certain Don Liniers, a French Bourbon naval officer now in Spanish service who had been absent from Buenos Aires, returned on the pretext of visiting his family. Having reconnoitred the meagreness of the British garrison, Liniers recrossed to Montevideo, combined with other officers including a certain Pueridon and Sobramente at Cordoba, and set in motion a *reconquista*.

By mid-July Beresford anticipated trouble and informed Popham who brought his ships closer to prevent a junction of Liniers and Sobramente. Strong winds and shallow water prevented any of the larger men-of-war from aiding the land forces in the events which were now to become a British disaster. On 1 August Beresford defeated Pueridon outside Buenos Aires in a skirmish, but was soon afterwards besieged by larger forces under Liniers which, despite the winds which had frustrated Popham's dispositions, had crossed from Montevideo (3). Lying offshore, Popham was unable to embark Beresford's wounded while Beresford's men stood to arms throughout the night of 11 August. They were overwhelmed on the 12th and with casualties mounting, Beresford asked for terms, which were granted. The

little army threw down its arms and were marched inland.

Popham, who had received some reinforcement from an anxious Baird at the Cape, now sought to blockade Montevideo, but the shallows prevented him achieving anything (4) and he dropped down the north bank to land Brigadier-General Backhouse and a small force of troops, seamen and marines at Maldonado, which they took without difficulty on 29 October (5). The small island of Goritti, which covered the entrance was forced to surrender, and town and island were held as a small British base.

As a result of Popham's action and its economic potential, the British government had reluctantly decided to make a virtue of necessity. Popham was relieved by Rear-Admiral Stirling who arrived with a small troop convoy in early January 1807; he was followed by Brigadier-General Auchmuty who prepared to capture Montevideo and then recross the Plate and retake Buenos Aires. Maldonado was abandoned, though Goritti was left with a small garrison. The troops, seamen and marines were re-embarked and taken upstream to be landed on 16 January eight miles east of Montevideo. On the 25th the guns opened fire on the walls of the city which were breached by 2 February. Before dawn on the 3rd, the city was stormed and fell (6). Little occurred until May when Auchmuty was replaced by Craufurd, who was superseded in turn by Lieutenant-General Whitelocke, brought out in the *Polyphemus*, 64, flying the flag of Rear-Admiral Murray to whom Stirling became second.

It was now decided to proceed against Buenos Aires. Once again the ships of the fleet did little to help the troops, who landed on 28 June at Ensenada de Barragon, below Quilmes. They immediately suffered from lack of supplies on a march of three days and Whitelocke's operations were no better arranged than his logistics. Attacking on 5 July, Craufurd's light division was quickly captured in the streets and the brigadier, held in Liniers' headquarters, was forced to endure bombardment from Murray's ships. By the end of the day Whitelocke had determined that at a loss of 2500 men, the cost of his attack was too great. Moreover, his resources were quite inadequate to subdue a country which, while it might be generally opposed to the distant rule of Madrid, was hostile to the even more distant rule of London. While the Navy was preparing to land the battering train, the white flag of truce was hoisted ashore. Whitelocke acquiesced to Liniers' suggestion that prisoners should be exchanged, the attack be discontinued and the British evacuate Spanish territory within two months. Whitelocke submitted; it was the best that could be achieved and it did at least release Beresford's unfortunate men held up-country.

Murray's squadron waited in the Plate to embark all the prisoners, the ships leaving as they loaded for Britain or the Cape and their supplies ran out. In the aftermath of the disaster, orders were received from London to mount fantastical expeditions to Peru and Chile on the back of the assumed subjugation of the Plate provinces. The ultimate consequence of attempting to open new markets in Spanish America was the ruin of those speculators who had come out from Britain in anticipation of making their fortunes. To ensure the safe evacuation of these men and their families, Admiral Murray was obliged to leave the frigate *Nereide*, the sloops *Charwell* and *Hermes* and the cutter *Olympia*. On 14 September Murray's squadron left, 'cursing the hour they entered the river'.

Only a few months later, on 2 May 1808, the whole Spanish nation rose against the impositions of the French military occupation. By August, Rear-Admiral Sir Sidney Smith, now commanding His Britannic Majesty's ships and vessels off Brazil had re-entered the Rio de la Plata, where a squadron was to be maintained for the next fifteen years, allies of the sovereign power.

Popham, the instigator of this absurd fiasco, fared better than Whitelocke. Inept but realistic, the lieutenant-general was cashiered as 'totally unfit and unworthy to serve His Majesty in any military capacity whatever'. Portland's new Tory ministry made him the scapegoat for defeat (7). Popham had escaped lightly, court-martialled aboard *Gladiator* at Portsmouth in March, before the surrender and while expectations of export markets were still alive. He was lucky, for he had friends in high places. His conduct was 'highly censurable; but in consideration of circumstances' the court 'doth adjudge him to be only severely reprimanded'. It was to scarcely blemish this impudently resilient officer's career.

The GHOST of BYNG

1

Ships of the Royal Navy: the 64-gun ship

THE 64 was an 'economy' battleship and for major navies the smallest acceptable unit of the line of battle. The principal weakness of the type was the main battery of 24pdrs, whereas the rest of the line from the largest three-decker to the standard 74 were equipped with 32pdrs in the British fleet and 36pdrs in the French. This meant that any 64 was always a weak link in the battle line and a source of concern to the admiral commanding. This had become recognised during the American Revolutionary War and neither Britain nor France built such ships thereafter (1). The type remained popular with second rank navies, like those of the Baltic states and, especially, the Netherlands, and although France built no more of the type for her own navy she acquired others from her satellite states like Venice and Holland. Therefore, British 64s were often concentrated in the squadrons opposing those powers.

Year	No in Sea Service	No in Ordinary or Repairing
1793	2	28
1797	28	2
1799	22	4
1801	21	6
1804	8	12
1808	19	2
1810	11	1
1811	9	0
1814	1	0

Because of a large building programme put in hand during the American War, there were still thirty 64s available in 1793 (2). Natural attrition reduced the numbers gradually during the war, but many were captured – mainly from the Dutch, but three from Denmark and two originally built for the Knights of St John at Malta! But very few of these were acceptable cruisers, and those not hulked were usually reduced to duty as troopships or store vessels. However, such was the rapidly escalating commitments of British fleets that in 1796 five of the largest East Indiamen building on the Thames were purchased and converted into 64-gun ships (3). They had their ports rearranged to take twenty-six 24pdrs instead of the twenty-eight 18pdrs they were designed for. They were longer in proportion than purpose-designed 64s, but nevertheless were deemed inadequate warships, being slow and unwieldy, thanks to their capacious mercantile hull form – there were known derisively in the fleet as 'sugar and tea ships'.

Because of the weak broadside of the 64 there was a tendency to keep them out of the principal battle fleets if at all possible. Even in 1794 when all manner of battleships were in short supply, Lord Howe's Channel Fleet did not contain any 64s, and in the period of close blockade 64s were only very rarely assigned to such duties. As the country's front line of defence against invasion, the Channel Fleet clearly had first call on the best ships, but the 64 also disappeared from other strategically impor-

2

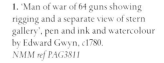

1. 'Man of war of 64 guns showing rigging and a separate view of stern gallery', pen and ink and watercolour by Edward Gwyn, c1780. NMM ref PAG3811

2. 'HMS Lion 1794. A Sixty Four', coloured etching after an original by W M, no date. NMM ref PAD5995

3. Lines and profile draught of the York ex HEIC Royal Admiral, 1795. NMM neg DR1209

4. Portrait of Raisonable, 64, watercolour by Lt Samuel Walters, who served in the ship on the East Indies station and during the ill-fated attack on the Plate. Merseyside Maritime Museum ref N98.0287

tant squadrons: by the middle of 1797, for example, the Earl of St Vincent's Mediterranean Fleet had only one, and even when assigned to a particular command the 64 was often detached on convoy and other duties outside the battle line, so were unpopular commands for ambitious captains. At that time the greatest concentration of 64s was with Admiral Duncan's North Sea fleet – ten ships, or exactly half his nominal line of battle – followed by Rear-Admiral Rainier's East Indies command of six, with four 74s and four 50s. Both were expected to face Dutch rather than French opponents, Duncan off the coast of Holland itself, and Rainier concentrating on Dutch colonies at the Cape and the Far East. The Dutch navy's ships tended to be smaller, since it was essentially a trade protection force, and at the battle of Camperdown in October 1797 there were seven 64s on each side.

Probably the last campaign in which 64s took part in large numbers was Copenhagen in 1801: nine were originally allotted to Parker's command, although only three went into action with Nelson's division. Once again the choice of ship type was determined by the numbers of similar vessels in opposing fleets; both Denmark and Russia – the planned next target after the Danish fleet had been dealt with – favoured smaller ships, and the inshore emphasis of Baltic operations suggested that shallow-draught and handy ships would be at a premium. Three went back to Copenhagen with Gambier in 1807, and Saumarez was assigned two 64s when a permanent fleet was sent to the Baltic in the following year. They played a big part in the Danish 'mosquito war', being a form of headquarters ship: Leyden, for example, was assigned eighteen lieutenants, most of whom were to command the gunboats that were attached as 'tenders'.

Although 64s were considered too weak for Channel service where the enemy battle line was composed of 74s and larger, in other areas the 64-gun ship had its uses. They were often handier and more weatherly than larger battleships, and could be employed on detached duties where more powerful opposition was unlikely. From a distance they looked like any other two-decker so could be used to maintain a presence off lesser ports, to lead small colonial expeditions, and to provide cover for the more important convoys. Agamemnon, Nelson's professed 'favourite ship', was very active under his command, and in the Mediterranean demonstrated some of the variety of roles performed by 64s outside the battle line. That the 64 was superior to any frigate was proved beyond doubt by Agamemnon's routing four of them (plus a brig) in October 1793; the 64's handiness was well illustrated by her hounding of the 80-gun Ça Ira in March 1795; and in the spring of 1796 under Nelson's broad pendant the ship led a detached squadron of one other 64, two frigates and two brigs to harrass the coast around Genoa and blockade the port.

The number of 64s in sea service began a steep decline in 1809-10, when the first of the large programme of 'Surveyors' class' 74s began to commission. Thereafter the remaining 64s took over from some 50s as distant-station flagships (4), saw more duty as convoy escorts, or were relegated to auxiliary status.

4

1

Brisbane and Curaçao

'WATCHING the motions of the enemy' necessitated constant observation on all enemy ports, one of which was the Spanish port of Havana, Cuba. In August 1806, shortly before her encounter with Leissègues' *Foudroyant*, HMS *Anson*, 44, lay off Havana in company with *Arethusa*, 38, Captain Charles Brisbane. Early on the morning of the 23rd they sighted a Spanish frigate, the *Pomona*, beating up for the entrance against a strong current in a light breeze. The *Pomona* had on board a quantity of specie and a cargo of valuable goods which she had loaded at Vera Cruz. Seeing the two British ships, and being unable to reach Havana, she bore up and headed inshore to anchor under the guns of Moro castle on the adjacent coast (1). The batteries mounted in the castle amounted to about eleven long 36-pounders; moreover the Spanish authorities at Havana, anxious for *Pomona*'s cargo and having observed her plight, sent ten gunboats out to her assistance.

2

3

4

Hauling anchor cables out through after gunports, Lydiard and Brisbane prepared to anchor close to the Spanish frigate but in the delay occasioned by the light wind, the gunboats got into a line protecting *Pomona*. Moreover, much of the specie had been taken off by the governor of Havana and the Spanish admiral commanding the dockyard, both of whom left the *Pomona* as the British ships drew close. At about 1000, the *Anson* anchored by the stern and engaged the gunboats, each of which bore a long 24-pounder, while *Arethusa* anchored between *Anson* and *Pomona* and concentrated her gunfire on the Spanish frigate (2). The aim of the gunboats' guns proved inaccurate, though red-hot shot occasionally came from the shore batteries and this started a fire aboard *Arethusa* which was quickly doused. After just over half an hour of this cannonade the *Pomona*'s colours came down, the frigate was taken possession off and afterwards purchased into the British fleet as the *Cuba* (3).

Captain Charles Brisbane's *Arethusa*, again in company with *Anson*, was to feature in one of the most remarkable exploits of the war. In the fall of 1806, Vice-Admiral Dacres commanding the Jamaica station, sent Brisbane

5

3. 'The Capture of the Pomona . . . blowing up of Coxima Castle by Two Frigates under the Command of Sir Charles Brisbane. 1. . . . 2. Anson engaging gunboats . . .', watercolour by Sir Charles Brisbane, no date. *NMM neg A2282*

4. 'Capn. Sir Charles Brisbane, Knt.', stipple engraving by Henry R Cook after an original by James Northcote, published by Joyce Gold, 31 August 1808. *NMM ref PAD3413*

5. 'The Conquest of the Island of Curacoa by Four Frigates under the Command of Sir Charles Brisbane &c &c – viz Arethusa Latona Anson and Fisguard. 1. Sr C. B. leading his men to storm Fort Amsterdam . . . 6. Dutch Commodore in possession. 7. Surinam in possession', watercolour by Sir Charles Brisbane, no date. *NMM neg 2268*

6. 'The Conquest of the Island of Curacoa by Four Frigates under the Command of Sir Charles Brisbane &c &c – viz Arethusa Latona Anson and Fisguard. 1. Sr C. B. leading his men to storm Fort Amsterdam . . . 6. Dutch Commodore in possession. 7. Surinam in possession', watercolour by Sir Charles Brisbane, no date. *NMM ref PA16996*

6

(4) with a frigate squadron to take Curaçao from the Dutch. Accordingly, Brisbane left Port Royal on 29 November 1806 with *Anson* and the *Latona*, 38. On 23 December they were joined by *Fisgard* off Aruba Island, whereupon Brisbane made known his intention of attacking Curaçao on New Year's Day. The attack was to be mounted on St Anne which was on the southeast coast of the island, exposed to the trade wind under the influence of which the squadron would run in.

An hour after the turn of the year the ships hove to and hoisted out their boats to take them in tow; then at 0500, with the wind easterly, they squared away to head for the narrow entrance between Fort Amsterdam on the eastern side of the entrance and the batteries on the western. Moored athwart the small harbour lay the 36-gun Dutch frigate *Kenau Hasselaar*, supported by the corvette *Suriname* of 22 guns and two armed schooners. Beyond, on a hill named the Misselburg was a series of fortified positions dominated by Fort Republiek which commanded the whole port.

At daylight Brisbane approached the entrance in *Arethusa* with *Latona*, *Anson* and *Fisgard* in line astern. The Dutch wisely ignored Brisbane's flag of truce and opened fire immediately, while a temporary wind-shift caused the *Fisgard* to ground briefly on the western side, but the other vessels got into the positions assigned by Brisbane and anchored (5). At this time, such was the confinement of the port, that *Arethusa*'s bowsprit stuck over the town wall. Holding his fire and insouciantly leaning

upon the *Arethusa*'s main capstan, despite the fire of the Dutch ships and batteries, Brisbane wrote a note to the governor, giving him five minutes to surrender and dispatching it by runner. The governor ignored the note and the Dutch gunners plied their weapons. At 0615, Brisbane hauled down the flag of truce and the British ships delivered three or four broadsides. In the wake of this, Brisbane soon afterwards boarded the *Kenau Hasselaar*, hauling down her colours himself before leaving Captain Wood of the *Latona* to warp alongside and take possession. At the same time, Lydiard of the *Anson* captured the *Suriname*. Having within minutes secured the ships in the harbour, all four captains were pulled ashore in their boats and 'at the rush' swept through several fortified positions, including Fort Amsterdam where 60 pieces of cannon lay, and on to the citadel and the town, all of which submitted (6). The party then returned to their ships which had meanwhile sprung themselves into a position to return the fire of Fort Republiek, centre of Dutch resistance. After half an hour's bombardment the fort's guns fell silent and before noon much of the island, was in British hands.

Brisbane's dashing exploit cost the Navy only 3 killed and 14 wounded; the Dutch lost severely, nearly 200 men, with Captain Evertsz of the *Kenau Hasselaar* being killed and Captain van Nes of the *Suriname* lying among the badly wounded. Brisbane and Wood received knighthoods and the first lieutenants, as was customary, were made commanders.

The West Indies, 1807-1812

THE protection of trade in the West Indies was best achieved by the denial of hostile havens to enemy privateers. On 21 December 1807 Rear-Admiral Cochrane sailed from Barbados and, as a consequence of Tilsit, seized the Danish islands of St Croix and St Thomas (1, 2). The French, however, still held Guadeloupe, Martinique and Guiana. In addition, San Domingo remained under the tricolour, though threatened by the neighbouring hostile black states of Haiti, and after May 1808, by the Spaniards of Puerto Rico.

French attempts to succour their West Indian islands were rarely successful, though individual cruisers remained dangerous to the safe passage of British merchant ships, and were far from easy targets, even for the superior force increasingly mustered against them. The relentless pursuit of known enemy cruisers was a cornerstone of British operations. In January 1807, the boats of *Galatea* took the corvette *Lynx* off Caracas after a fierce action, while on 27 March 1808, the boats of *Ulysses*, 44, *Castor*, 32, *Hippomenes*, 18, and *Morne Fortunee*, 12, attacked Marin harbour, Martinique, in which lay the *Griffon*. Despite capturing a battery, the combined fire of the other defences and brig foiled them and *Griffon* was not taken until 11 May, after a furious fight off Cape San Antonio, Cuba, with *Bacchante*, 20 (3).

This inexorable rise in British naval power in the West Indies placed the remaining French colonies under siege. In 1808 the plight of Martinique was desperate. In August 1808 three corvettes, *Diligente*, *Sylphe* and *Espiègle* loaded with supplies for Martinique, were chased in the Bay of Biscay by *Comet*, 18, which forced *Sylphe* to strike. On the 16th the remaining corvettes encountered *Sibylle* which took *Espiègle*, though *Diligente* again escaped until caught by *Recruit* off Antigua on 6 September. A hot action followed, but *Recruit*'s main mast fell, whereupon Commander Lemaresquier raked his enemy and made for Martinique, leaving *Recruit* to limp back to Carlisle Bay, Barbados.

More stores were sent out from Cherbourg in the corvette *Cygne* and two schooners. Observed off the Pearl Rock by the gunbrig *Morne Fortunee* on 12 December 1808, the arrivals alerted the frigate *Circe*, the sloops *Stork* and *Epervier*, and the schooner *Express*. One of the French schooners was driven ashore on St Pierre, *Cygne* and the remaining schooner were cannonaded by *Express*, *Stork* and *Circe* while a boat attack was repulsed with heavy losses (4). The following day *Cygne* began working her way along the shore towards St Pierre, but with the arrival of the 18-gun sloop *Amaranthe* the attack was renewed, aided by the boats of *Circe* and *Stork*. Despite a

1. Christianstaed, St Croix engraved by Baily after an original by Pocock published by Joyce Gold, 30 April 1811 (Plate CCCXXXV from the *Naval Chronicle*, Vol XXV). *NMM neg D9278*

2. 'View of the Harbour of St Thomas', engraved by Baily after an original by Pocock, published by Joyce Gold, 30 September 1811 (Plate CCCXLVI from the *Naval Chronicle*, Vol XXVI). *NMM neg D9267*

3. 'Action between HMS Bacchante & French Brig Le Griffon', aquatint engraved by Baily after an original by Lt Evans, published by Joyce Gold, 30 April 1813. *NMM ref PAD5771*

4

5

heavy supporting fire from guns ashore, *Cygne*'s crew finally abandoned her and the remaining schooner to destruction by the British.

The duty laid upon a British commander to 'do his utmost' encouraged attack, but prize money and ambition also drove officers to rashness that risked failure. Lieutenant Bennett of the 12-gun brig *Maria*, cruising off Guadeloupe on 29 September 1808, chased and engaged the 22-gun *Départment des Landes*, which bore a large crew and heavier guns. Bennet was overwhelmed and killed. The authority vested in any commanding officer was an important component in the Royal Navy's ability to

accomplish what it did, particularly with small men-of-war. The mixture of official coercion with ambition and opportunity, undoubtedly encouraged men like Bennet to take risks, while this influential cocktail imbued most of the officers in the Service. But if example is the essence of leadership, then lack of it could have disastrous results. A few days after *Maria*'s capture, Commander Gregory of the 18-gun *Carnation* encountered the 16-gun brig corvette *Palinure* off the northeast coast of Martinique. A furious fire-fight ensued, Gregory was killed, his two lieutenants severely wounded, the master mortally, and several other officers became casualties including the marine officer. Equally damaged, *Palinure* drifted down onto *Carnation*. Although Boatswain Triplet fought on at the head of a few men, the French captured *Carnation*, for without leadership most of the British crew fled below led by the sergeant of marines, John Chapman (5).

But the strategic tide ran against the French. A raid on Samanha Bay, San Domingo, by the frigates *Franchise*, *Daedalus* and *Aurora*, and the sloops *Reindeer* and *Pert* in November 1808, wrecked the defences and robbed enemy privateers of another secure haven. A few days later the 64-gun *Polyphemus* cut out a man-of-war schooner on the same coast, though a raid by the boats of *Heureux*, 16, on shipping at Guadeloupe on the 28th was defeated.

In the new year offensive military operations were begun against French Guiana and Martinique. Rear-Admiral Sir Sidney Smith, now the British naval commander in South American waters, ordered Captain Yeo to take a small, allied expedition to raid French Guiana. At Belem, at the mouth of the Amazon, Yeo in the ship sloop *Confiance*, 22 took under his command the Portuguese 64-gun ship *Infante Dom Pedro*, the brig *Voador* and some small craft. Embarked were 800 Portuguese and Brazilian soldiers under Lieutenant-Colonel Marques. Yeo captured Appruague, Guiana, on 15 December 1808, then advanced on the French colonial capital of Cayenne, situated on an island between the Cayenne and Mahury Rivers (6). Yeo entered the Mahury on 6 January 1809 and that evening set off in ten canoes with about 250 seamen and marines from both the British and Portuguese ships to attack the defending forts, with Commander Salghado of the *Voador* following after dark with the bulk of the troops. The canoes were upset in the surf, but Yeo took the battery at Fort Diamant, while Colonel Pinto seized that at Degard des Cannes. However, the Portuguese cutters *Lion* and *Vinganza* had discovered two other posts further up the Mahury and Yeo promptly re-embarked and successfully assaulted both posts.

By now Hugues had counter-attacked at Desgard des Cannes and at Fort Diamant, but his troops were held at bay for about three hours before the French withdrew from before both places. Next day a flag of truce was sent upstream to seek terms, but was fired upon from a fort defending Governor Hugues' house, which was stormed by the Anglo-Portuguese with the bayonet, routing the garrison. Thereafter Cayenne was summoned on 10 January and capitulated on the 14th. The territory was added to Brazil, though after the war most was returned to France. On 13 January the French frigate *Topaze* appeared with reinforcements for Hugues. Boldly approaching with 25 of his crew and a score of natives, acting master James Arscott of the *Confiance* and two midshipmen, drove off the heavier enemy.

The reduction of Martinique was ordered by the government in London. On 28 January 1809, Rear-Admiral Alexander Cochrane left Barbados in the 98-gun *Neptune*, with five two-deckers, *Ulysses*, 44, seven frigates and a further twenty-eight sloops, gunbrigs and schooners – practically the whole naval force deployed in the Caribbean – and an overwhelming 10,000 troops embarked in numerous transports commanded by Lieutenant-General Beckwith. Vice-Admiral Villaret-Joyeuse, the captain-general, had at his disposal 2400 regular soldiers and an uncertain militia of 2500. The coasts were protected by about 290 guns and in Port Royal lay the frigate *Amphitrite*, 40, which successfully made the passage from Cherbourg. Having fought off her interceptors, the corvette *Diligente* lay at St Pierre and the captured British brig *Carnation* was at Marin.

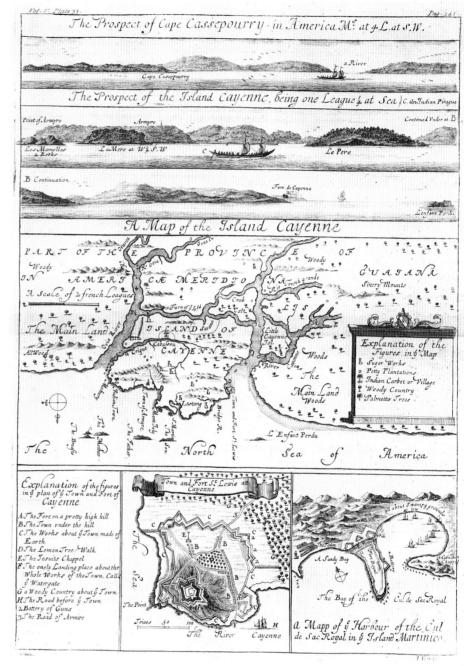

Troops were landed at Pointe Sainte Luce, Cape Solomon and Baie Robert, seamen going ashore under Captain Cockburn of *Pompee* to assist with the guns. The invaders encountered no resistance from the militia, driving the regulars back on Fort Desaix. A heavy bombardment of Pigeon Island (Ilot aux Ramiers) in Port Royal Bay was supported by both Cockburn ashore and with fire from *Æolus*, *Cleopatra* and *Recruit*; the fort fell on 4 February. Cochrane now stood into the bay with the fleet and the French set fire to *Amphitrite* as they had burnt *Carnation* on the appearance of the British at Marin. St Pierre and *Diligente* were taken on the 9th as Fort Desaix was invested, and Port Royal itself was occupied on the 10th. The bombardment of Fort Desaix began on the 19th

6. 'The Prospect of Cape Cassepourry in America . . .; The Prospect of the Island Cayenne . . .; A Map of the Island Cayenne; Town and Fort St Lewis at Cayenne; A Map of ye Harbour . . . Island Martinico', engraving and etching by Jan Kip, no date.
NMM ref PAH3050

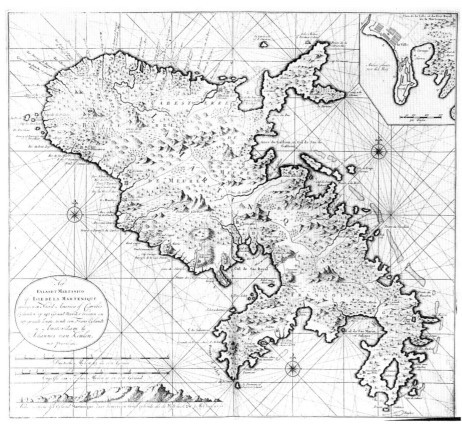

7

8

and continued until a parley was beat at noon on the 23rd. The negotiations failed and fire recommenced until white flags were hoisted on the 24th, whereupon Martinique fell into British hands (7). While Villaret-Joyeuse went home to be broken by a court-martial in Paris, British naval justice was visited on the hapless, captive crew of the *Carnation*. Sergeant John Chapman of the marines was hanged for cowardice and thirty-two seamen and marines were transported to Botany Bay.

Further attempts to supply the beleagured islands

were frustrated. In January 1809 the frigate *Melampus* captured the French brig *Colibri* off Barbuda and the corvette *Hébé*, laden with flour for San Domingo, was caught in the Bay of Biscay by the British frigate *Loire*, 38. Earlier, in December, *Loire* had had a brush with the French frigate *Topaze*, 40, as she escaped from Brest on her way to Cayenne. Intimidated by Arscott she made instead for Guadeloupe where she was seen by the British squadron running to anchor under the batteries of Pointe Noire on 22 January 1809. That afternoon *Cleopatra*, 32, stood in to engage her and she resisted until *Jason*, 38, and *Hazard*, 18, arrived and compelled her to surrender.

The odds were now heavily against the French. The 40-gun *Junon*, having for some time been lying in Les Saintes, broke out on 7 February only to be pursued by the brig sloop *Superieure*, 14. The overwhelming imperative of escape now had the powerful *Junon* fleeing from the aptly named *Superieure*, formerly a French schooner. On the following day the British frigate *Latona* joined in the windward chase, but the following morning, the two British ships were well astern with little prospect of bringing their quarry to battle. Then the frigate *Horatio* and sloop *Driver* appeared on the opposite tack and Captain Rousseau was obliged to run off before the wind to avoid the trap, only to be headed off by *Latona*. Rousseau decided to accept the better odds offered by *Horatio* and passing the 38-gun frigate on the opposite tack, exchanged shots. Rousseau wore ship immediately, but was out-witted by *Horatio* which wore so smartly that she raked *Junon* as Rousseau hauled up again on the starboard tack, whereupon both ships came to close action. *Horatio* now sustained disabling damage aloft and *Junon*, hulled by *Horatio*, disengaged. The pursuit now resumed, with *Latona* and *Driver* too far away to assist *Superieure*, which fired into the passing French frigate. But the damage inflicted by *Horatio* now told against *Junon*; *Latona* slowly overhauled her and with *Driver* supporting, opened fire. Rousseau boldly tried to rake by tacking, but lost his main and mizzen masts in the attempt, ending a spirited defence against a greatly superior force and with the loss of one-third of his men (8). *Junon* was taken into the Royal Navy.

A final effort to succour Martinique was made by Commodore Troude, who left France with three 74s, *Courageux*, *Polonais* and *D'Hautpoult*, and two frigates, *Félicité* and *Furieuse*, reduced as storeships. Troude reached Martinique unmolested but, learning of its capture, slipped into Les Saintes. The presence of the French vessels resulted in Cochrane ordering the islands taken, and on 14 April troops and two howitzers were landed by Captain Beaver of *Acasta*. During the night Troude's three 74s sailed, but were observed by *Hazard* and reported to Cochrane. Offshore with *Neptune*, were *York*, *Pompee*,

Polyphemus and *Recruit*, and a general chase began. *Pompee* and *Recruit* overhauled Troude's *D'Hautpoult* and opened fire. Cochrane's *Neptune* then came up, but the French ships drew away with only the *Recruit* hanging onto them throughout the night, opening fire and annoying the heavier French ships until compelling them to yaw and discharge broadsides at her (9). By the evening of the 15th, *Pompee* had again caught up and forced the French to scatter. *D'Hautpoult* steered west-northwest with *Pompee* in pursuit, *Neptune* and *Recruit* followed *Courageux* and *Polonais*. The chase ran into the 16th, with the frigates *Latona* and *Castor* joining *Pompee*. Before dawn next morning, *Castor* was close enough to disable her until *Pompee* arrived to bring Troude to close action. British ships were now arriving from every point of the compass and at 0515, Troude submitted.

Courageux and *Polonais* got away, returning to Cherbourg, but *Furieuse* and *Félicité* were not so fortunate, though they slipped out of Les Saintes on the night of the 15th. Discharging their desperately needed cargoes at Guadeloupe, they sailed from Basse Terre on the night of 14 June but were chased until, on the 18th the *Latona* caught and captured the *Félicité*. *Furieuse* ran on until 5 July when, in mid-Atlantic she encountered *Bonne Citoyenne*, 20. Commander Mounsey skilfully handled his fast, former French corvette, and in seven hours fired 129 broadsides to the *Furieuse*'s 70. Then, having exhausted his ammunition, worked athwart *Furieuse*'s hawse to board, whereupon *Furieuse* struck. Mounsey afterwards brought both ships into Halifax (10).

British attention now focused upon San Domingo where General Ferrand's troops were not only under threat from the neighbouring black states, but from their former allies, the Spanish in Puerto Rico. A Spanish force landed on San Domingo and Ferrand shot himself after his defeat at Palo Hincaldo on 7 November. The Spanish invested San Domingo city, supported by Cochrane's squadron and in May 1809 troops under Major-General Carmichael arrived from Jamaica. San Domingo surrendered on 6 June and many of the garrison, black and white, were evacuated to New Orleans — to fight the British again under Andrew Jackson in 1815.

Of all former French Antilles, there remained only Guadeloupe, supplied intermittently by French frigates. In the autumn of 1809 *Renommée* and *Clorinde*, both of 40 guns, and the former 40-gun *Loire* and *Seine*, reduced to *flûtes* of 20 guns, were sent out, only to be chased off Antigua on 13 December by *Junon* and the sloop *Observateur*. Deceived by Spanish colours and the private signal, *Junon* was greeted by a devastating broadside from *Renommée*, and after a stout resistance against the whole French squadron Captain Shortland surrendered, but his ship had to be set on fire by her captors. The *Observateur*

9

escaped to inform Captain Ballard of the *Blonde*, 38, who concentrated his force of the *Thetis*, 38 and the 18-gun sloops *Hazard*, *Cygnet*, *Scorpion* and *Ringdove* between Les Saintes and Guadeloupe (11). Early on the 17th the trap was sprung as *Castor*, 32, arrived with the French in chase astern. Seeing the British squadron ahead, they ran for Anse le Barque with Ballard after them. Commander Dowers of the *Ringdove* impetuously stormed and carried a battery without loss and next day Ballard was now joined by the 36-gun frigate *Freya* and the 74-gun *Sceptre*. On the 18th the British attacked in force, but *Renommée* and *Clorinde* slipped away to the northward. *Sceptre* and *Freya* engaged the shore batteries, which were also attacked by a landing party from the sloops under Cameron of *Hazard*, while *Thetis* and *Blonde* fired on the two frigates *en flûte*. Both soon struck, but catching fire, their cargoes were lost.

But the noose was drawing tighter all the time. *Melampus* had taken the brig *Béarnais*, 16, off Guadeloupe on 14 December; *Rosamond*, 18, seized her consort the *Papillon* on the 19th; on 11 January Ballard sent *Scorpion* into Basse Terre to bring out the 16-gun brig *Oreste* and on the 21st, Hayes of the *Freya* fell upon some vessels in Baie Mahaut. Finally, on the 27th, Rear-Admiral Cochrane brought Lieutenant-General Beckwith and 7000 men

10

from Martinique, successfully landed them and marched across the mountains to corner General Ernouf in Basse Terre. Ernouf's troops were disaffected; many dispersed and he could only rely upon one line regiment. After a few days of skirmishing, he capitulated on 6 February. In the succeeding fortnight Beckwith and Cochrane mopped up the remaining small Dutch colonies of St Martin, St Eustatius and Saba. So, with the exception of Haiti, the entire West Indies was in the hands of Great Britain or her new ally, Spain.

A last bizarre event concluded the war in the West Indies. The Royal Navy respected both the adjacent Haitian states of King Christophe and President Pétion as independent sovereign nations. In early 1812 a renegade of Christophe's navy, a former privateersmen named Gaspard, was illegally raiding trade in the 44-gun frigate *Améthyste*. She was the former French *Félicité*, taken by the

Latona and sold to King Christophe. In February Gaspard's pirates were in the Bight of Léogane while Captain Yeo, now commanding the frigate *Southampton*, was lying at Port au Prince. Yeo slipped to sea under cover of darkness on the 2nd and challenged Gaspard's legitimacy the following day. Gaspard responded with a broadside, precipitating an action in which *Southampton* shot away *Améthyste*'s main and mizzen masts, causing fearful losses and killing Gaspard. After her surrender, the refitted *Améthyste* was restored to King Christophe.

The Royal Navy's numerous cruisers everywhere dashed the hopes of the French, despite the enemy's gallantry and skill, and guaranteed the deployment of British troops wherever it was considered necessary. In a climate highly destructive to shore-bound garrisons, the actions of the Royal Navy robbed France of the economic value of her sugar islands.

11. Chart of Guadeloupe by William Faden, from *West Indies Atlas* (London c1808).
NMM neg A4431

11

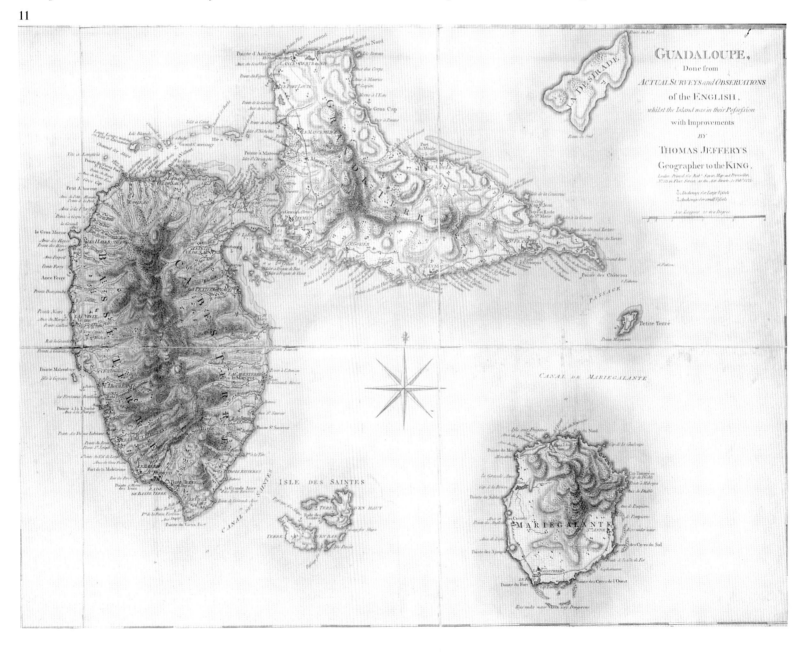

1

The East Indies, 1806-1808

IN 1806, the situation east of the Cape was complex. The area was subject to two admirals, Troubridge and Pellew, an unhappy circumstance in itself. In addition to protecting the movements of both the East India Company's ships and the Country trade, the presence of the French at Île de France and a Dutch squadron in the East Indies, stretched available resources, and the facilities available to maintain men-of-war were inadequate. The graving dock at Bombay was too small, though a replacement was under construction, and in the spring of 1806 Troubridge was examining the possibility of creating a dockyard at Penang (1). Eventually the frigate *Malacca* was launched there in 1809, although a proposed 74 was cancelled. A mutiny at Vellore required the assistance of Pellew's marines and deferred any attempt to reduce Île de France during 1806.

The Dutch squadron in the East Indies was divided between Batavia, the Dutch colonial capital in western Java, and Griessie, near Sourabaya in the east. Dutch men-of-war were used for trade protection and the suppression of piracy, so the British cruisers threw them on the defensive. The 36-gun frigate *Pallas* and two richly laden Indiamen were captured south of Celebes in late July 1806 by the British frigate *Greyhound*, 36, and sloop *Harrier*, 18. Even greater success was enjoyed by Captain Peter Rainier, of the *Caroline*, 36: a few months earlier he had been a mere midshipman, but his uncle was a former Commander-in-Chief and Rainier attained post-captaincy in June 1806 at the age of just twenty-one. On 18 October, Rainier found the frigate *Maria Reijgersbergen*, 36, together with the 14-gun sloops *William*, *Maria Wilhelmina* and *Zeeploeg* and the 'colonial' vessel *Patriot*, of 18 guns all at anchor in Batavia roadstead. The frigate *Phoenix* was not far distant and several gunboats were in the vicinity, but

Rainier engaged *Maria Reijgersbergen*, opening a heavy fire and forcing her to strike her colours after half an hour's cannonade during which her consorts offered little or no assistance. Rainier was able to carry off his prize from under the noses of the Dutch and the ship was purchased into the Royal Navy as *Java* (2).

The following month Pellew himself appeared off Batavia. The rear-admiral flew his flag in *Culloden*, 74, having with him three two-deckers, two frigates and a brig. On the way, Pellew took *Maria Wilhelmina*, arriving in the roadstead on the 27 November to find the *Phoenix*, *Zeeploeg*, *William*, and *Patriot* still passively anchored. They had been joined by the 18-gun *Avonturier* and some vessels of the Dutch East India Company. Pellew's squadron took the Dutch by surprise; while the *William* struck her colours to the *Terpsichore*, commanded by Pellew's 17-year-old son Fleetwood (3), the remainder cut their cables and ran into the shallows. The crew of the *Phoenix*

2

3

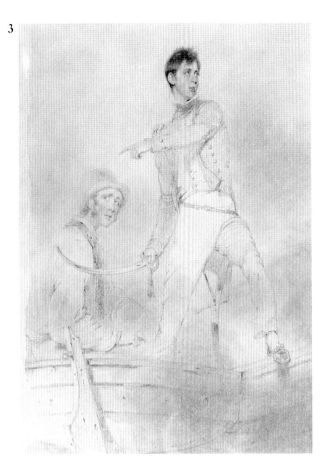

sion to unite the command under his flag. Troubridge was recalled but the old and leaky *Blenheim* and the equally crazy *Java* foundered in heavy weather with the loss of all hands, including Troubridge himself. Pellew was left with his flag in *Culloden*, with his forces spread around India, off Batavia, at Penang, Sumatra and cruising in the South China Sea, and even on convoy duty between the Persian Gulf and the Red Sea. However, there was one relief, when the Admiralty assigned the blockade of Île de France to the admiral at the Cape. Pellew could now contemplate removing the Dutch from Java.

To take Java, the new Governor-General, Lord Minto, would only release a battalion of the 30th Regiment, but Pellew had strengthened his squadron by two prizes, one of which was the 12-gun privateer *Jaseur*. The second was the Dutch corvette *Scipio*, taken by the *Psyche* on 31 August while the latter was reconnoitring the coast of Java and bought into the Service for £4725. At the time *Psyche* was commanded by Pellew's son Fleetwood who had shifted from the *Terpsichore* (4). With the troops embarked in Madras Roads on 17 October, Pellew proceeded to Malacca, leaving for Java on 20 November, reinforced by *Powerful*, 74, the frigates *Fox* and *Caroline*, and four sloops. His prime objective were the Dutch ships of the line and he knew that two, the *Revolutie* and *Pluto*, still lay at Griessie, near Sourabaya in the east of Java.

scuttled her and all the British could achieve was to destroy the remainder. However, Vice-Admiral Hartsinck's four ships of the line had eluded Pellew and, dispersing his squadron, he retired to Malacca.

Here, on 1 January, he learned of the Admiralty's deci-

Pellew's ships arrived in the Madura Strait on 5 December to be joined by *Psyche*. The admiral summoned the governor of the fort at Griessie to surrender, but this was refused and Pellew began lightening *Culloden* and *Powerful*. Silencing a 12-gun battery at Sambilangan, the

4

squadron passed into the shallow river and began to work its way upstream (5). Arriving at Griessie, Pellew found the *Revolutie* and *Pluto*, the sheer hulk *Kortenaar* and the Indiaman *Rusthoff* had been scuttled, and he had to content himself with setting fire to what remained of them above water (6). The guns and stores at Griessie were also destroyed and the battery at Sambilangan was demolished.

Back in Madras on 10 February 1808 to rumours of a French overland expedition to Persia and India, Pellew became alarmed that an accompanying French fleet would soon be in the Indian Ocean. Captain Ferrier of the *Albion* had sailed for the Persian Gulf with *Phaeton* and *Dedaigneuse* four days earlier. Pellew went to Bombay, followed by complaints of French cruisers and corsairs which had enjoyed considerable success in his absence. Despite 'intersecting the Bay [of Bengal] in every direction', only the *Russell* had been successful, seizing the privateer *Adele* on 5 December. Though glad to have relinquished the blockade of Île de France, Pellew complained to the Admiralty, 'no information can reach me but by very uncertain Channels respecting the arrival and departure of the Cruizers, and for the most part, the first Intelligence of their appearance in the bay [of Bengal] is announced by their success'.

On the one hand were privateers, of whom Robert Surcouf was the most active and most feared; on the other were the large national frigates *Cannonière* and *Sémillante*. The latter had fought an action with *Phaeton* and *Harrier* off the Philippines in August 1805 which had prevented her crossing the Pacific to Mexico. Thereafter she retired to Île de France, making several successful cruises, but in March 1808 she fought a fierce and inconclusive action with the British frigate *Terpsichore* in which *Sémillante* was so badly damaged that she was judged unfit for further service as a cruiser, and had to be sent home to France.

Meanwhile, in August 1808, the *Cannonière*, returning from the South China Sea, joined the damaged *Sémillante* at Port Louis, to be blockaded in early September by the 22-gun ship *Laurel* which had arrived from the Cape with stores for the ships she expected to find offshore. Instead, Captain Woollcombe invested the French port and retook a Portuguese ship which had been taken by the

5

French and was making for Port Louis. Aboard were some French ladies who had taken the opportunity of effecting a passage from the neighbouring island of Bourbon and Woollcombe sent in a boat to Decaen to arrange for their landing. Complying, Decaen sent out the second-captain of *Cannonière* to assess *Laurel* and when she was close inshore on 12 September, *Cannonière* emerged to engage her. Up to now Woollcombe knew only of the *Sémillante* in Port Louis, but Woolcombe ordered *Laurel* to engage as the darkness gathered. The wind was light and *Laurel* raked *Cannonière* but then, although *Cannonière*'s shot flew over the heads of the sloop's company it utterly destroyed the *Laurel*'s rigging and after an hour and a half, Woollcombe struck his colours, having inflicted material damage on the hull of the *Cannonière*. Captain Bourayne returned the swords of Woollcombe and his first lieutenant, William Woodman, having sustained casualties of 40 men out of 420 embarked, against the *Laurel*'s 9 wounded out of 150 men. The *Cannonière* was also condemned, sold and loaded with a cargo valued at some £150,000. Unlike *Sémillante,* she failed to make a friendly port and was chased fourteen times in ninety-three days, evidence of the proliferation of British cruisers on her route. She was finally captured off Belleisle by the 74-gun *Valiant*, not far from the position where, on 12 April 1812, the *Laurel*, now renamed

6

7

Espérance was recaptured by the *Unicorn*, 32, rejoining the Royal Navy as *Laurestinus*.

The acquisition of *Laurel* was offset by the loss of a further French national cruiser, the corvette *Jena*, 18, a purchased former privateer. On 8 October 1808 she fell in with the 36-gun *Modeste*, which chased her for nine hours and after an action of one, compelled her to strike. This effectively wiped out a French force in the Indian Ocean, but not before malicious letters had been sent to London impugning Pellew.

Pellew knew all this but had other matters to worry him. The alliance of Portugal with Britain persuaded Lord Minto that the Portuguese territory of Macao must

be taken and held under British protection on the same terms as Goa, though the territory itself was not held under the same conditions. Pellew proposed that his relief, Rear-Admiral Drury, should command the expedition prior to taking over the East Indies station. Drury, whose force included Company troops and artillery, was to be advised by a Select Committee of supercargoes and afterwards to suppress piracy along the south coast of China where the 'ladrones' were said to be increasing in audacity.

No message had been passed from Minto to the Viceroy of Goa for transmission to Macao (7), so that the appearance of Drury at the beginning of September

8

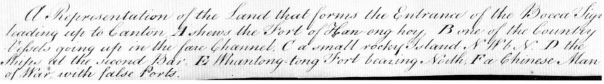

A Representation of the Land that forms the Entrance of the Bocca Sig[...] leading up to Canton, A shews the Fort of Han-ong hoy, B one of the Country Vessels going up in the fare Channel, C a small rocky Island N.W.b.N. D the Ships at the Second Bar, E Whantong-tong Fort bearing North, F a Chinese Man of War with false Ports.

caused consternation in both the Portuguese and the Chinese camps. The Company's financial balances were so precarious at this time that failure to load or any similar event would ruin it at a stroke, so under pressure from the Committee, Drury reluctantly agreed to the immediate occupation of Macao without explanation, which caused uproar, both in Macao and Canton. Drury worked his men-of-war upstream towards the Bogue (8) with a view to intimidating the Chinese and preventing their intervention, 'perceiving we were infringing and trampling under foot every moral law of Man and of Nations, and the poor defenceless Chinese infuriated to Phrenzy.'

But on 27 November 1808, matters came to a head. Drury, exasperated by the 'complex . . . crooked, left-handed, winding mode of proceeding', condemning the Committee for having prevented his 'conciliating the Chinese government to the aggression of occupying Macao', now proposed the concentration of all trade at Macao. The Emperor wanted Canton closed to the 'foreign-devils' and only the accruals to the viceregal treasury and the fortunes of the mandarins, combined with those of the Hong merchants remained to keep open this tenuous but vital source of income to the East India Company. Tension mounted and only Drury's self-control prevented a confrontation between his boats and a Chinese fleet blocking the river from ending in bloodshed.

Peking now took a hand: an imperial edict ordered the British out of Macao before they were ejected by the Chinese army. The Committee requested he withdrew his frigates from Whampoa (9) on 8 December and embark the troops from Macao. On 23 December Drury reported to Pellew the sorry business was at an end. 'Thus has finished the most mysterious, extraordinary and scandalous affair that ever disgraced such an armament.' He went on to reprobate the effect of placing political and diplomatic decisions in the hands of mercantile supercargoes. As for the pirates of the Ladrones Islands, Drury, believing Peking, reported they did not exist. They did, and in the succeeding century prospered exceedingly, requiring an extension of British seapower to extirpate them.

To placate the Portuguese, Drury extended British naval protection to their trade and the general delays caused by the affair cancelled the customary December sailing of the 'China fleet'. Instead the convoy was to sail in March 1809. Leaving an escort for this, Drury sailed for Penang, where he relieved Pellew about 3 January 1809 and went on to Madras. Pellew sailed in *Culloden* for Galle, joining a convoy which was dispersed off the Île de France in a gale. Four Indiamen foundered and *Culloden* suffered damage. The remnants reassembled at the Cape and continued, arriving in the Channel in early July. Pellew struck his flag at Spithead on the 10th: 'He had made his fortune at the price of a five years exile'.

4. 'Captain Fleetwood Pellew in the Psyche 36, captures the Dutch armed merchantman Resolutie and the Dutch corvette Scipio near Sumarang 31 August 1807', aquatint and etching after an original by Nicholas Pocock, no date
NMM ref PAH8054

5. 'Sir Ed Pellew's squadron standing into Grisse', anonymous black & watercolour pen & ink, no date.
NMM ref PAH3823

6. 'Town of Grisse Fallen from Dutch 1807', black & watercolour pen & ink by John Fraser, 1807.
NMM ref PAH3824

7. 'Macao from Penha Hill', coloured lithograph engraved by Sarony & Co after an original by Chinnery, no date.
NMM ref PAH2769

8. 'Entrance to Bocca Tigris', watercolour by Sir Frasmus Gower, from his manuscript log 'Nautical Observations on a voyage to China', 1793. NMM ref GOW/2.
NMM neg D9232

9. 'Whampoa in China . . . This View is Taken from Danes Island, looking towards Canton, embracing Whampoa & Junk rivers', coloured aquatint engraved by Edward Duncan after an original by William John Huggins, published by the artist, 1838.
NMM ref PA10239

9

1

Piémontaise

2

EAST Indiamen could usually defend themselves against privateers but were no match for frigates, or even a well-manned naval sloop. However, this did not prevent the more stubborn from trying: a celebrated example involved the 36-gun *Warren Hastings*, Commander Larkins, and the French 40-gun frigate

Piémontaise, Captain Epron. On 21 June 1806, *Warren Hastings* was alone off the island of Réunion in the southern Indian Ocean, homeward bound from China, when she sighted a strange sail during the late forenoon. Captain Epron's frigate wore British colours, but when Larkins received no reply to the private signal, he cleared for action as *Piémontaise* ranged up on his port quarter (1). Epron elected to attack from the lee side to disable the Indiaman which he wanted as a prize; at the same time the *Warren Hastings*, heeling towards her attacker, was robbed of much of her own firepower. Hoisting the tricolour, the French frigate swept past, cannonading the Indiaman, which responded. She then tacked back and forth, often at very close range, gradually destroying the Indiaman's rigging. Only the main mast was left standing with its topsail set, but the braces shot through. The mizzen's falling encumbered the working of the after upper deck guns, the lieutenant's gunroom was set on fire, the tiller rope was damaged and even the surgeon's instruments were swept away by a ball passing through the sickbay. *Piémontaise* had lost her own main topsail, but with her much heavier armament and manpower, she now overwhelmed the Indiaman (2).

Despite putting up a gallant fight for over four hours, Larkins surrendered, his disabled ship colliding with the

Frenchman as she lowered her boats to take possession. This was construed as a deliberate act by the boarding officer, Lieutenant Moreau; he dashed on board and stabbed Larkins. In a frenzy, his followers knifed the surgeon, the second officer, a midshipman and a boatswain's mate. These men were said to be the worse for drink, the only explanation for the conduct of Moreau and his party, whose assault Larkins survived, despite injury to his liver. Epron took his prize in tow and arrived at the Île de France on 4 July.

Epron's *Piémontaise* was active for some time, but ran out of luck in March 1808 while lying in wait for some late-sailing Indiamen off Cape Comorin. Captain Hardinge of HM frigate *San Fiorenzo* had orders to escort the dilatory ships which she met early on the 6th. Seeing the British frigate, *Piémontaise* ran, but shortly before midnight Hardinge closed sufficiently to exchange broadsides. After ten minutes engagement, Epron had inflicted sufficient damage to the British ship's rigging that he escaped. Undeterred, *San Fiorenzo* caught up with her quarry again at dawn on the 7th and at 0625 Epron wore to open fire at a range of half a mile. Hardinge replied, swung board-to-board as Epron continued to aim at *San Fiorenzo*'s tophamper and Hardinge the hull of the *Piémontaise*. After two hours the British frigate's masts and sails were wrecked, and at 0815 *Piémontaise*'s fire ceased and she made sail eastwards, with pumped water pouring from her scuppers.

Hardinge's men laboured all day to make good their ship's rigging. At midnight, moonlight revealed the *Piémontaise* in sight, and by 0900 *San Fiorenzo* bore down upon her enemy, who hoisted false colours but did not seek to run. Hardinge threatened to cross Epron's stern to weather him, whereupon Epron hoisted his true colours and made sail, with Hardinge once more in chase. But *Piémontaise* was now waterlogged and sluggish. Frustrated, Epron turned towards his pursuer and the two frigates re-engaged. Hardinge was killed by *Piémontaise*'s second broadside and command of *San Fiorenzo* fell upon Lieutenant Dawson. For eighty minutes the two frigates fought it out until Epron hauled his colours down.

Piémontaise had besides a large crew, numerous lascars from prizes able to assist in working his ship. Nevertheless Epron lost 49 killed and 92 wounded, while besides her captain, *San Fiorenzo* had 13 killed and 25 wounded. Despite Epron's numerical advantage, compounded by the manpower problems confronting the British, the superior sailing of the *San Fiorenzo*, and the industry of her company in refitting her, ultimately secured their victory, combined as it was with gunnery unaffected by the degeneracy increasingly common in the larger ships. In Epron's defence, he expended all his 18- and 8-pound shot, being reduced to using 36-pounder carronades. Nevertheless, he was defeated by a foe who made light of the French tactic of disabling and relied on a more brutal annihilation.

Dawson took his prize in tow after her masts fell on the 9th (3), arriving at Colombo on 13th. Only four years old, *Piémontaise* was purchased into the Royal Navy as the *Piedmontaise*. Dawson was made a post captain, but died in 1811.

1. 'Situation of the Honble East India Compys ship Warren Hastings . . . & the French Frigate La Piemontaise . . . on June 21st 1806 . . .', coloured aquatint engraved by J Jeakes after an original by Thomas Whitcombe, no date.
NMM ref PAH8046

2. 'Situation of the Honble East India Compys ship Warren Hastings . . . & the French Frigate La Piemontaise . . . on June 21st 1806 . . .', coloured aquatint engraved by J Jeakes after an original by Thomas Whitcombe, no date.
NMM ref PAH8047

3. 'To the memory of Captain George Nicholas Hardinge . . . three Actions . . . with La Piedmontaise French Frigate, near the Island of Ceylon, 8 March 1808 . . . representing . . . San Fiorenzo & her Prize, after the Action, is inscribed by N Pocock', coloured aquatint and etching by Nicholas Pocock and James Bennett after an original by Nicholas Pocock, published by the artist, September 1809.
NMM ref PAH8064

3

2

1

The Bombay Marine

IN addition to its cargo carriers, the Honourable East India Company possessed a small private navy, the Bombay Marine. In 1812 this comprised the 24-gun frigate *Mornington*, the smaller ship sloops *Aurora*, *Ternate*, *Benares*, *Teignmouth*, *Mercury* and *Prince of Wales*; the brig sloops *Nautilus*, *Thetis*, *Psyche*, *Vestal*, *Ariel* and *Antelope*, the ketch *Rodney* and the schooners *Sylph* and *Zephyr*. Having scrapped or lost four bomb vessels between 1808 and 1812, a further bomb vessel, the *Thames*, was added in 1814. Occasional additional cruisers were taken up from trade when required, such as the *Malabar* which was temporarily on the establishment in 1812.

The Bombay Marine was regulated by a superintendent, it possessed its own dockyard at Bombay under a master-attendant, and its 100-strong officer corps was commanded by a commodore stationed at Surat. This position was held in rotation by the senior captains who were paid £2500 annually and ranked with a colonel in the Bengal Army. Ordinary captains, known as second captains, were paid around £500 per annum and ranked below the commander of an Indiaman. The lascar-manned force bore lieutenants, midshipmen and volunteers, some of whom were deserters from the Royal Navy and fuelled a long-running antipathy between the two services. Active in protecting the Company's interests against either pirates or the actions of Indian princes, the usual cruising ground for the Marine's vessels was on the Malabar coast and they rarely doubled Cape Comorin. They owed a duty to protect the Indian-owned Country trade to Persia and Arabia, but the Bombay Marine also supported the Royal Navy and carried out punitive raids in the Arabian Seas against nests of pirates. In one respect it was ahead of the Royal Navy: it actively encouraged surveying and systematically produced numerous charts

3

4

—indeed, the Company's first official hydrographer, Alexander Dalrymple (1), was appointed in 1779. Even after he became the first Hydrographer to the Admiralty sixteen years later, he continued to work for the East India Company at the same time.

The incessant internecine warfare of the Arab tribes living on the mountainous coasts of Oman and Muscat, their tradition of extensive seafaring and natural rapacity, promoted piracy in the Persian Gulf. Arab dhows and bhagalas frequently disturbed the Country trade from Bombay to Bussorah (Bushire, now Bandar-e Bushehr) at the head of the Persian Gulf and Muscat. The loss of the merchant brigs *Shannon* and *Trimmer* in 1805 was followed by the fitting of the latter as a pirate by her captors. In July, the *Mornington* appeared off the coast with a demand for the return of the *Trimmer* and was attacked by upwards of three dozen craft. Only her guns saved her and the position of the British Indian trade was demonstrably precarious.

Delicate diplomacy was necessary and a treaty was signed at Bandar Abbas on 6 February 1806 with one local sheik, Sa'id. But the complex nature of Arab politics did not augur for stability and in June 1807 the French secured an agreement for a consular presence at Muscat. In the era of Tilsit a French mission was said to be in Tehran and the safety of the Country trade in the Persian Gulf was under increasing threat. The Governor-General of India, Lord Minto, had sent embassies to the courts of the Punjab, Afghanistan and Persia (Iran) while the *Albion*, 74, and frigates *Phaeton* and *Dedaigneuse* cruised in the Gulf in 1808, though this did not deter the pirates. Minto's mission to Tehran found the French well established and returned to Bombay to find a diplomat from London bound on the same mission in the *Sapphire*. Sir Harford Jones secured the enthusiastic services of the ruthless and arrogant Captain Corbet of the frigate *Nereide*, then completing repairs. Taking Jones on board and the naval sloop *Sapphire* and Bombay Marine's schooner *Sylph* under his orders, Corbet sailed for Bussorah, the *Nereide* contemptuously racing ahead of her consorts and arriving on 14 October.

As a result of this curious conduct, on 21 October, *Sylph* was captured by an overwhelming force of Arab craft, including large bhagalas. Most of *Sylph*'s crew were massacred. Extraordinarily, the capture occurred within sight of Corbet who was now returning to Bombay and he counter-attacked as darkness set in, managing to retake *Sylph*, but the event clearly demonstrated that the shifting alliances of the sheikhs had made them masters of the lower Gulf. Their ambitions extended further: in April of the same year, 1808, the Company's schooner *Lively* had run into four pirate dhows cruising off Gujerat and driven them off. They later turned up off Surat, but were suffered to go free, such was the unwillingness of the authorities to provoke the Arabs. Bombay Marine officers had been severely censured for taking action, even in their own defence, for most of the small cruisers were inferior in size and manpower to the large Arab bhagalas.

A larger force of some fifty Arab vessels next appeared off Sind; a Country trader, the *Minerva*, was captured, her master and crew killed, and the ship refitted as a pirate. Moreover, the two largest of the Company's cruisers, *Mornington* and *Teignmouth*, were in constant action against a combined Arab fleet of over 60 large bhagalas, some 800 smaller dhows and a force estimated at 19,000 men. The government at Bombay therefore determined upon a punitive raid to extirpate this piracy in the autumn of 1809, under the influence of the northeast monsoon. The main force was provided by the Bombay Marine, and consisted of the Company's 24-gun frigate *Mornington*

1. 'Alexr Dalrymple by Geo Dance 18 Jul 1794', soft ground etching engraved and published by William Daniell after an original by George Dance, 1 July 1809.
NMM ref PAD3115

2. 'Sixteen Views of Places in the Persian Gulph . . . Forces . . . Against the Arabian Pirates No. 6. The Wall & Beach near Rus ul Khyma, with Troops preparing to land . . . 13th Nov 1809', coloured aquatint engraved by I Clark after an original by R Temple, published by W Haines, April 1813.
NMM ref PAF4798

3. 'Sixteen Views of Places in the Persian Gulph . . . Forces . . . Against the Arabian Pirates No. 7. The Troops landing at Rus ul Khyma . . . 13th Nov 1809', coloured aquatint engraved by I Clark after an original by R Temple, published by W Haines, April 1813.
NMM ref PAF4799

4. 'Sixteen Views of Places in the Persian Gulph . . . Forces . . . Against the Arabian Pirates No. 10. A View of Linga or Lung, from the Sea, during the destruction of the Dows &c Novr. 16 1809', coloured aquatint engraved by I Clark after an original by R Temple, published by W Haines, April 1813.
NMM ref PAF4802

5

under Captain Jeakes, with the *Aurora, Ternate, Mercury, Nautilus, Prince of Wales, Ariel, Fury* and the bomb ketch *Stromboli*. These vessels were reinforced by the naval frigates *La Chiffone*, under Captain Wainwright who was to act as commodore, and the *Caroline*. The troops consisted of a body of Company sepoys from the 2nd Native Infantry, a battalion of the 65th Foot, the flank companies of the 47th Foot, eight 6-pounders and two howitzers of the Bombay Artillery, a small detachment of cavalry, 268 men of the Bombay Marine Battalion and some pioneers, all under Lieutenant Colonel Smith of the 65th.

Well briefed and having sent some of the frigates and Company cruisers on ahead, Wainwright and Smith sailed on 17 September. Once at sea the following morning, the *Stromboli* proved so rotten that her over-loaded state resulted in her foundering with considerable loss of men and matériel. Moreover, progress was slow, delayed

by the need to take on water at Muscat and to detach several ships to protect a convoy of Country merchantmen. To compound this confusion, intelligence gained from the friendly Sheikh Sa'id was discouraging, with news of Bedouin reinforcements and an opposition of 20,000 men. Wainwright, aided by a drawing provided by a Persian merchant, determined to attack the main base of the enemy at Ras-el-Kaima, where he arrived on 11 November. The captured *Minerva* and a force of dhows came out, then turned tail, the *Minerva* running aground only to be boarded and burnt, but the Arabs were entrenched in strength with stone defences and artillery. Hampered by the loss of their artillery in *Stromboli*, the shallow approaches now prevented the heavier frigates closing to bombard. For three hours on the 12th the smaller sloops and ship's boats armed with guns, anchored and fired on the enemy positions, while offshore Smith made his preparations for assault.

6

At 0200 on the 13th, the troops scrambled into the squadrons' boats and were pulled inshore to lie alongside the anchored sloops (2). At dawn, the main body were to make for the southern end of the defences, while Lieutenant Leslie of *Chiffone* with two gunboats and a small body of troops, put off for the port at the northern end to mount a diversion. The appearance of Leslie's boats from their cover, drew off the Arabs, whereupon Smith's main force broke from their hiding and dashed for the beach. Before two companies were ashore, however, the Arabs counter-attacked, but were checked by grape and canister from the boat carronades, allowing Smith's grenadiers and light companies to form and establish a beachhead at the point of the bayonet (3). There followed a fiercely contested action as the troops slowly fought from house to house, setting fire to the dry matting of many small cadjan huts. Covered by the smoke carried ahead by a southerly wind, the British-Indian troops slowly advanced and by mid-afternoon had taken the sheikh's palace.

As soon as possible, the squadron's seamen pulled into the port where they found over fifty craft, of which thirty were large, powerful bhagalas. These were all burnt, as were the warehouses filled with looted merchandise, while the magazines were blown up. By nightfall Ras-al-Kaima lay under a pall of smoke. During the following morning the troops re-embarked while taunted by the distant Arabs.

On the 17th twenty large craft were set on fire at Linga (4) and on the 26th eleven more were burnt at Laft, on Qishim Island. This attack was bungled and while the attacks at Ras-al-Khaima and Linga had resulted in trifling losses of 5 killed and 34 wounded, the affair at Laft caused 70 casualties.

By Christmas 1809, the whole force had returned to Muscat and on 3 January 1810 a further attack was made to recover a fort at Shinas (5) to cement the accord with Shiekh Sa'id. The troops were then returned to Bombay, though naval operations continued for some time in an attempt to root out every piratical vessel. This was limited in its success, for the presence of inlets unknown to the British ensued that the greater proportion of the Arab fleets survived.

Nevertheless, this involvement in the Persian Gulf, allied to a realisation of its limitations, stimulated an increased desire for better charts of the region. After the first tentative efforts of the Bombay Marine (6), the full resources of the Royal Navy's expanding hydrographic service continued the business of surveying the Persian Gulf and the Red Sea which had been started by Home Popham and his assistant David Bartholomew in 1801-2. Bartholomew, who had begun his service in the merchant marine, was first lieutenant of *Sapphire* in 1808, when she bore Harford Jones east. He subsequently carried out surveys in the Gulf the results of which were privately published in London in 1810.

Less durable was the suppression of the pirates. The Company's cruisers were diverted east to assist the Royal Navy in operations off Java, though the *Benares* and *Prince of Wales* showed the flag in 1811 and the naval sloop *Hesper* was in the Gulf the following year. Attacks, however, resumed, mainly on Country ships, but the Company's cruisers were not always exempt, *Aurora* being one victim (7). The Bombay Marine continued to be active against these successful commerce raiders and by 1812 the tide was beginning to turn with the occupation of Medina by the Ottoman Turks. In the event it was to be the power of The Porte, rather than Paris that was prevail in the hinterland of Arabia, while the British reached their accommodations with the Trucial States in due course.

5. 'Sixteen Views of Places in the Persian Gulph . . . Forces . . . Against the Arabian Pirates No.16. The Storming of Shinass, Jany 3d 1810', coloured aquatint engraved by I Clark after an original by R Temple, published by W Haines, April 1813. *NMM ref PAF4808*

6. 'Island of Faroun near the head of the Sea of Akabah . . . showing the HEIC's surveying vessel Palinurus', watercolour by Robert Moresby, no date. *NMM ref PAF5971*

7. 'Attack on HEICS Aurora by pirates, 1812: end of the action', oil painting by Thomas Buttersworth (1768-1842), no date. *NMM ref BHC1085*

7

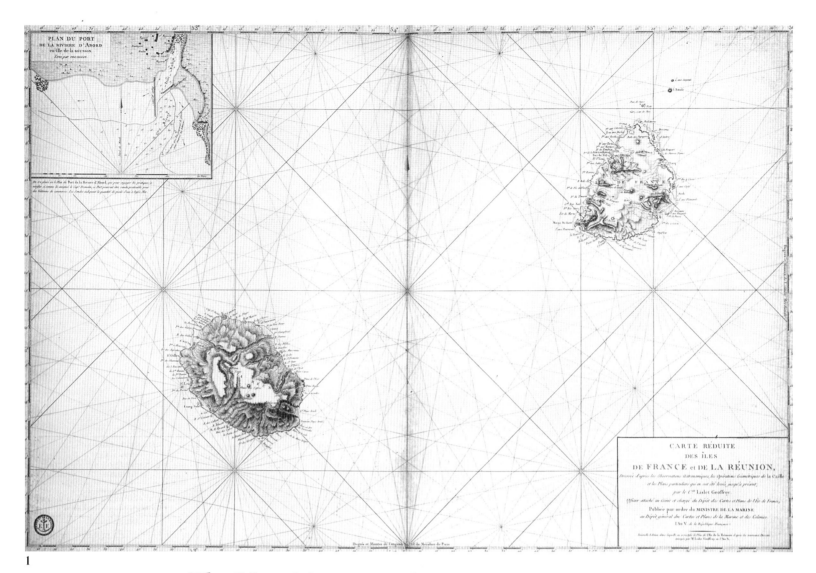

1

The Mauritius campaign

1. 'Isle de France et Reunion', chart by
Lislet Geoffroy 1797 from *Hydrographie
Francois . . .par M Bellin*, Vol 2 (Versailles
1756-1802). Official French
compilation by the ingenieur-
hydrographe du Dêpot de Marin.
NMM neg D9233

ILE de France, Île de Bourbon and Rodriguez (1) are situated close to the homeward route of Indiamen from India and China, and provided a formidable base from which the French could wage their *guerre de course*. Entry and exit from the Mauritian ports was relatively easy in the steady trade winds which confronted the blockaders with constant blowing weather; and 'The longest period which the ships . . . have hitherto been able to maintain their station,' Pellew reported, 'has been ten weeks for, altho always victualled for six months, the length of the passage [from India] occupies the whole of the remaining period', to which he adds 'exclusive of the impracticality of preserving the Health of the Crews for a greater length of time.'

Once the Cape was in British hands and the blockade was based there, British domination of the area reduced the flow of supplies to the islands. However, Governor Decaen had a ready supply of manpower for his cruisers, for blockaded merchantmen provided additional sea-

men, as did deserters from prizes. Vice-Admiral Bertie relieved Stirling at Cape Town in August 1808 with orders to tighten the blockade. Bertie stationed Captain Rowley off Île de France in *Raisonable*, 64, with *Grampus*, 50, *Nereide*, 36, *Laurel*, 22, *Cormorant*, 20 and the 18-gun sloops *Otter* and *Harrier*.

Reinforcements also reached Decaen with arrival of the new frigates *Manche*, 40, *Caroline*, 40, *Bellone*, 44, and *Vénus*, 44, whose commander, Hamelin, was designated commodore. Between them, these powerful ships captured a number of Indiamen, a few small warships (including the Portuguese frigate *Minerva*), and attacked the Company's factory at Tappanooly in Sumatra. It was clear that the British blockade was failing, despite the occupation of Rodriguez by Lieutenant-Colonel Keating and 600 men from Bombay, intended to provided the blockaders with a source of wood, water, vegetables and poultry.

Sea-time, however, bred hardiness and on the night of

14/15 August, the boats of *Otter* cut out a lugger from under the guns of Rivière-Noire. Nesbit Willoughby, *Otter*'s commander, was a cantankerous man. Dismissed from the Navy in 1801, reinstated in 1803 he had finally been promoted on merit in April 1808 to command *Otter*. Wounded so many times he was called 'the Immortal', his raw courage was unquestioned, as were his resource, ability and cruelty.

When *Caroline* returned to the islands with her two prizes, Rowley had just ceased chasing the escaping *Bellone*, which left Port Louis on 17 August 1809. Aware of Rowley's presence, Billiard of *Caroline* slipped into St Paul's on Bourbon. Hearing this, Rowley decided to cut her out, called up 368 troops from Rodriguez and prepared a careful assault. It was to be commanded by the notoriously brutal Corbet of *Nereide* who would lead men from *Sirius*, *Otter* and *Sapphire*, and the Company's schooner *Wasp*. The troops under Keating were supported by seamen and marines under Willoughby and all embarked in *Nereide* which left Île de Bourbon after sunset on the 20th, with the squadron's boats hoisted in jury davits. At daylight *Nereide* signalled the landing effected, and rejoined the squadron offshore. Shortly afterwards the Union flag flew above one of the batteries and the ships closed the shore to bombard *Caroline* (2). By 0830 the town was taken and *Caroline* and her prizes, the Indiamen *Streatham* and *Europe* together some smaller vessels, were in British hands (3). On the 22nd French troops were seen on the coast road and Willoughby landed with seamen and marines to destroy a government godown containing the silk from the Indiamen worth £500,000. He coolly re-embarked and on the 23rd it was learned General Desbrusleys, commandant of the island's forces, had shot himself. A truce was arranged and the British removed all stores and prize cargoes from the warehouses before

2

retiring. The *Caroline*, built at Antwerp in 1806, was commissioned by Corbet as *Bourbonnaise* and Willoughby replaced him in *Nereide*.

On 29 December the newly arrived British frigate *Magicienne* recaptured the Indiaman *Windham* as the latter tried to make Port Louis, but on 2 January 1810, while Rowley's squadron lay uncharacteristically becalmed offshore, a coastal breeze allowed *Bellone* and *Manche* to slip into Port Louis with their prizes *Minerva* and *Victor*, and the Indiamen *Charlton* and *United Kingdom*, only to be followed later by Hamelin in *Vénus*. Rowley now retired to the Cape, leaving Lambert of the *Iphigenia* to continue the blockade with *Magicienne*, *Sapphire* and a handful of sloops until the cyclone season forced them to withdraw. In their absence, on 14 March 1810, Decaen sent Captain Duperré to sea again in *Bellone*, with the recommissioned *Minerva* (now *Minerve*) and the ex-British sloop *Victor*.

2. 'Attack on St Paul's Island of Bourbon., Septr 21st 1809. By the British Squadron under Commodore Rowley consisting of HM Ships Raisonable Boadicea Sirius Nereide Otter & E.I.C Schooner Wasp and the and Forces under Lt. Col. Keating 56th Regiment. The advanced British Frigate is the Sirius Capt Pym raking the French Frigate La Caroline. The first Battery was taken by Lt Cottel, commanding R Marines & Lt Knight 56th per Orders of Lt Col Keating', coloured aquatint engraved by C Calvert after an original by Captain Charles Leonard Irby, published by Edward Orme, no date. *NMM ref PAD5787*

3. 'The capture of Saint Paul near the Isle de Bourbon, 21 September 1809', oil painting by Thomas Whitcombe (c1752-1824), 1812. *NMM ref BHC0593*

3

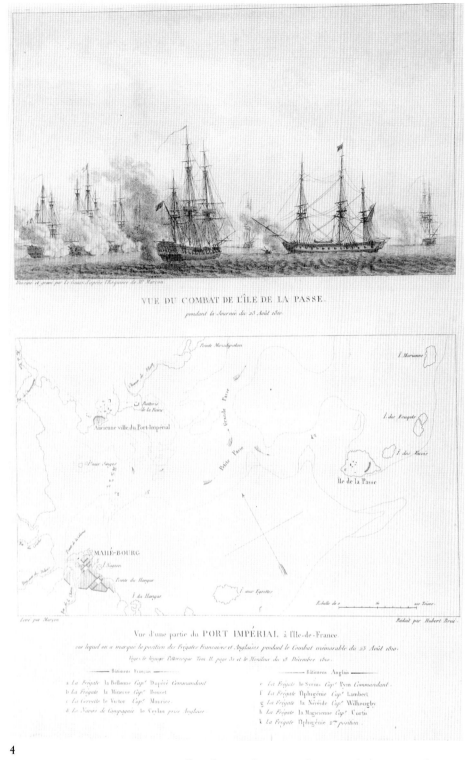

VUE DU COMBAT DE L'ÎLE DE LA PASSE.
pendant la Journée du 23 Août 1810.

Vue d'une partie du PORT IMPÉRIAL à l'Île-de-France.
au lequel on a marqué la position des Frégates Françaises et Anglaises pendant le Combat mémorable du 23 Août 1810.

4

response to Decaen's appeals, *Astrée*, 36, had just arrived and *Mouche* was on her way from France. By the beginning of July, Drury's *Diomede* and *Ceylon* had escorted the troop convoy to Rodriguez. The blockade was withdrawn and thrown into the assault on Bourbon, the troops landing at Grande Chaloupe, west of St Dénis, the island's seat of government, and at Rivier des Pluies, some three miles further east. On the 8th the French governor sued for terms and as soon as the island was taken, *Sirius, Iphigenia, Nereide* and *Staunch* resumed the blockade of Île de France.

In the interim before the main assault on Île de France, it was decided to occupy Île de la Passe, in the entrance to Grand Port (4) and subvert the population with persuasive leaflets. A landing was effected on 13 July by Pym of the *Sirius* who left Willoughby in charge and returned to cruise off Port Louis. From the 17th Willoughby was active in raiding and leafleting, suffering no casualties in the process. These auspicious events were rapidly changed on the forenoon of the 20th when the *Bellone*, *Minerve* and *Victor* appeared with their prizes, the Indiamen *Windham* (taken for the second time) and *Ceylon*. Though trapped, Willoughby hoisted French colours and a private signal he had found in a captured signal book, encouraging the ships to approach. As the *Victor* passed *Nereide*, Willoughby shifted his colours and opened fire. *Victor* immediately struck, anchoring under *Nereide*'s quarter, but on *Minerve* and *Ceylon* opening fire as they passed, she weighed and followed. Neither *Nereide*'s guns, nor those of Île de la Passe had much effect. Willoughby's predecessor, Corbet, a brutal commander whose crew had mutinied the previous year, though a punctilious ship-handler, had neglected gunnery practice, while Willoughby had done little to remedy the deficiency.

Duperré, still outside in *Bellone*, directed *Windham* to stand away to the westwards, then bore down towards the entrance. As she passed into Grand Port, *Bellone* fired into *Nereide*, and Willoughby sent off an officer in the ship's launch to request reinforcement from Pym. In the meantime he ordered the mortars on Île de la Passe to fire, forcing the French to move further up the harbour. Pym was busy retaking *Windham* at Rivière Noire, when her prize crew revealed something of the situation at Grand Port. Pym therefore sent *Windham* to Rowley at St Paul's and made for Île de la Passe. Rowley in turn dispatched *Magicienne* to Port Louis to pick up Lambert's *Iphigenia* and *Staunch* with orders to rendezvous with him off Grand Port.

At Grand Port, Duperré had formed his ships in a crescent protected by coral reefs, with springs on their cables enabling them to command the approach to the inner anchorage. Approaching Grand Port, Pym now fell in

Rowley's raid on St Paul's persuaded Minto and Drury that the Mauritian islands might be taken. Troops and transports for an assault on each island with a two month interval would be provided by Madras. Rowley's, or rather Bertie's ships would undertake the operation and they had resumed the blockade after the cyclone season at the end of March 1810.

While *Vénus, Manche* and the corvette *Entreprenante* were in port, *Bellone, Minerve* and *Victor* were still at large, and in

4. 'Vue du Combat de l'Isle de la Passe pendant le Journee du 23 Aout 1810. Vue d'une partie du Port Imperial a l'Ile de France sur lequel on a marque la position des fregates Francaises et Anglaises pendant le Combat memorable du 23 Aout 1810', coloured etching engraved by Le Gouaz after an original by himself and Marcon, no date.
NMM ref PAD5795

5. Unidentified action, pencil and wash sketch attributed to A D'Etroyer. The composition is identical to a coloured lithograph of the Grand Port action by A Mayer, engraved by Sabatier and published by Lemercier; the National Maritime Museum has a copy of this, ref PAH8086.
Peabody Essex Museum, Salem MA ref 15191

6. 'N. J. Willoughby', anonymous stipple engraving, no date.
NMM ref PAD4298

7. 'Combat de Grande Port (Ile de France) (24 Aout 1810)', steel engraving by Chavane after an original by Gilbert, published by Diagraphe et Pantographe Gavard, no date.
NMM ref PAF4778

with Willoughby's boat and next morning, the 22nd, arrived off Île de la Passe. Pym sailed in and *Nereide* weighed in his wake in what was to be a foolhardy attack. *Sirius* soon missed the unmarked channel and grounded. Willoughby immediately anchored *Nereide*, but *Sirius* was not refloated until early on the 23rd when she was re-anchored close to *Nereide*. By mid-afternoon *Iphigenia* and *Magicienne* had joined, and all four British frigates resumed the attack. *Nereide* led and was to anchor between *Victor* and *Bellone*; *Sirius* was to anchor directly abeam of *Bellone*; *Magicienne* between the captured Indiaman *Ceylon* and *Minerve*, with *Iphigenia* abeam of the latter.

As they approached, *Sirius* and then *Magicienne* ran aground. *Iphigenia* dropped her stream anchor astern, ran ahead and let go her bower under-foot, by which time she was abreast of the *Minerve*. She opened fire at pistol shot with a furious intensity, reserving her quarter guns for the *Ceylon* (5). Willoughby, realising the original plan was wrecked, fired into the much heavier *Bellone*, anchoring *Nereide* with a spring upon her cable. Shore artillery now joined in, and the smoke and noise of the cannonade rolled over Grand Port.

As night began to fall, *Ceylon* drifted aground out of the line. Then, her cable shot away, *Minerve* did likewise, fouling *Bellone*'s cable and forcing her aground. She still fired into *Nereide*, and the battering of *Nereide* continued until all her guns were disabled and her stern was on the bottom. At about 2245 Willoughby sent a boat to *Bellone*, 'to say we had struck, being entirely silenced and a

dreadful carnage on board'. As the 25th dawned *Nereide* fell to the French, all but 52 of the 291 men on board her being killed or wounded; Willoughby himself had lost an eye (6).

During the 25th *Magicienne*'s crew burned and abandoned her while the *Iphigenia* warped out with the intention of rendering assistance to *Sirius*, but the latter was fast aground and was also set on fire, to explode before noon (7). Pym sent a boat to inform Rowley of what had transpired, and it reached Bourbon early on the 27th with the dismal news. Meanwhile *Vénus*, *Manche* and *Astrée* under Hamelin had got out of Port Louis, and appearing off Grand Port at about 1700 demanded the surrender of *Iphigenia*; after the dispatch of a boat to Bourbon, Lambert capitulated.

Rowley in *Boadicea* did his best to recover from the disaster but the situation deteriorated further when Corbet, now commanding *Africaine*, 38, unwisely attacked *Iphigénie* and *Astrée* off Port Louis before *Boadicea* could come up. Corbet was killed and *Africaine* struck to Bouvet, although Rowley was able to retake her shortly afterwards. On 17 September the frigate *Ceylon*, 32, on her way to join Rowley from Madras was also captured off Grand Port by *Vénus* and *Victor*, and again Rowley was called upon to retrieve the situation. *Vénus* lay-to to defend her prize, directing *Victor* to escape, and engaged *Boadicea* as she approached, but after ten minutes' action, Hamelin surrendered. Taken back to St Paul's Bay, *Vénus* was recommissioned as *Nereide*, though she was in poor condition; *Ceylon* was also recaptured.

By October the second invasion force was assembling at Rodriguez. An impatient Vice-Admiral Bertie, despairing of promised troops from home, took advantage of the arrival of the brand new frigate *Nisus* from Britain, hoisted his flag and left Table Bay on 4 September 1810. On meeting Rowley on 15 October, Bertie shifted his flag into *Africaine* and with *Nisus*, *Boadicea*, *Nereide* (ex-*Vénus*), *Ceylon* and *Staunch*, reconnoitred Île de France, receiving fire from the batteries at Port Louis. Bertie then left Rowley with *Boadicea*, *Nisus* and *Nereide* and ran on to Rodriguez.

Rowley had been busy carrying out preparations for invasion, leaving nothing to chance. The landing was to be under the direct command of Captain Beaver of *Nisus*, specially sent out from home with a reputation for such operations. Under cover of darkness Lieutenant Street of the *Staunch* had carried out an assiduous survey of the north coast of Île de France assisted by Lieutenant Blakiston of the Madras Engineers and the masters of *Boadicea* and *Africaine*. There was a natural break in the rocky coast at a point covered by the island known to the British as Gunner's Quoin, behind which lay the undefended beach of Mapou Bay. Unfortunately one of *Nisus*'s boats had been captured, but the approach to Mapou Bay was secretly buoyed the night before the invasion.

Bertie, at Rodriguez with the army commander, General Abercromby, finally gave orders for the expedition to sail without the Cape division on the 22 November. The force under Bertie now consisted of his flagship *Africaine*, 38, *Illustrious*, 74, *Cornwallis*, 44, the 38-gun frigates *Boadicea*, *Nisus*, *Clorinde*, *Menelaus* and *Nereide*, and the smaller *Phoebe*, *Doris*, *Cornelia*, *Psyche* and *Ceylon*. There were also four sloops, the gunbrig *Staunch*, the armed ship *Emma*, and three hired auxiliaries. Most of the 6848 soldiers were embarked in transports, though this figure includes the fleet's marines. The first wave consisted of 1555 men in forty-seven boats from the squadron. Twelve further boats were armed with either the frigates' boat carronades or 6-pounders, with two bearing small howitzers, all manned by 160 seamen and artillerymen. The gunboats were disposed to cover the two main divisions each of which carried a scratch battalion of infantry made up largely of the light and grenadier companies of the 12th, 33rd, 56th, 59th Regiments. The boats formed 'a most magnificent and interesting spectacle' as they left the squadron about two hours after noon on 29 November 1810 when 'the breeze . . . [was] particularly favourable, and the day one of the finest that could be chosen' (8).

The landing was unopposed, though the retreating enemy exploded a magazine at Fort Malartic in Grand Bay not far off. There was some confusion and Beaver lost his signals book through his gig being swamped while towing astern of *Nisus*. All the troops were ashore by 2030, the advance guard having moved off under Keating three hours earlier. They skirmished with the retreating garrison from Fort Malartic and halted for the night (9) before resuming the march at daylight as the second wave of troops landed. When Keating reached the Tombeau River beyond which lay Port Louis, he halted to await the rest of the force, expecting a battle for possession of the island. Here the British were reconnoitred by Decaen who dashed up on his horse and collected a slight graze from a musket ball for his trouble. The French general had at his disposal only about 2000

8

9

10

11

regular troops of all arms, the remnant of the garrison of Bourbon, his own original troops and marine artillery from the ships in port, though many of these were in the seaward defences of Port Louis. There were about 3000 militia, but Decaen could not rely on these confronting the regular British infantry, even if stiffened by his own regulars. These men, mostly creoles, had endured neglect from France and the utmost privation under Decaen. Their desire to defend the honour of the emperor was not great. Decaen himself had long ago despaired of seconding his master's grandiose plans to invade India, and felt himself to be abandoned while his contemporaries made reputations in Europe. Moreover, Port Louis was indefensible from a land attack and could not withstand a siege (10), but Decaen formed his troops up outside Port Louis under the command of his deputy, Vandermaesen.

Abercromby's advance was supported on the seaward flank by *Nisus*. The frigate's boats kept the troops supplied direct from the sea and provided Abercromby with a floating headquarters. On 1 December 1810, he confronted Vandermaesen and mounted a turning movement followed by a frontal assault, upon which Vandermaesen's men broke and fled. The following morning Decaen sent out a flag of truce. 'After much

extravagant bravado and insolence on the part of Governor de Caen [sic], the Isle of France was surrendered by capitulation on the 3rd,' wrote Beaver, who regretted their being 'allowed to march with their arms, the eagles and fixed bayonets.' But Abercromby and Rowley were not so fussy; hurricanes were not unknown in December and while they possessed overwhelming force, for on the 2nd the troops had arrived from the Cape, time pressed. Since the objective had been achieved and the Mauritius, as it must now be called, was no longer in French hands, the parading of a few discredited eagles was not of much consequence.

The French frigates *Bellone*, *Vénus*, *Manche*, *Minerve*, *Astrée* and *Iphigénie* were all taken, as was the corvette *Victor*, the brig *Entreprenante*, two dozen French merchantmen, the East Indiamen *Ceylon*, *United Kingdom* and *Charlton* and some other prizes (11). The battered hulk of Willoughby's *Nereide* was also retaken but abandoned as unserviceable. The gun embrasures contained 209 serviceable heavy cannon and among the prisoners were about 500 disaffected Irishmen. Willoughby and his colleagues and ship's company were liberated, as was the unfortunate Commander Matthew Flinders, whose long days of unjustifiable captivity were over, though he was a broken man.

8. 'Isle of France No. 1. View from the Deck of the Upton Castle Transport, of the British Army Landing', coloured aquatint engraved by I Clark after an original by R Temple, published by W Haines, April 1813. *NMM ref PAF4779*

9. 'Isle of France No. 2. A West View of the Moulin a Poudre, where the British Army halted', coloured aquatint engraved by I Clark after an original by R Temple, published by W Haines, April 1813. *NMM ref PAF4780*

10. 'Isle of France No. 5. The Town, Harbour, and Country, Eastward of Port Louis', coloured aquatint engraved by I Clark after an original by R Temple, published by W Haines, April 1813. *NMM ref PAF4783*

11. 'Isle of France No. 6. The Town of Port Louis, from the West of the Harbour', coloured aquatint engraved by I Clark after an original by R Temple, published by W Haines, April 1813. *NMM ref PAF4784*

1

Tamatave

ON 5 January 1811 French colours lured a French vessel into Port Louis. Smartly relieved of her dispatches, they revealed three further frigates were bound for Mauritius with troops to reinforce the former Îles des France and Bourbon. Beaver, senior officer after Bertie's departure for the Cape, ordered *Phoebe*, *Galatea* and the sloop *Racehorse* to intercept them; but the French ships did not leave Brest until 2 February and the wait was to be long. Meanwhile Beaver sent the 18-gun sloop *Eclipse* to seize the tiny French post of Tamatave, on the Madagascan coast, which was taken and garrisoned on 12 February. Having survived a cyclone which struck on 18/19 March, Beaver sailed to occupy the Seychelles

before going to Madras to load specie to refloat the economy of Mauritius. *Astraea* returned to Port Louis and thus Schomberg was senior officer when the French finally appeared.

Under Commodore Roquebert of the *Renommée* were the other 40-gun frigates *Clorinde*, Captain St Cricq, and *Néréide*, Captain Lemaresquier. Roquebert made his landfall at Grand Port, where he learned the islands were now British. The following morning he ran into *Phoebe*, *Galatea* and *Racehorse* and the British gave chase, Captain Losack of the *Galatea* sending off a boat to Port Louis to inform Schomberg. The French commodore threatened the closely chasing *Phoebe*, but Captain Hillyar refused to

2

engage, fell back on his consorts, and allowed Roquebert to escape. Already on half-rations, Roquebert's ships now veered away in search of provisions, and on 19 May, descended upon Tamatave, surprising the tiny garrison.

Hillyar's squadron was disaffected by this turn of events. *Galatea*'s company requested Losack that he chase the enemy, and Losack remonstrated with Hillyar, who refused, and the squadron returned to Port Louis on the 12th. Here, however, Schomberg took command and arrived off Tamatave at dawn on 20 May 1810. The light offshore breeze was failing and it was late afternoon before any action was possible. The ensuing engagement was to be frustrated by intermittent airs in which the British lost all formation, though the zephyrs favoured the French. *Clorinde* led *Renommée* and *Néréide* in line on the port tack, with the British line, led by *Astraea*, straggling on the starboard (1). An exchange of distant broadsides at long range was followed by a calm. The British now drifted out of formation, *Astraea* came to a standstill, while *Renommée* and *Clorinde*, astern of *Phoebe* and *Galatea*, were able to rake.

Néréide engaged *Astraea* and Schomberg signalled *Racehorse* to ply her sweeps and place herself athwart *Néréide* to rake, but *Racehorse* failed to accomplish this. *Néréide* slowly worked clear of *Astraea*, joining *Renommée*'s attack on *Pheobe*. At twilight, a little breeze sprang up and Hillyar worked *Pheobe* across *Néréide*'s stern and within half an hour silenced her but had to disengage as *Renommée* and *Clorinde*, their sails filling, came to Lemaresquier's assistance.

These two had severely shattered *Galatea*. Losack had tried towing and sweeping round to bring his guns to bear, only to lose two boats and then find the French ships veered away to assist *Néréide*. It was now dark and

Losack was in distress, but Roquebert, having extricated Lemaresquier, bore away northwards. Having effected repairs, Schomberg ordered a pursuit and by 2200 *Astraea* was in a fierce fire-fight with *Renommée* which struck her colours as *Racehorse* approached (2). *Astraea* and *Phoebe* now went in chase of *Clorinde* but St Cricq ran and Schomberg and Hillyar were compelled to abandon their efforts when *Phoebe*'s fore topmast fell at 0200 on the 21st.

On the 25th, *Néréide* reached Tamatave and after riding out a gale, Schomberg followed, sending *Racehorse* under a flag of truce to summon her. *Néréide* and Tamatave were relinquished on condition *Néréide*'s company were exchanged. This was agreed and the last French post in the east was given up (3).

Losses on both sides were severe; Roquebert and Lemaresquier were killed and *Galatea* was severely damaged. St Cricq took water at the Seychelles, provisions at Diego Garcia, and in September reached France. In March 1812 St Cricq was cashiered for failing his commodore and disobeying his orders to go on to Java. Napoleon afterwards remarked that he should have been shot.

There was some rancour among the British squadron over Losack's conduct, a manifest injustice hinging upon the technicality of his failing to haul his ship's head round after he had reported *Galatea*'s state to Schomberg, but owing more to his argument with Hillyar a few days earlier. There was no court-martial, but the affair was unfortunate; *Galatea* was the most damaged ship and her butcher's bill the longest. The French prizes were purchased, but since the captured *Vénus* had been renamed *Nereide*, *Néréide* was commissioned as *Madagascar*, while *Renommée* replaced the lost *Java*.

1. 'Commencement of Captn Schomberg's Action off Madagascar, May 26th 1811. HMS Astraea from a drawing by Mr Beechey', aquatint engraved by Thomas Sutherland after an original by Sir William Beechey and Thomas Whitcombe, no date. *NMM ref PAD5803*

2. 'The Action Renewed by Night. Astraea Tamatave. From a drawing by Mr Beechey', aquatint engraved by J Bailey after an original by Sir William Beechey and Thomas Whitcombe, no date. *NMM ref PAD5802*

3. 'Surrender of Tamatave. From a drawing by Mr Beechey, coloured aquatint engraved by Thomas Sutherland after an original by Sir William Beechey and Thomas Whitcombe, no date. *NMM ref PAD5805*

3

1

The foundations of seapower: the merchant marine

THE numerous merchant vessels by means of which British trade prospered were owned and managed by small 'houses', largely overshadowed by the remnants of the old joint-stock companies. The majority of British merchantmen, whether they were Whitby 'cats' carrying coal to the Baltic and returning with timber, flax and turpentine, West Indiamen (1) bringing sugar, rum and molasses to the bonded warehouses of London, the rakish slavers of Liverpool, engaged in the notorious triangular trade with West Africa and the Antilles, or the overseas 'Country' traders of the Indian and China Seas, were a vast, disparate collection of vessels. It is impossible to gauge the exact size or manpower of the merchant marine of the day, but studies indicate approximately 24,500 merchantmen

2

were in deep-water, coasting or short-sea voyages, fishing and foreign colonial trade in the western hemisphere by the end of the war in 1814. The majority of these vessels were only of 200-300 tons burthen. A second merchant fleet of so-called 'Country' vessels, built and owned in India by British and Parsee interests, serviced the Far East, the two separated by the exclusive Indiamen of the Honourable East India Company.

British bottoms were engaged upon several distinct trade routes: foreign trade, trade between Britain and Ireland, the Isle of Man and the Channel Islands which was listed as 'foreign coastal', trade between Ireland and countries other than Great Britain, foreign cross-trades and the coastal and local trade of Great Britain and her possessions overseas. With the exception of the cross trades, the others were either fully or partially protected by the Navigation Acts. An expedient relaxation of the latter admitted American ships on 'British' routes, enabling the merchant marine of the young United States to blossom, augmented as it was by the demand for North American timber to make up the shortfall from the restricted and riskier resources of the Baltic. In 1801 only 3000 loads of squared timber were imported from America, as opposed to 159,000 from northern Europe. By 1811, increased demand, the effects of the Continental System and tariffs favourable to Canadian produce, caused North American imports to have risen to 154,000 loads, with Baltic derived cargoes amounting to 125,000. Much of the vacuum which American shipping filled was caused by the outbreak of the Peninsular War in 1808. Large numbers of British ships were diverted to trooping and the carriage of cavalry remounts, guns, stores, ammunition, uniforms for not only British and Hanoverian troops, but also the Portuguese army under allied command. Wellington's insistence on the self-sufficiency of the Allied army created this demand and underwrote the ultimate success of military operations in the Iberian Peninsula. It was not only a largely unappreciated service, it was also undramatic and virtually unrecorded.

The Navigation Acts, established in the seventeenth century, secured the majority of the carrying trade for British ships and a monopoly of colonial markets for British goods. This made Britain the entrepôt for colonial produce, thus generating a re-export trade and vastly enriching British merchants. On the other hand it bred complacency and inhibited both social reform and ship development. Although British ships were compulsorily registered under an Act of 1797, this was a purely bureaucratic measure. The archaic and restrictive tonnage measurement rules severely hampered hull development until their abolition long after the war when the entire shambling structure of British shipping was overhauled in response from market forces generated largely in the United States. Instead, a series of strictures, which included greater regulation of pilotage and quarantine and the protection of the Navigation Acts, were laid upon shipping around the turn of the century. Their only purpose was to maintain the government income essential to the prosecution of the war.

In addition to the widespread disregard for the upkeep and improvement of ships, there was a corresponding neglect of the proficiency and welfare of their officers and crews. Shipowners had no interest in ship husbandry or navigation, their sole concern being to run up freight rates and run down costs. Parsimony and disinterest brought its own retribution. There were no certificates of competency and while many were first-rate seamen, it was commonly said that a merchant master had 'come in at the hawse-pipe and went out through the cabin window'. The subordinate mates, 'holding a certain rank in society, with emoluments very unequal to the wants of a family . . . generally resorted to illicit trade, as a means of bettering their condition'. Shipping losses were consequently huge and as often due to incompetence as to barratry and other malpractices. Lack of education and regulation was only part of the picture, however. The Admiralty's Hydrographic Department had only been founded in 1795 and it was ten years before a systematic production of charts was begun; moreover the provision of sextants, chronometers and the charts themselves were often beyond the means of a master or mate, assuming he had the knowledge to benefit from their possession.

There were significant exceptions to this situation and they were marked. The cabotage and seamanship of the small barks and brigs (2) plying the North Sea with coal to Europe or London (3), had their own trade association which existed to maintain standards of seamanship to minimise losses. An able seaman had to pass an oral examination which included in addition to the traditional skills of a seaman, a knowledge of ship-handling. It was by this thorough induction into the mechanics of manoeuvre, that their colliers could work the tides up through the congested Thames, making stern boards, turning short round by means of an anchor and generally proceeding where other vessels were quite incapable of going.

The East India Company, offering significant returns in the form of social cachet and the potential to make a substantial sum of money, recruited from the middle classes, taking in unemployed naval officers when circumstances put them on half-pay. Ruling India as a private fiefdom, the Court of Directors made treaties, appointed governors and raised their own armed services. Its fleet of merchantmen were built in yards at

3

Limehouse, Blackwall and Deptford, paid for by syndicates of private speculators, known as 'The Shipping Interest' and chartered into the Company's service. These capitalists influenced both the shipbuilders and the Directors and by operating a closed, hereditary ring, resisted the temptation to compete and ensured that their own profits were high and the Company's were almost non-existent.

Indiamen were contracted for six or seven round voyages and their sizes varied according to their specific trade, the largest, of 1200 tons being employed in the China trade (4). The smallest class of 500 tons ascended the difficult Hooghly to Calcutta to load valuable cargoes of silks and cotton 'piece-goods'; 800-tonners

4

5

loading bulk cargoes of 'gruff-goods', rice, saltpetre and sugar. The legitimate private trade of the officers, added coral, amber, pearls, emeralds, sapphires and rattans to the list. The China trade was balanced with outward cargoes of wool and tin, combining with raw cotton and opium from India to pay in part for the cargoes of tea loaded at Canton for London. The defence of India and maintenance of the strategic posts at Bengal's expense during the war, virtually wiped out profits, and the Company relied more and more upon the increasingly popular fashion of tea-drinking for its increasingly meagre profits.

The passages of Indiamen were subject to the monsoons, steady winds created by the annual shift of high pressure over the land masses of central Asia. The favourable wind for the outward passage was the southwest monsoon which blew from May to October and brought the rains to India; the homeward passage was made under the influence of the northeast monsoon, between November and April. However, these meteorological phenomena were complicated by the prevalence during August and September of typhoons in the South China Sea and cyclones in the Indian Ocean. It took about two months to make Table Bay, but when the monopoly was lifted in 1813, passage times decreased, commanders driving their ships harder to combat the inevitable competition.

Acting as 'feeders' to the Indiamen, the Parsee builders of Bombay constructed fine, teak ships on the European pattern to carry cotton goods, pepper, sandal wood and opium to China. Tea, porcelain, silks and satins came on the return passages with additional cargoes being loaded and discharged at Malacca. The value of the China trade in these 'Country' ships amounted to 10 millions sterling between 1806 and 1808. These vessels were of surprising tonnage, many over 500 and some over 1000 tons. Opium was carried in smaller, faster vessels, usually by the Burmese at Rangoon, but later at Calcutta. Trade extended also to the Persian Gulf and round the Indian coast. Country ships were commanded and officered by Europeans and either owned by British, often Scots, companies, underpinned by Parsee capital, or by wholly Parsee firms. The reputed fortunes made in oriental shipping were more likely to be made in Country ships engaged in opium trading, than Indiamen, and Country

6

ships were not only larger than the generality of contemporary European merchant ships, they were notably faster and, being of teak, or with teak frames, much longer lived. Apprehension and concern as to the superiority of these 'native-built' ships was voiced by Captain Sir Joseph Cotton, a former commander, then East India Company Director and Deputy Master of Trinity House. Appreciation of these advantages resulted in a few naval vessels being ordered from Parsee yards.

The protection of this and all trade under the convoy system was a responsibility of the Royal Navy, but required the co-operation of the merchant masters. A few fast, well-armed merchantmen were permitted to sail as independent 'runners' under Admiralty licence, but the vast majority were governed by the compulsory Convoy Acts and conformed to the imposed disciplines of naval control. It entailed a complex organisation which started on the home coast with fortnightly 'coastwise convoys'. Most relevant to the post-Trafalgar period, however, was the network linking the Baltic, from the rendezvous off Malmo and thence via Vinga to either Leith or Longhope in Orkney, from whence ships diverted to Glasgow and Liverpool. Orkney was also a rendezvous for shipping to and from Archangel. Other Baltic convoys ran from the Thames and Hull, with cruisers protecting the seasonal expeditions of whalers and ships of the Hudson's Bay Company. Additional convoys were sailed with military stores for the Peninsula.

Generally the system worked well and although about 7000 vessels were captured from convoys between 1803 and 1815, in relative terms this amounted to little more than half of one per cent of vessels in convoy. More vulnerable were stragglers, with losses of some 7 per cent. Occasionally, however, disaster struck, as with severe weather in the winter of 1810-11, when a series of gales scattered convoys in the North Sea, tore the Goodwin lightvessel from her moorings and drove cruisers into shelter and the Channel Fleet into Torbay. That summer had also seen Danish gunboats decimate two convoys. In July 1810 a convoy bound for Longhope lost 42 ships and in August another 47 were taken from a 200-strong homeward bound convoy off the Naze of Norway. Losses in this case amounted to £425,000.

In addition to the brigs and ships making up the mass of merchant shipping, were the smaller craft employed as coasters (5) and in the fisheries, of which the most important was that of the herring (6), but which were supplemented by cod-fisheries, oyster dredgers and shrimpers, as well as the deep-water whaling industry (7). Unique to the estuary of the Thames, was the spritsail barge which exported horse manure from the stables of the capital to the fields of East Anglia, bringing lime mortar, bricks and hay in return (8).

7

Upon the masters, mates and seamen of the British merchant marine throughout the Napoleonic War rested the great burden of maintaining the commercial wealth upon which their country depended for its means to fight. The social inferiority of the seaman generally, ensured by the rollicking image of the Jolly Jack beloved by an indulgently amused public and fostered by the songsters, lampooners and printsellers, made of him a cynosure when he enjoyed his brief shore-leave. His curious dress and language, his drunkenness and debauchery were marked even in an age of excess and drew upon him a fascination which also kept him at arms' length. This image obscures a considerable collective expertise which, for all the groundings and founderings, corruption and malpractices, amounts to an expression of seapower as eloquent, if not as prominent, as those 'storm battered' men-of-war referred to in Mahan's memorable phrase.

8

1. 'A frigate close-hauled', anonymous watercolour, c1780. Despite the formal title, the ship is actually a West Indiaman.
NMM ref PAD8478

2. '1789: The Brig Vigilant of Hull Capt George Orton', watercolour by Reuben Chappell, no date.
NMM ref PAG9972

3. 'Merchant shipping off Harwich, 1776', grey wash by Francis Swaine, 1776.
NMM neg 1642

4. 'British East Indiamen, Anchoring in Table Bay at the Cape of Good Hope', aquatint and etching by Robert Dodd after his own original, published by Robert Sayer, 1 May 1788.
NMM neg 2816

5. 'Loading Barrels onto Coastal Traders', watercolour by Nicholas Pocock, c1800.
NMM ref PAD8796

6. 'Herring fishery', engraving by Mathias de Sallieth after an original by Hk Kobell, 1780. This is the Dutch fleet but the British equivalent looked very similar.
NMM ref PAF7399

7. 'Whale fishing', engraving by Mathias de Sallieth after an original by Hk Kobell, 1780.
NMM ref PAF7397

8. 'A hooy schip laden', pen & wash by Gerrit Groenewegen, c1790. A stack barge laden with hay.
NMM ref PAD8414

Capture of Amboyna and Banda, 1810

BLOCKADE of the French possessions in the southern Indian Ocean was the responsibility of the admiral commanding at the Cape of Good Hope and news of the capture of the Île de France in December 1810 reached Madras on 25 January 1811. This ought to have removed all anxiety from the minds of the British, but Louis Bonaparte's refusal to enforce the Continental System in his vassal Kingdom of Holland, had caused his imperial brother to annex the kingdom. The Dutch thus lost control of Java and the French frigates *Meduse* and *Nymphe* left Nantes on 28 December 1810 carrying General Jansen to replace the Dutch Governor, General Daendels. The corvette *Sappho*, sailed from Bordeaux at about the same time and while an 80-gun ship was allocated to Java, the frigates *Renommée*, *Clorinde* and *Néréide* sailed in February 1811. Due to call at Île de France, they were ignorant of its capture.

Meanwhile Minto wished to 'purge the Eastern side of the globe of every hostile or rival European establishment'. Even before the fall of Île de France, Drury had been carrying out a steady reduction of Dutch islands.

On 9 December 1810, Captain Tucker in *Dover*, 38, with *Cornwallis*, 44, and *Samarang*, 18, anchored off Amboyna in the Moluccas. Amboyna was heavily fortified with Victoria Castle mounting over 200 guns. More artillery lay in the Wagoo battery, an offshore piled outwork, and the elevated works at Wannetoo and Batto-Gautong. Tucker anchored in Laetitia Bay for several days making his preparations, while the Dutch scuttled three ships in the harbour and added their crews to the defenders.

On the 16th, having lowered boats on the offshore side of his ships and filled them with seamen (1), marines and a detachment of the Madras European Regiment, Tucker's squadron weighed as if to depart, disappointed. By keeping their sails a-flutter the ships edged obliquely across the bay towards a selected landing place under fire from the batteries (2). At the appropriate moment the ships bore round, engaged the batteries and, slipping the boats, put 400 men ashore. These stormed and carried the Wannetoo battery then scrambled across difficult country to force the Dutch and native gunners to abandon Batto-Gautong. With these guns taken, Tucker's ships anchored in Portuguese Bay as night fell. Commander Spencer of the *Samarang*, now landed with a party of seamen and marines with two small field pieces which he brought to bear on Wagoo and the pile battery, driving out their garrisons. With the guns of Batto-Gautong, fire was opened on Victoria Castle. The governor sued for terms. Of the three vessels sunk in the inner harbour, the 12-gun brig *Mandarin* was afterwards raised.

In the succeeding days Tucker received the surrender of Harouka, Saparoua, Nasso-Laut, Bouru, Manipa, persuading the sultan of Gorontale to substitute British for Dutch colours at his trading post. Subsequently Tucker appeared off Manado and secured the garrison's surrender, following which Copang, Amenang, Kemar and

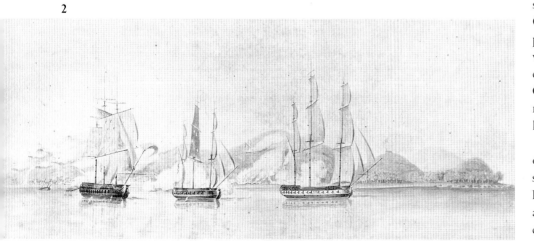

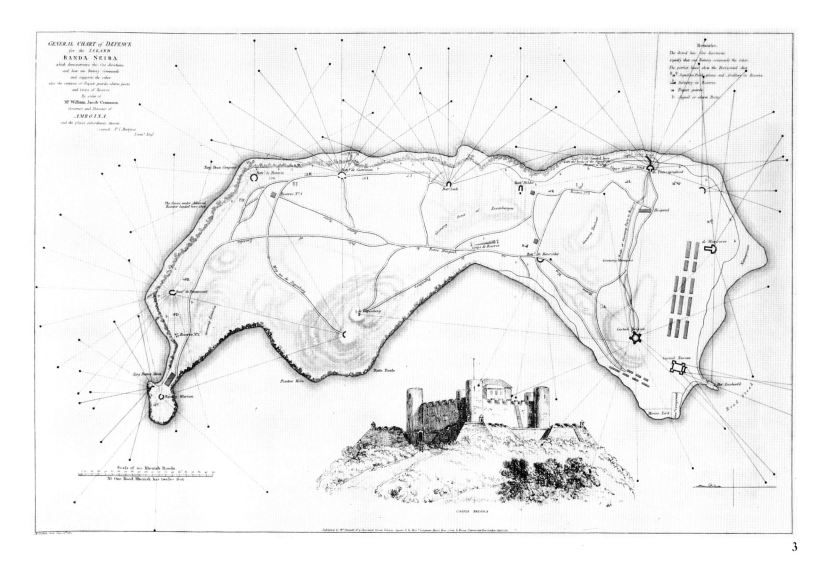

GENERAL CHART of DEFENCE
for the ISLAND
BANDA NEIRA
which demonstrates the fire directions
and how one Battery Commands
and supports the other
also the customs or Piquet-guards alarm posts
and Corps of Reserve
By order of
Mr William Jacob Cranssen
Governor and Director of
AMBOINA
and the places subordinate thereto

CASTLE BELGICA

3

Tawangwoo submitted. The *Cornwallis*'s boats cut out the Dutch naval brig *Margaretta* from a bay on the north side of the island of Amblaw and by May a garrison of 100 men of the Madras European Regiment was embarked for Amboyna in the frigates *Caroline* and *Piedmontaise*, the sloop *Barracouta* and the refitted *Mandarin*.

At Madras, Cole of the *Caroline* had been given *carte blanche* to seize other Dutch possessions on his way and decided to attack the fortified island of Banda Neira, the seat of Dutch government in the eastern end of the archipelago (3). Scaling ladders, bombardiers and two field pieces were loaded at Penang and Cole was joined by *Samarang* off Singapore. Here he learned Banda Neira was defended by 700 regular soldiers plus 800 militia. This induced Cole to take a circuitous route without charts, coasting north of Borneo and through the Balabac Strait into the Sulu Sea; then heading southeast across the Celebes Sea, Cole fetched New Guinea on 21 July, turning southwest through Pitt Passage to beat up to Goram (Ceram) where he embarked two Moluccan pilots. A haze now favoured the secrecy of the final approach to Pulo Banda and in the afternoon of 8 August the squadron hove-to and hoisted out the boats within sight of the island of Rosensgen. After sunset the ships filled their sails and stood towards their objective (4). But they lost the element of surprise, for a full moon rose, the haze vanished and they were fired upon from Rosensgen. Cole hove-to again until after moonset when the night became dark and squally; Cole boldly decided to continue, he himself leading the loaded boats towards the eastern extremity of Great Banda (5). The conditions however rapidly dispersed the boats and their 400 men; by 0300 on the 9th only Cole and Kenah (of the *Barracouta*) were still in touch. At this time the two frigates and the *Barracouta* loomed out of the night with the news that more boats were close astern and, having rounded some up, Cole pressed on.

Banda Neira was mountainous and well fortified. Guns were mounted in prepared positions one of which, the Voorzigtigheid, was directly facing Cole as he splashed ashore with about 140 seamen and marines and 40 men of the Madras infantry. It was not long before dawn but the nature of the weather had lulled the Dutch garrison, though they were at their posts. Cole advanced

4

1. 'Amboyna captured from the Dutch by a squadron under Sir Edward Tucker Feb 1810 3rd view', watercolour by Lieutenant Richard Vidal, no date. *NMM ref PAH4085*

2. 'Amboyna captured from the Dutch by a squadron under Sir Edward Tucker Feb 1810', watercolour by Lieutenant Richard Vidal, no date. *NMM ref PAH4086*

3. 'General Chart of Defence for the Island of Banda-Neira. View of Castle Belgica', coloured etching by M Graham, published by William Daniell, 15 October 1811. *NMM ref PAG9057*

4. 'View of the Island of Banda-Neira . . . Captured by a force landed from a squadron under the Command of Captain Cole in the morning of the 9th August 1810', coloured aquatint after an original by Captain Christopher Cole, published by William Daniell, 16 October 1811. *NMM ref PAG9056*

5. 'Capture of the Island of Banda, Augt 9th 1809. From a plan by Sir C. Cole', coloured aquatint engraved by Thomas Sutherland after an original by Thomas Whitcombe, no date. *NMM ref PAD5792*

stealthily and carried the battery at the point of the bayonet. He now pushed on for the citadel, Fort Belgica, but the assult faultered when the British party found their scaling ladders too short to reach the inner ramparts. At this point the gates were opened to admit During, the colonel-commandant and his staff. They were promptly rushed by the British; During fell severely wounded, whereupon the British 'swept the ramparts like a whirlwind'. As the sun rose 'the day beamed upon the British flag'.

The short-handed ships offshore had had a difficult night. Frequently having to douse their topsails to avoid running into each other in the fiercely gusting wind, uncertain of their exact position, endangered by the proximity of the off-lying islands, they had run into Cole

at about 0300 and later rounded up the dispersed boats. At daylight they were uncertain of the position ashore when they were fired upon by the lower batteries, but this was quickly silenced by shot from Fort Belgica itself where a small British Jack flew above Dutch colours. Cole now sent a message to the Dutch governor saying the town of Nassau would be cannonaded unless a capitulation was made. This was forthcoming and as the ships and lost boats of the squadron came into the harbour, the garrison lay their arms down on the glacis of Fort Belgica.

After a fierce fight on 31 August 1810, Captain Tucker of the *Dover* took the island of Ternate. With the Moluccas in British hands, there remained only Java to complete Minto's grand design.

5

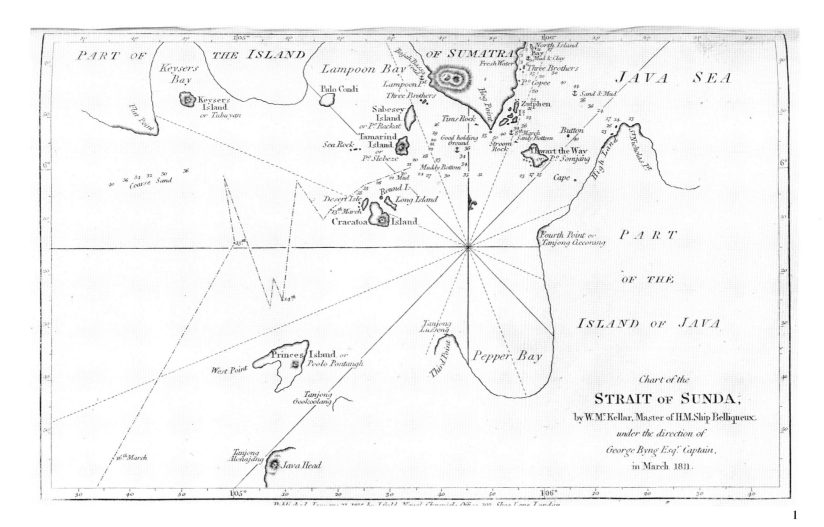

1

The conquest of Java and triumph in the East

BEFORE he died on 6 March 1811 Vice-Admiral Drury had planned an operation against Java, but in April preparations were put in train under Commodore Broughton. On 18 May Cole of the *Caroline* arrived at Penang escorting the first division of troops, with Fleetwood Pellew in the *Phaeton* joining him with the second a few days later. Having joined up with the contingent from Bengal escorted by the senior naval officer, the cautious Broughton in the *Illustrious*, 74, the expedition sailed on the 11th, with 11,960 troops embarked, of which 5344 were European and the remainder sepoy, under Lieutenant-General Auchmuty; over 1000 sick were left behind.

British cruisers had been harrying Java for some time. On 23 May off Rembang, *Sir Francis Drake* had cut up a flotilla of Dutch gunboats, and Marrack (1), at the western extremity of Java where a strong fort and garrison of Dutch infantry were stationed, had been attacked by boats from the *Minden*, 74, and *Leda*, 36, who were blockading Batavia. A raid was carried out on Dutch gunboats under French colours by the 18-gun brig *Procris* on 30 July (2).

On 4 August Broughton's expedition arrived off the estuary of the Marandi River, carrying the first of the land breeze in to the selected landing point off Chillingehing, a dozen miles east of Batavia, where they anchored at 1400. The naval force now assembled was considerable, and *Leda*, *Caroline*, *Modeste*, *Bucephalus*, and the sloops *Procris*, *Barracouta*, *Hesper*, *Harpy*, *Hecate*, *Dasher* and *Samarang* provided covering fire. Commanded by Captain John Hayes in the *Malabar*, the Bombay Marine's cruisers *Aurora*, *Mornington*, *Nautilus*, *Vestal*, *Ariel*, *Thetis* and *Psyche* assisted. In six hours, 8000 men were landed before the enemy had mustered to oppose them and only the advance guard made contact with a brief skirmish between vedettes. General Jansen had recently arrived to take over the governor-generalship and immediately retreated into a complex of redoubts and fortified lines named Meester-Cornelis lying between two rivers and some nine miles inland from Batavia (3).

The *Leda* and small cruisers now worked into the Anjol, or Batavia River, while the deeper vessels of the squadron anchored off Tanjong Priok. The seamen pre-

1. 'Chart of the Strait of Sunda', by W McKellar, master of HM Ship Belliqueux under the direction of George Byng, Esq. captain, March 1811. Published by Joyce Gold, 1815 (Plate 429 from the *Naval Chronicle*, Vol XXXIII). *NMM neg D9261*

2. 'The Boats of His Majesty's Sloop Procris attacking and capturing six French Gunboats off the coast of Java on the 31st day of July 1811', coloured aquatint engraved by C Rosenburg after an original by William John Huggins, April 1837. *NMM ref PAH8085*

3. 'Plan of Batavia, in the Island of Java', published by Joyce Gold, 29 February 1812 (Plate 357 from the *Naval Chronicle*, Vol XXVII). *NMM neg D9273*

4. 'The City of Batavia in the Island of Java and Capital of all the Dutch Factories & Settlements in the East Indies', coloured engraving and etching after an original by Jan Van Ryne, published by Robert Sayer, c1780. *NMM ref PAH2743*

5. HMS Akbar Augst 10th 1815', watercolour by Admiral Sir George Black, no date. *NMM neg X1387*

2

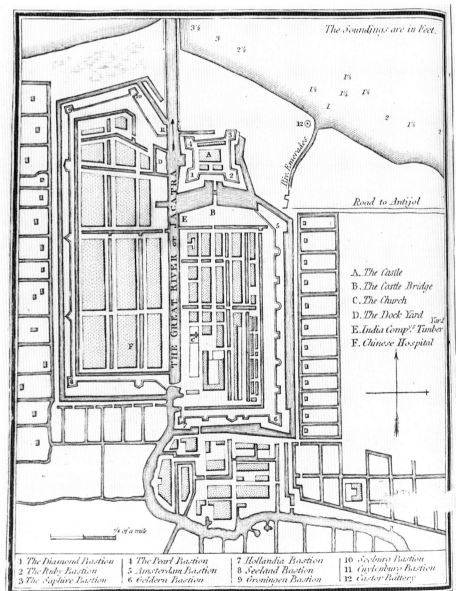

3

The Soundings are in Feet.

Road to Antijol

Riv. Emeralds

THE GREAT RIVER OF JACATRA

A. The Castle
B. The Castle Bridge
C. The Church
D. The Dock Yard
E. India Comp.'s Timber Yard
F. Chinese Hospital

⅛ of a mile

1 The Diamond Bastion	4 The Pearl Bastion	7 Hollandia Bastion	10 Seeburg Bastion
2 The Ruby Bastion	5 Amsterdam Bastion	8 Seeland Bastion	11 Cuylenburg Bastion
3 The Saphire Bastion	6 Geldern Bastion	9 Groningen Bastion	12 Castor Battery

Published by Joyce Gold, Naval Chronicle Office, Shoe Lane, London, February 29.th 1812.

pared a bridge of boats for the army to cross the river and an advance was made after a flag of truce had announced that all private property would be respected. On the 8th a deputation of citizens agreed to surrender Batavia at discretion, placing themselves under British protection (4).

The following day Rear-Admiral Stopford arrived to take command, having taken the unusual step of not relieving Rear-Admiral Bertie at the Cape as his orders stated, but heading on eastward on hearing of Drury's death and the operations against Java. His flagship, the *Scipion*, 74, which in addition to the ships previously named, joined the *Lion*, 64, *Akbar*, 44, the frigates *Presidente*, *Hussar*, *Phoebe*, *Doris*, *Cornelia* and *Sir Francis Drake*, the transports and captured gunboats, made the fleet number almost one hundred vessels.

The army ashore was affected by sickness and the fleet's marines were required to reinforce the troops before the advance on Meester-Cornelis resumed the next day. At Weltervreeden the Dutch guard were routed and on the night of the 20th, ground was broken before the entrenchments. Seamen assisted in throwing up siegeworks and moving the artillery into position, operations which, on the 22nd, a Dutch sortie failed to disrupt. A tremendous fire was then opened from the Dutch position which faltered on the 23rd and was resumed by both sides on the 24th. The mutual destruction was severe and at midnight on the 25th the British made a frontal assault which carried Meester-Cornelis with further frightful losses, although General Jansen made good his escape.

While the expeditionary force was taking Meester-Cornelis, Stopford had sent *Akbar*, *Phaeton*, *Bucephalus* and *Sir Francis Drake* east to Sourabaya where were lying the new and powerful 40-gun French frigates *Méduse* and *Nymphe* which had brought Jansen out from France. *Akbar*

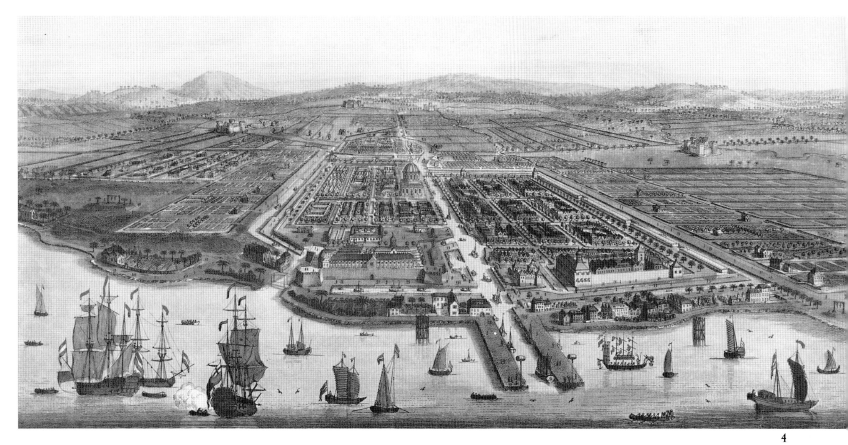

4

(5) and *Bucephalus* blockaded the eastern end of the Madura Strait, the other two frigates the western, but *Akbar* left soon afterwards. Warned by Jansen on 3 September of the disaster at Batavia, the two frigates, under Commodore Raoul of the *Nymphe* got under weigh, observed by Captain Pelly of the *Bucephalus*. Pelly was joined on the 4th by *Barracouta* and both vessels gave chase to the northeast. In the succeeding days the *Barracouta* dropped astern but the 36-gun British frigate maintained contact. At 0600 on the 12th, the three ships

5

6

6. 'Watering at Panoonbangan during British Expedition to Northern Borneo and Java', anonymous graphite drawing, no date. *NMM ref PAH0138*

7. 'Jamsetjee Bomanjee, Indian shipbuilder, showing plan and construction of Minden 74 guns, built Bombay 1810', lithograph engraved by J R Jobbins after an original by G Bragg, no date. *NMM ref PAG6494*

7

were in sight of Pulo Laut on the southeast point of Borneo, whereupon Raoul wore round with the obvious intention of embaying Pelly between Pulo Laut and Borneo, but Pelly wore in turn and the chase was reversed to the west southwest. *Nymphe* now overhauled *Bucephalus* and at 1300 opened fire with her bow-chasers, Pelly responding with his stern guns. *Nymphe* had to yaw a little, allowing *Méduse* to catch up, and both French frigates loomed on either quarter of *Bucephalus*, *Nymphe* to port, *Méduse* to starboard. But the pursuit by Raoul's frigates was half-hearted. Seeing two shoals ahead, Pelly sought to pass between them and lure the French after him, but *Nymphe* and *Méduse* turned away and gave up the chase, eventually reaching Brest safely on 22 December 1811.

Meanwhile, by the beginning of September, the fort at Samanap on Madura, over which the French flag had been raised, had been seized by men from the *Sir Francis Drake*, *Phaeton*, *Dasher* and some marines from *Hussar*. A French officer was also in command at Cheribon, and it was thought Jansen was seeking refuge there, so Stopford embarked a force of the *Lion*'s marines in the frigates *Nisus*, *Presidente* and *Phoebe*, and the sloop *Hesper*. On landing at Cheribon, Captain Warren of the *Presidente*, with the aid of his gig's crew, seized General Jamelle of Jansen's staff together with some other officers. Thereafter the frigates, their seamen and marines mopped up the minor posts occupied by the Franco-Dutch (6) while some seamen actually served as 'Marine Light Dragoons' in the pursuit of Jansen which finally caught up with him at Salatiga, 343 miles east of Batavia. Here, on 18 September 1811, he surrendered the valuable colony of Java.

By this time Stopford had left the area and Broughton reported the conquest of Java to the Admiralty. He com-

plained of the climate and the severe losses to his squadron due to sickness, losses which exceeded those inflicted by the enemy and which were the true price of British seapower in the eastern seas. *Illustrious* lost 71 men due to sickness off Java, the squadron losing 230, and these persisted in the seven frigates and two sloops which Broughton left in the Java Sea and which remained until March 1812.

From this period the war in the east was effectively over, the much diminished squadron guarding the trade against any incursion of the French or the Americans. The danger from American cruisers required *Doris*, *Modeste*, *Bucephalus*, *Cornelia*, *Procris*, *Barracouta* and *Samarang* to be nearer home and news of war with America reached Bombay via Frankfurt and Muscat on 4 January 1813. The command was consequently reduced to one 74, ten frigates, five sloops, a hospital ship at Penang and a sheer-hulk at Bombay The new flag-officer, Vice-Admiral Sir Samuel Hood, arrived at Madras on 5 April 1812, and set about establishing a naval base in the secluded and beautiful harbour of Trincomalee, not merely for its security, but because it lay in a Crown Colony rather than within the territory of the Honourable Company. Meanwhile the new teak-built Third Rate *Cornwallis* was launched at Bombay with Hood in attendance and some new frigates were laid down there at the Wadia shipyard (7). Hood made a cruise to Penang in the summer of 1814 in the *Minden*, but died at Madras in December, having contracted malaria

At the time of Hood's death, the East Indies squadron had increased to four Third Rates, eleven frigates, two ship sloops, and eight brigs. It was the remotest of stations on which a flag officer commanding had enjoyed considerable powers. Patronage and purchase had lain within his gift and his squadron profited considerably from prize money. Hood's main problems, like those of his predecessors, had been satisfying the commercial pressures of the Calcutta merchants, maintaining the complements of his ships and keeping in touch with them on their dispersed cruising grounds as he sought to cover the trade and execute those military operations he deemed necessary. His men-of-war were poorly maintained, short of supplies and had to make do and mend with what local stores were available. His ships and men bore little resemblance to the prints and plates circulated about the drawing rooms of London. Elderly, passed-over lieutenants were subordinated to young commanders with acting commissions, and marines were in constant short supply. Yet this distant and exigent collection of ships, hard pressed to fulfil so much, succeeded in reducing any enemy presence in the Far East, and thereafter held the Indian and China Seas until the end of the war.

Part III

EXPLOITING SEAPOWER IN EUROPE

IF we except the blockade of the main naval arsenals of France (and its subsidiary block-ade of Spain, which ceased in the summer of 1808), as the cornerstone of British naval policy with worldwide implications, the campaign in Europe centres on three theatres. In the centre, and indissolubly linked with the economic war, lay the struggle in the North Sea and English Channel; in the south, the prosecution of the war in the Mediterranean basin, with its impli-cation for the east, put extraordinary demands on Collingwood and his successors; and in the north, between 1807 and 1810, the complexities of the Baltic required an equal amount of diplo-matic skill and was largely a war of defence. For the admirals commanding in the Baltic and the Mediterranean, the days of forcing a fleet engagement on the enemy were over. Colling-wood was criticised for not having achieved it on one occasion, but by 1807-8, British sea-power lay not so much in winning battles, but holding fast to the advantages won by Trafal-gar. It was this empowerment that was Nelson's great legacy to his colleagues and successors.

But in asserting the legacy of Trafalgar as British naval supremacy, it is easy to overlook the problems in home waters. The economic war was a real one: privateers which attack merchant ships do not grasp the imagination of naval historians intent upon chronicling more momentous events, an attitude reflected at the time by the lack of promotion to meritorious naval officers who fought fierce and bloody actions against daring and courageous French corsairs. Officers engaged in these tasks were usually those with little social influence and few expectations, consequently, given the vital nature of the war they fought within the greater conflict, they are perhaps the unsung heroes of British naval history. There was also evidence of Napoleon's ultimate naval ambi-tion in home waters with the plans for enlarg-ing Antwerp, and the building of Cherbourg as an important naval base enclosed by its new breakwaters. The fiasco of the great expedition

against the Schelde was a failed attempt against the former, while a small squadron had to be permanently assigned to watch the latter. Squadrons of varied force were also required to watch the Texel, Helgoland, Boulogne and the Channel ports. Invasion craft still kept the British twitchy, and the Martello tower build-ing programme continued along the southeast coasts, with the great redoubts of Harwich and Eastbourne being finished by 1809. What was called the North Sea station extended from Selsey Bill to the Shetlands, but the complica-tions of convoy work involved it with the less-er squadrons based at Cork in Ireland and the Channel Islands, though the ships assigned to these places came under the Commander-in-Chief of the Channel Fleet. The chief locations of the North Sea squadrons were the Downs, the Nore, Great Yarmouth Roads, the Texel, the Schelde and Leith.

Collingwood was C-in-C in the Mediter-ranean from the death of Nelson to the day

before his death in 1810, for he died on the first day of *Ocean*'s passage home after Cotton relieved him. His tenure of office coincided with the most difficult period in southern European waters. He had to pursue the main strategy of blockading Toulon, Cadiz and Cartagena; he had to protect Sicily and guard against invasion from the Bonapartist kingdom of Naples on the far side of the Strait of Messina. A substantial force of troops in Sicily allowed him to mount offensive operations against Naples, Spain and the French-held Ionian Islands. At the same time, he had to prevent French intrigues gaining control of the Turkish fleet, and in this he was badly let down by his subordinate Duckworth. During the period following the Dardanelles disaster, when the Ottoman Porte was allied with France,

The elaborate theatricality of the meeting on the raft at Tilsit is well captured in this nineteenth-century engraving for a published life of Napoleon.   Chatham collection

Collingwood stayed his hand and maintained communications with Constantinople, a wise course of action which ultimately bore fruit. On the other hand he pursued a vigorous policy of dominating the Adriatic, even though both sides of that long gulf were in the enemy's hands, and in the end it was the Royal Navy which systematically reduced French influence in the Balkans.

Throughout his command Collingwood, and his successors Cotton and Pellew, kept up a cruiser war against trade and military communications in which a number of frigate commanders distinguished themselves. After the Spanish insurrection of May 1808, although the character of operations on the Peninsular coast altered, the resources required did not, and the Mediterranean squadrons played their part in supporting both Wellington and the Spanish guerrillas. However, the principal involvement of the Navy in the Peninsula was in its overall protection of the supply lines to Lisbon, the evacuation of Moore's troops at Coruña and the services of a detached squadron nominally under Lord Keith as C-in-C of the Channel Fleet, which co-operated with the guerrillas along the north coast of Spain.

'View of Isaac's Bridge, the Winter Palace and the Admiralty, St Petersburg', coloured aquatint and etching by Christian Gottlieb Hammer, published by Rittners Kunsthandlung, Dresden, no date. The attitude of the Russian court was to play an ever larger role in the diplomacy of the Napoleonic War. NMM ref PAI0140

Oddly, the event most influential on strategy in the Mediterranean, and the cause of the formation of the Baltic fleet, was a meeting in a small town on the Polish-Lithuanian border. On 25 June 1807, Napoleon and Tsar Alexander I met on a decorated *pont volant* moored in the River Nieman at Tilsit. Eleven days earlier Napoleon had decisively beaten the Russian army at Friedland, the Tsar had sued for an armistice and the summit meeting had been arranged. Nursing hostility against the Turks, the shallow Alexander had been upset by the refusal of Britain to make another loan and he was overheard to greet the Emperor of the French with the words, 'I loathe the English as much as you do', to which Napoleon made the swift rejoinder, 'Then why are we fighting?'. Thereafter the two men withdrew for a private negotiation, emerging after three hours to announce the conclusion of a public treaty of peace, though what they had agreed to was a secret alliance.

Napoleon was to abandon the Turks to Alexander, who would also have a free hand in the Baltic in exchange for Polish territory intended to form the Grand Duchy of Warsaw, and Prussia would relinquish Westphalia as a kingdom for Jérôme Bonaparte. But other articles were agreed secretly between the two emperors, and they were intended to starve Britain by the ruthless application of the Continental System, while her naval supremacy was to be eroded. This great objective was to be achieved by several initiatives. An aggressive

programme of shipbuilding was to be put in train in all the major ports under Napoleonic hegemony; the Russian navy was to reinforce the French, and this combined fleet was to be further augmented by seizing the fleets of neutral Portugal and Denmark.

By an intelligence *coup*, these secret articles were soon known about in London. A British military mission under General Hutchinson was serving with the Russian general staff but its officers were kept away from Tilsit, as was the British ambassador, Lord Granville Leveson-Gower, who was at the time isolated at Memel on the coast. But the anglophile aristocrat Count Vorontzov and a British agent named Colin Mackenzie quickly acquainted themselves with the secret concordat. There is circumstantial evidence to suggest that Mackenzie was the mysterious spy who lay concealed in the *pont volant* and eavesdropped on the conversation of the two emperors. Mackenzie was at Copenhagen on 10 July where he spoke to Garlicke, the British minister, before crossing to Tönning. A few days later he was in London and his news confronted London with a strategic imperative upon which it acted with great speed and decision.

In due course the Royal Navy escorted the Portuguese royal family and its fleet into exile in Brazil, Admiral Seniavin was blockaded in the Tagus and Grieg's squadron left isolated and impotent in the Adriatic. But the most urgent problem was the Danish fleet. With Bernadotte's Army Corps poised to invade Denmark,

the ultimate mastery of her men-of-war was a matter that could brook no delay and an expedition was sent to seize the fleet at Copenhagen.

Thereafter the Baltic situation became complex: Britain continued to require the commodities known as 'naval stores', which had to run the gauntlet of hostile Danish waters, while waging her own economic war against the Continental System. This she did with considerable success, but Alexander was also proactive and urged Gustavus IV Adolphus of Sweden to join the embargo on British trade. This was rejected, Swedish iron and timber largely filling the void left by the loss of Russian suppliers. The unstable Swedish king's mental state was such that war erupted between Sweden and Russia on the one hand and the Danes on the other. The Russians invaded and annexed Finland in February 1808 while by then Denmark's crown prince had succeeded his incapable father as Frederick VI and was firmly in the Franco-Russian camp. Intending to invade Sweden with his own forces and Bernadotte's Corps, Danish aspirations perished when the *Prinds Christian Frederick*, one of Denmark's last pair of serviceable line of battle ships, was destroyed by *Stately* and *Nassau* on 22 March and Romana's division was evacuated by Keats's squadron in August.

Meanwhile a British fleet under Vice-Admiral Saumarez entered the Baltic, whither British troops had been sent, some 7000 men stiffening the Swedish garrison in Stralsund, although greater co-operation proved impossible with the difficult Gustavus. But the loss of Finland (and with it the huge inshore flotilla, or *skärgårdsflottan*, of mainly oared craft) and occupation of the Åland Islands, combined with Gustavus's mental instability to provoke the king's deposition and his replacement by his uncle Charles XIII in March 1809. Broadly, Charles was opposed to Britain, and wished France to persuade the Tsar to give up Finland, but Napoleon had no desire to upset the Tsar and demurred, while the shifting perception of the Swedes was that the loss of Finland could be offset by the acquisition of Norway and that Britain would support and indeed aid this ambition. Swedish negotiations with Russia, France and Denmark to end hostilities were therefore most delicate, and while Sweden avoided a declaration of war against Britain, she

agreed to subscribe to the Continental System. However, in September 1809 the final Swedish attack faltered and Sweden gave up Finland, assuming a half-heartedly hostile posture to Great Britain.

But a British fleet was hereafter present in the Baltic during the ice-free summer months. Saumarez enforced a blockade so effective that, irrespective of edicts from Paris and St Petersburg, Baltic trade adapted, since no trade with Britain meant no trade at all. Despite the successes of Danish naval interference, it was commercial power which won, though the initial strangulation of trade seemed most effective, annual clearances at Königsberg, for instance, falling from 1000 to 50. The whole of the Baltic trade, even in Britain, was largely in the hands of mercantile houses of German and Scandinavian origin which were bound by a network of religious, marital, financial and commercial interests, powerful agents providing the very 'machinery of resistance'.

Such mutual interests could only find encouragement under the protection of the British fleet at sea, but needed assistance of a more fraudulent kind in port. Consequently there grew up a complicated charade in the production and abuse of false papers and flags of convenience. Documents 'proving' neither a ship nor her cargo had the remotest connection with Britain were widespread, confusing both the imperial *douaniers* and the commanders of privateers. Licences, however, had to be issued to ships seeking convoy by the Royal Navy and the incompatibility of these twin and simultaneous deceptions was solved most easily by the strict control of ships in convoy whereby the deception practised towards the Napoleonic authorities had little consequence once the ship had sailed, but that towards the British possessed inherent advantages. Any ship straying from a convoy, unless with sworn good reason (in which case she should in any case repair to a rendezvous), would thereafter be suspect and condemned as a prize. The British took about 400 'hostile' merchant ships during the period, an interdiction of enemy coastal trade roughly equivalent to their own total losses in numbers, though not in value. Since there was little point in proceeding anywhere other than to or from a British port, the system worked and commerce was entirely disguised until renewed imperial enforcement of

the Continental System by the Fontainebleau Decree of October 1810.

This coincided with the election of Bernadotte as crown prince of Sweden, an event which Napoleon expected would result in a declaration of war by Sweden on Britain. Saumarez handled this crisis with consummate skill, maintaining a constant reassurance in what remained of the navigable season of 1810 and throughout 1811 (a year of great economic stress on both sides) that Swedish interests, not to mention her essential imports, were best served by the friendship of Britain. His advocacy of tolerance was backed by private assurances, so that London took little notice of the cosmetic declaration of war which accompanied the ice in the Baltic at the close of 1810. Despite some confiscations of British cargoes in Scanian ports, which were 'a mask only to the real sentiments of the Swedish court towards Great Britain', the anticipated hostility of Bernadotte did not materialise, for the new crown prince was warming to the idea of inheriting an integrated kingdom of Norway *and* Sweden. Throughout the period of 'hostility', Saumarez's ships made use of undefended anchorages on the Scanian coast in perfect safety.

France's opposition to Sweden's annexation of Norway was based on her long-standing alliance with Denmark and her final occupation of Swedish Pomerania in January 1812, so Bernadotte was able to conclude a treaty with Russia at Örebro on 12 July 1812, less than three weeks after Napoleon's Grand Army had crossed the Nieman. Later he met Alexander at Åbo in Finland.

Saumarez's wise and temporising policy avoided the Swedes being forced into a hostile corner as Denmark had been. Though not always understood in London, where his judgement was sometimes doubted, Saumarez's achievement was remarkable. Rising to high command at a period when the tasks of an admiral were no longer the vigorous pursuit of enemy fleets, Saumarez, on the northern flank of Europe, employed his fleet to facilitate the entire trade of the region and to successfully maintain and nurture a delicate and shifting web of political intrigue and aspiration. In this his contribution was as surely a manifestation of British seapower as that of Collingwood and Pellew on the southern flank in the Mediterranean.

1

2

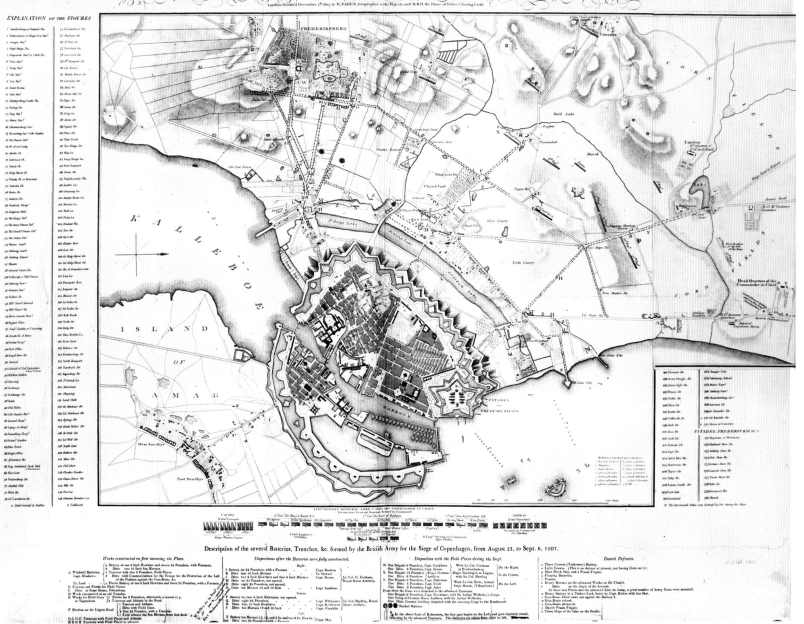

3

Copenhagen, 1807

WHEN, as a consequence of Tilsit, Denmark became a vassal-state of France, the interruption of Baltic naval supplies would be an easy matter for the enemy, while the potential combination of the Russian and Danish fleets would provide thirty-six ships of the line to which could be added eleven more, wrested from an isolated Sweden. Perhaps more important was the pool of experienced manpower available, for the Danish government required every seafaring man to serve six years when called upon. A registration scheme included 20,000 able seamen, with 4000 constantly 'regimented for sudden occasions and kept in constant pay at Copenhagen'. By this means 'the Danish fleet is very easily and quickly manned'.

Moreover, with a peaceful Europe dominated by two despots acting in amiable concert, the prospect of invasion loomed once again in London, a prospect with a revitalised and perhaps more realistic chance of success than hitherto. It was a situation the British Government needed no debate over, though the Opposition were kept in total ignorance of the plans now afoot. Experience of a northern coalition had been telling during the War of American Independence, and since the turn of the cen-

tury Denmark had twice figured in a similar scenario, though on this occasion she was to be an unfortunate victim. By 14 July an immediate embargo was laid on the movement of coastal shipping and orders sent to the Admiralty, War Office, Navy and Transport Boards for a swift mobilisation. On 19 July the Government committed itself to the dispatch of an expedition. An envoy was sent to ask Denmark to accept an alliance with Britain and voluntarily 'deposit' her fleet for safe-keeping, otherwise her fleet would be seized. The means to do this were meanwhile assembled in Yarmouth Roads and Admiral Gambier, appointed to the command of the sea forces, was given a carefully constructed timetable to enable him to act without further orders.

On 25 July 1807, Gambier sailed with seventeen of the twenty-five ships of the line and twenty-one of the eventual forty frigates, sloops, bomb vessels and gunbrigs intended for the service. In addition, no less than 377 transports were massed to convey 25,000 troops, many of them Hanoverians of the King's German Legion. In anticipation of the Crown Prince of Denmark's refusal to surrender his fleet, the expedition's orders were to cut off the island of Zealand and seal off the Danish capital from

4

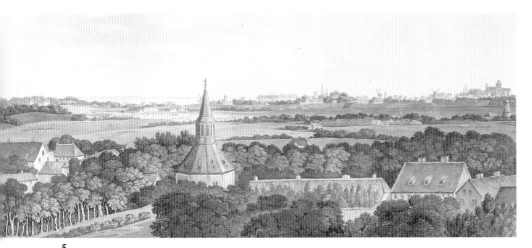

5

6

From Vinga a squadron was detached under Commodore Keats to cruise in the Great Belt and seal Zealand off from Fünen and the west. Keats, in *Ganges*, 74, had with him *Vanguard, Orion, Nassau,* and the frigates *Sybille*, 38, *Franchise*, 36, *Nymphe*, 36, and ten gunbrigs. A few days later Keats was joined by his old ship, the *Superb*, into which he shifted his broad pendant.

Gambier's main fleet passed the castle at Cronborg with an exchange of salutes on 3 August to anchor at Elsineur Road at about the same time that Francis Jackson, the British envoy, was futilely putting London's terms to Crown Prince Frederick at Kiel. A single Danish frigate, the 32-gun *Frederickscoarn* lay at anchor, but on the night of the 12th she slipped her cable and steered towards Norway, then a fief of the Danish crown. At the time, the Danish *Prindts Christian Frederic*, 74, and *Prindcesse Louisa-Augusta*, 64, were lying in Norwegian ports and Gambier detached the *Defence* and *Comus*, 22, in pursuit. Running ahead, *Comus* slowly overhauled *Frederickscoarn* in light airs around midnight on the 14th. After the Danish frigate refused to submit to detention, in the absence of a declaration of war, a battle ensued in which *Comus* ran alongside and boarded her. British casualties were trivial, while the unfortunate Dane, though overwhelming in numbers, lost 12 killed and 20 wounded, and struck her colours.

At Elsineur (Helsingør), the arrival of the British fleet had been welcomed by the inhabitants who sold local produce to the ships. The 'men of war and transports appeared like a forest' (1). On the morning of 15 August the ships weighed and moved south again, towards Vedbaek where they reanchored while Rear-Admiral Essington in *Minotaur* led a division south towards Copenhagen. Next day the troops began to land unopposed. Gambier now sent a proclamation to the Danes announcing his intentions. The situation of Denmark, under the influence of increased French power, made it 'absolutely necessary for those who continued to resist French aggression, to take measures to prevent the arms of Neutral Powers from being turned against them', pleading that the British had arrived in overwhelming force 'in self-defence', but also to impose the maximum coercion possible and thus, it was piously hoped, to avoid bloodshed. Of the Danish fleet 'we ask deposit, we have not looked to capture . . . if our demand be amicably acceded to, every ship belonging to Denmark shall, at the conclusion of a general peace, be restored to her, in the same condition and state of equipment . . .'

From Copenhagen the same day came an order sequestring all British property, particularly ships in Danish ports and a week later the unprovoked attack on the *Frederickscoarn* was known of. By this time the army ashore had brushed with the Danish defences in the

reinforcements by the main Danish army which was in Schleswig-Holstein confronting Bernadotte.

The mobilisation of this huge expeditionary force at such short notice is a remarkable tribute to the organisational capability of the whole apparatus of naval and military management, and it demonstrates the decisive understanding of seapower now enjoyed by the British. By 1 August the main body of the fleet was off Vinga, near Gothenburg. Here the main body of troops from Britain caught up on the 7th. The following day a second troop convoy arrived with Hanoverians from Rügen and the army commander, Lieutenant-General Lord Cathcart. By the middle of the month the total fleet consisted of Gambier's flagship, the 98-gun *Prince of Wales*, eighteen 74-gun and six 64-gun ships of the line. In addition to her flag captain, *Prince of Wales* bore as Captain of the Fleet, or chief-of-staff to Gambier, the person of Sir Home Riggs Popham. It was an unpopular appointment about which several senior captains complained.

form of the *Landværn*, or landguard and operations by the navy in support of the army ashore had ended any pretence at peaceful coercion. More troops and guns were being landed south of the city in Kiøge Bay; Copenhagen was being ruthlessly invested.

The defence had been entrusted to General Peyman supported by Steen Bille, the chamberlain, a distinguished officer who commanded the naval forces. On 10 August Crown Prince Frederick had arrived to encourage the citizens, but he left with King Christian VII on the 12th, to rejoin the army at Kiel. By the time of the declarations of the 16th, the 2500 regular troops in Copenhagen had been reinforced by the seamen and a levy of armed citzenry totalling no more than 12,000 in a city whose population was about 100,000.

The defences consisted of the Trekroner Fort, a pile battery guarding the mouth of the canalised harbour which ran through the city centre. A second offshore battery lying in front of the citadel and supported by the arsenal, giving a total of 174 heavy guns and 25 mortars. These fixed posts were augmented by the blockship *Mars*, 64 guns, and a flotilla of *praames*, or flat-bottomed gunboats, whose heavy artillery added about another 120 guns to the seaward defences (2).

Within the dockyard port lay sixteen sail of the line and twenty-one sloops in ordinary, three 74-gun ship's building on the stocks, one of which was almost completed. The condition of these ships was later represented by the British government's opponents as being largely worthless, but it was the Danish government's policy to maintain a fleet in being, nominally of a strength of thirty-six of the line.

On 17 August a becalmed British merchant brig was taken off Copenhagen by gunboats and in the succeeding days skirmishes occurred between Danish gunboats and British gunbrigs and bomb vessels. During the period in which the army was investing the city, Gambier directed Captain Puget of the *Goliath* to take under his command a

7

force to close the seaward approaches to the port while the artillery dug batteries into position to command the area. The establishment of these emplacements was being hampered by fire from Danish gun-vessels. The brig sloops *Hebe, Cruizer* and *Mutine* accordingly covered the disposition of the bomb vessels *Thunder, Vesuvius, Aetna* and *Zebra* close to the Trekroner fort. With them went the gunbrigs *Indignant, Kite, Pincher, Urgent, Tigress, Safeguard, Fearless, Desperate*, three small armed transports and ten launches equipped with mortars. For four hours these vessels exchanged a furious fire with the Trekroner fort and other enemy guns, both ashore and afloat, which could be brought to bear on them. Having sustained some losses in killed and wounded and endured a degree of damage, the British ships withdrew under cover of the now commissioned shore batteries (3).

As Cathcart's forces drew the noose tighter round the hapless city, Danish gunboats made periodic attacks on the British in Kiøge Bay and Danish shells blew up the armed transport *Charles* (4). On 1 September, having completed their preparations, Cathcart and Gambier again offered Peyman terms for the 'deposit' of the Danish fleet in British hands, an offer which was again

8

1. 'The Siege of Copenhagen, Plate 1 ... the English Fleet & Transports preparatory to & during the Bombardment of the Windmill Battery & the Village of Fredericsberg', coloured aquatint engraved by Robert Pollard and Joseph Constantine Stadler after an original by Captain Cockburn, published by Boydell & Co, 2 November 1807. *NMM ref PAH8059*

2. 'A Plan of the City of Copenhagen, with the adjacent ground showing the positions of the several batteries erected by the British during the Siege in September 1807 commanded by Lieutenant General Lord Cathcart', coloured etching published by W Faden, 4 December 1807. *NMM ref PAG9046*

3. 'The Siege of Copehhagen, Plate 4 ... the Island of Amak & the Coast of Sweden, the Advanced Squadron under Sir Samuel Hood, with the British Batteries & Danish Gun Boats engaging', coloured aquatint engraved by Robert Pollard and J Hill after an original by Captain Cockburn, published by Boydell & Co, 2 November 1807. *NMM ref PAH8060*

4. 'Admiral Gambier's Action off Copenhagen, 1807', watercolour by Thomas Buttersworth, c1813. *NMM ref PAH9512*

5. 'The Siege of Copenhagen, Plate 2 . . . View taken from the top of the Royal Palace of Fredericsberg, represents the City of Copenhagen previous to the Bombardment', coloured aquatint engraved by Robert Pollard and J Hill after an original by Captain Cockburn, published by Boydell & Co, 2 November 1807. *NMM ref PAH8060*

6. 'Bombardement de Copenhague, du 2 u 5 Septembr 1807. Vue considerable Flotte Anglaise commandee par l'Amiral Gambier', coloured aquatint and etching after an original by I Laurent Rugendas, published by the artist, no date. *NMM ref PAH8055*

7. 'Copenhagen. A View of Copenhagen, with the British Forces taking possession under the Command of Sir Home Popham and Genl Murray', engraving published by J Ryland, no date. *NMM ref PAF4764*

8. 'The Last Act of the English', engraving by Eckersberg, no date. *NMM ref PAF4762*

9. 'The Justitia captured at Copenhagen 1807', black & watercolour pen & ink by Nicholas Pocock and Livesay, no date. The frigate alongside is also a prize and shows off her uniquely Danish 'Hohlenberg' stern. *NMM ref PAG9735*

9

rejected (5). Next day the bombardment began, mainly from the artillery emplacements ashore, but with some shells thrown into the city from the bomb vessels. Fire ceased early on the 3rd, but recommenced that evening, though less intensively in the hope that the Danes could be brought to terms. This not being the case, a furious resumption took place on the morning of the 4th and a large and valuable wood yard was ignited by red-hot shot (6). The city was now gradually set on fire and on the evening of 5 September, Peyman asked for a 24-hour truce. This was refused, but an officer was sent to Peyman to insist that the British objective remained the surrender of the Danish fleet and on the 6th, Major-General Sir Arthur Wellesley, Captain Sir Home Popham and Lieutenant-Colonel George Murray were appointed to treat with Peyman.

On the morning of 7 September 1807, Peyman agreed that the British should take possession of the citadel, dockyard, the ships of war and their stores (7). The Danish ships had to be removed and within six weeks the citadel and dockyard were to be restored while the entire British force was to have quit the island of Zealand, all prisoners having been exchanged. Losses among the invaders were minimal, and Danish casualties among combatants amounted to about 250, but some 2000 civilians were killed and many more rendered homeless. Peyman had taken no advantage of offers to permit the city to be evacuated, which was much regretted by the religious Gambier.

The victors necessarily took the spoils. The dockyard was so well organised that it took only nine days for the seamen of the fleet to rig fourteen sail of the line, plug the few scuttling holes cut in them, warp them out and anchor them in the roadstead. In the six weeks allowed them, three further ships of the line were take to sea with all the frigates and sloops, though the blockship *Mars* and *Dithmarschen*, 64, were condemned and destroyed. Of the 74s on the stocks, two were dismantled and the most useful timbers shipped out, while the planked up hull of the third was sawn up (8). Two smaller *praames*, *St Thomas* and *Triton*, were also destroyed. Gambier's fleet sailed on 21 October with its prizes, although *Neptunos* grounded on Hven and had to be burnt, and all but two of the twenty-five gunboats foundered in bad weather crossing the North Sea. The Danes had extinguished their lighthouses and to aid Gambier's passage, the fireship *Prometheus* was moored as a lightvessel off the Skaw.

Gambier returned home, announcing that he had brought the fleet of Denmark 'to add to that of England' (9). This consisted of the 80-gun ships *Christian VII* and *Waldemar*, the 74s *Danmark, Norge, Arve-Prindts Frederick, Justitia, Kron-Prindts Frederick, Odin, Prindsesse Sophia-Frederica, Skiold, Prindsesse Carolina, Fyen, Trekroner, Krondprinsesse Marie,* and the 64-gun *Seiherre*; the 38-gun frigates *Perlen* and *Rota*, the 36s *Freya, Havfruen, Iris, Venus, Nayaden* and *Nymphen*. In addition were two 20-gun ships, *Fylla* and *Lille-Belt*, two 16-gun ship sloops *Elven* and *Eyderen*, seven 16-gun brigs *Allart, Delphinen, Glommen, Gluckstadt, Mercurius, Nid-Elvin* and *Sarpen*, and the 14-gun brig *Flewende-Fisk*. Another brig, *Brevdrageren*, and the 12-gun schooner *Ornen* were destroyed as useless. However, only four of the captured ships of the line were found to be worth recommissioning in the Royal Navy, the much-admired *Christian VII*, (of which a copy, HMS *Cambridge* was ordered), the *Danmark, Norge* and *Prindsesse Carolina*, along with some of the frigates and sloops. The most valuable acquisitions were, of course, the bulk of the naval stores, though the ordnance was largely useless due to incompatible calibres. The benefit to Britain was what Denmark and thus Napoleon had been deprived of; much was made of the unfitness of the line of battleships to serve their captors, but they would have been invaluable at the very least as armed troopships for an invasion.

While Gambier's fleet had lain idly coercive off Zealand, Keats's ships had been more active. On the withdrawal of the King's German Legion from Stralsund the town had fallen to the French. This news persuaded Gambier to detach part of Keats's squadron to blockade Rügen. The remainder patrolled over 200 miles of coastline. Danish reinforcements crossing the Great Belt were minimal and, insofar as their influence on events around Copenhagen were concerned, futile. By the onset of winter a much reduced force, consisting of *Vanguard* and a handful of lesser cruisers were left in the Kattegat.

1

Helgoland and Anholt

THE annexation of the Danish island of Helgoland was small in itself, yet significant in terms of the economic warfare enshrined in the opposing edicts of the Continental System and the Orders in Council. After Tilsit, Helgoland had been blockaded by Captain Viscount Falkland in *Quebec*, 32, with the gun-brigs *Lynx* and *Sparkler*. On 30 August Falkland received secret orders via the packet *British Fair* from Vice-Admiral Russell commanding the North Sea squadron, to summon the island. This failed until the appearance of Russell in the 74-gun *Majestic* on the afternoon of 4 September 1807 persuaded the governor to surrender (1).

Helgoland was placed under the temporary governance of Lieutenant D'Auvergne of *Majestic*, until Edward Nicholas and a small garrison of the Royal Veteran Battalion arrived. Thereafter Helgoland supported a detachment of sloops which effectively blockaded the adjacent estuaries of the Elbe, Jade, Weser and Ems and provided a location for trading companies which, licensed by the Foreign Office, constructed warehouses in the lower-town (2). From these a mutually lucrative clandestine trade was opened with Bremen, Hamburg (3), Emden and Delfzijl. Communications with London by means of a packet service to Harwich enabled Helgoland to be a 'listening post' and secret rendezvous for intelligence operations.

The extinguishing of the lighthouse on the Danish island of Anholt in the Kattegat compromised navigation in the approaches to The Sound. In the spring of 1809, the Admiralty decided to occupy Anholt and relight the lighthouse. Accordingly, Vice-Admiral Saumarez detached the 64-gun *Standard*, the frigate *Owen Glendower*, three sloops and a brig to take the island. On 18 May 1809, Captain Selby of the *Owen Glendower*, stormed the beaches with a party of seamen and marines, defeating the garrison and accepting its surrender. Anholt was duly commissioned as one of His Britannic Majesty's 'ships' under the command of Captain Maurice who had formerly commanded HMS 'Diamond Rock' off Martinique and served as governor of the captured island of Marie Galante. Like Helgoland, Anholt initially served as a depot for trade goods and for this reason the garrison of 350 marines and 31 marine artillery were tolerated by the dispossessed Danes. On the early break-up of the ice in the spring of 1811, however, and under the increasing severity of the Continental System, the Danish authorities grew hostile and determined to drive the British out. A force of two-dozen gun-vessels and

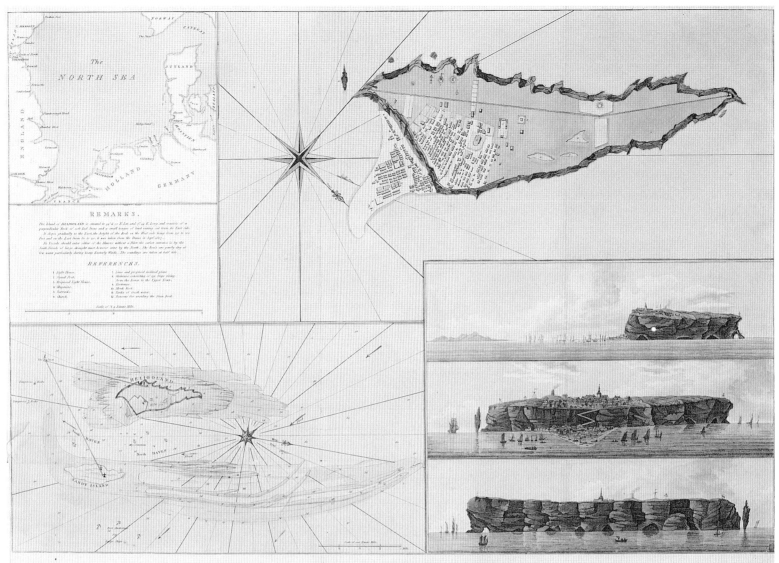

The ISLAND of HELIGOLAND, Views of the same and Chart of the Harbour.

2

troop transports were mustered in Gierrild Bay to storm Anholt with 1000 men under Major Melstedt.

On 24 March 1811, Lieutenant Holstein of the Danish navy landed under a flag of truce and reconnoitred the island on a pretext. Maurice was undeceived and had had word as early as 10 February that an attack was preparing. Holstein concluded Anholt could be taken and that the island's tender, the schooner *Anholt*, was of no account. The defences consisted of two strong-points, the lighthouse fort, Fort York, and the Massarene battery, with some outlying guns and the inhabitants' houses forming natural strong-points in an assault. Holstein did not know that on the 25th the frigate *Tartar*, 32, and the 16-gun brig sloop *Sheldrake* anchored to the north of Anholt.

The approaching flotilla was observed by the pickets before dawn on 26 March. Maurice and Captain Torrens of the Royal Marines left the prepared defences, determined to confront a landing. Forming line, the marine battalion, with six small howitzers, made for the sand dunes fringing Anholt's southern shore. To his alarm, however, Maurice found the Danes already ashore and extended in a line which convincingly outflanked his own. In the twilight Maurice prudently ordered a retreat, whereupon Holstein advanced on the howitzers, over-ran a single gun emplacement, hoisted the swallow-tail flag of Denmark and was on the point of taking the howitzers when he came under a withering fire from the marine artillery in the Massarene battery. Driven back in disorder, the Danes occupied two fisher-folk's houses before being driven out by shot from both the Massarene and York batteries. As full daylight broke the British regained their defensive lines with the howitzers, the Danes reorganised behind the cover of the dunes and their gun-vessels worked round to enfilade the British works.

A telegraphed signal from the lighthouse now alerted *Tartar*. Captain Baker ordered *Sheldrake* to remain where she was, weighed *Tartar*'s anchor and ran off to leeward to

3

double Anholt and its off-lying shoals. Meanwhile more Danish soldiers had landed on the northern shore, but were so assailed by shot from both batteries that they were pinned down in the sand dunes until they enfiladed the Massarene battery with a field gun. Under covering fire, Melstedt now ordered an assault, but the *Anholt* had worked into a position covering the open ground the Danes must cross, and the defensive musketry and gunfire from the British lines was devastating: Melstedt and Holstein were killed, Melstedt's second-in-command had both legs taken off and the assault failed. The Danes fell back calling out for quarter (4).

By now the *Tartar* was beating up from the east, causing consternation to the Danish vessels lying off the southern beach. They immediately weighed and headed for Anholt's western end. Abandoned, the Danish force occupying the southern dunes called for terms, but Maurice insisted on unconditional surrender. After the

Danes to the south capitulated, Maurice with a small and inadequate force went in pursuit of those falling back on the western beach. These were too numerous for Maurice and Torrens to attack, even with the support of howitzers, and they were suffered to embark without further loss.

Captain Baker failed to molest the gunboats which pulled easily through the shallow water as *Tartar* approached, nor was *Sheldrake* in a better position to interfere with the western embarkation, but once afloat the Danish vessels divided, eight gunboats and most of the transports steering for the Jutland coast, the remaining four gunboats and one transport making for the coast of Sweden. *Tartar* persisted in intercepting the former while *Sheldrake* gave chase to the latter. In the next hours she captured *Gunboat No 9* and *Lugger No 1*, and sank another gunboat. Meanwhile *Tartar* took two transports before shoal water compelled her to break off the pursuit.

4

1. 'Heligoland , or Helgoland . . . taken from the Danes by the British 1807', anonymous tinted lithograph, no date.
NMM ref PAI0117

2. 'The Island of Heligoland. Views of the same and Chart of the Harbour', coloured aquatint and etching published by G Testoline, 10 November 1810.
NMM ref PAI0116

3. 'Hamburgh', anonymous coloured aquatint published by Robert Bowyer, 1815.
NMM ref PAH2487

4. 'Defeat of the Danes, in the Attack on Anholt, March 27th 1811', coloured aquatint engraved by Clark and Jeakes after an original by R Turnbull, published by Edward Orme, 21 July 1811.
NMM ref PAH8095

1

Ships of the Royal Navy: the quarterdecked ship sloop

THE ship sloop evolved in the 1750s, when the frigate form was being introduced for Fifth and Sixth Rates. They became larger and less sharp lined, acquired an almost continuous lower deck, a full quarterdeck and forecastle, and adopted the three-masted ship rig. Not surprisingly, for a short while these vessels were called 'frigates' in official correspondence. They were usually around 300 tons and were armed with fourteen or sixteen 6pdrs (1), although a few larger vessels carried eighteen; needless to say, the introduction of carronades added six or eight of the smaller calibres to the quarterdecks and forecastles of the ship sloops. They proved more seaworthy, more habitable, longer-ranged and better armed than the old two-masted type, and the ship rig must have conferred some advantages in battle - three masts would have made them less vulnerable to damage aloft than two. But the one quality the new-style sloops did not possess was speed.

Ship sloops were rather like post ships in that they were seaworthy and more habitable than brigs but simply not as fast or weatherly (2). They could be easily overtaken by far more powerful frigates and a number were captured under these circumstances: *Alert* and *Hound* in 1794, *Peterel* in 1798, *Cyane* and *Ranger* in 1805, and *Favourite*

1. 'A Twenty Gun Ship', aquatint and etching by Robert Dodd after his own original, published by the artist, 1807. Despite the artist's description, the French-style quarter galleries identify the ship as an *Echo* class ship sloop. *NMM ref PAG9423*

2. 'His Majesty's ship Blossom off the Sandwich Islands', watercolour by William Smythe, 1824-28. As the smallest quarterdecked ship type, the sloop made a suitable and economical long-range exploration ship. *NMM ref PAF5964*

3. lines and profile draught of the *Towey*, 1813. These ships were later rerated as Sixth Rates, largely because of a lack of suitable commands for junior post captains. *NMM neg DR2676*

in 1806. Moreover, their sluggish sailing could result in the loss of other ships, like the *Africaine* in the Indian Ocean in 1810, surrendered because the British commodore could not assemble his force in time to prevent it, largely due to the slow progress of the *Otter.*

This failing was well known, both inside the fleet and to civilians. A contemporary pamphlet called *Remarks on the Form and Properties of Ships* criticised ship sloops as 'the worst kind of ship that can be imagined, either for peace or war, being not fit for attack, nor capable of defence even by running away.' As a result it was rare for any ship sloop of the traditional type to be employed by the main fleets, and certainly not in frontline roles. They were not weatherly enough for the Channel blockade, and were not fast enough or powerful enough to act as scouts for the battlefleet. When attached to fleet commands, they were usually to be found detailed to convoy merchantmen within that command's jurisdiction. They had a further drawback as a fleet cruiser, as Byam Martin discovered when commanding the *Tisiphone* in Hood's fleet in 1793: their masts were too short to make adequate repeating ships. It is perhaps indicative of the official view of the quarterdecked ships that they tended to retain their long 6pdrs on the main deck, where the larger brigs were quickly converted to 32pdr carronades: the ship sloops seem to have been regarded as the smallest viable independent cruiser (for which a mixed armament was more useful), and patrol and convoy work, especially on more distant stations, was their usual lot for most of the war.

Almost all the sloops attached to the Channel Fleet in the early years of the war were brigs. This was true of the detached squadrons as well as the main force: *Kingfisher* was with Cornwallis in 1795, *Childers* with the Quiberon expedition of the same year, and *Kangaroo* was the only sloop present in Warren's clash with Bompart in October 1798. High-profile forces like Kingsmill's Irish squadron had almost all brigs amongst its sloops, in contrast to Duncan's cinderella fleet in the North Sea that had many ship sloops (perhaps reflecting its heavy workload of convoys, and many small ports requiring blockade).

There were two significant, and very interesting, exceptions to the main fleet 'ban' on ship sloops. The Channel Fleet under Lord Howe contained a number of sloops which had been built during the American War as fireships of the fast and fine-lined *Tisiphone* class. Howe was an advocate of the fireship and may have been instrumental in the reintroduction of this type in the 1780s, which raises the intriguing possibility that they were in his fleet in the 1790s with similar employment in mind. They could be converted quickly and without the resources of a dockyard; one, the *Vulcan*, was certainly expended at Toulon in 1793 in her intended role, but the

Channel Fleet had no real opportunity for fireship attack.

The other type of ship sloop allowed a major fleet role in the 1790s was a new form of flush-decked vessel, initially entirely acquired by capture but from 1797 purpose-built as well. These latter were essentially brig hull designs given three-masted rigs, whereas most of the French prizes were more ship-like, but lacking substantial upperworks were more weatherly and usually faster. The Channel Fleet's *Scourge* was of this design, while the 500-ton *Bonne Citoyenne* was a particular favourite; she proved a very effective scout for the Mediterranean Fleet leading up to the battle of St Vincent, and in most respects was a good substitute for a frigate.

Quarterdecked Ship Sloops

Year	No in Sea Service	No in Ordinary or Repairing
1794	32	1
1797	43	2
1799	38	0
1801	34	0
1804	19	2
1808	49	3
1810	54	2
1812	50	1
1814	43	1

2

The flush-decked ships grew in numbers in the French Revolutionary War just as the quarterdecked ships declined, reflecting the fleet concerns of the period, and the willingness of the Spencer Admiralty to back innovation in ship design (only one quarterdecked type was ordered after 1795). With sloops, as with so many other classes, a regression began with the St Vincent administration; the 1802 programme included fourteen quarterdecked ships to a design of 1795, and succeeding admiralties built even more (3). This period was obsessed with the threat of invasion, and the good defensive qualities of the quarterdecked sloop may have seemed a better bet in the circumstances; certainly new building declined with the post-Trafalgar change in priorities. The flush-decked sloop also staged a small recovery towards the end of the war, thanks to the victories of the big American ship sloops, forcing the construction of similar ships.

3

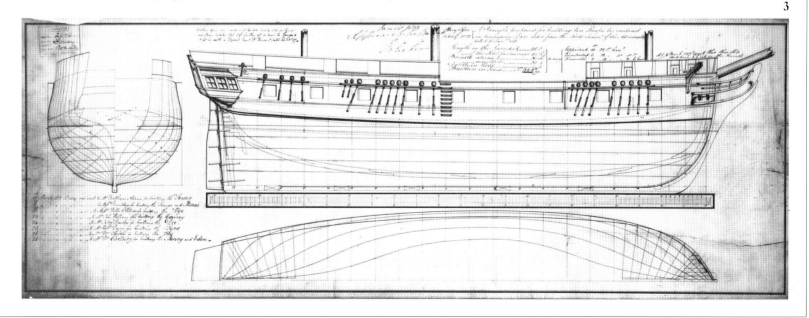

1

Saumarez and the Baltic, 1808-1812

THE provision of protection for the Baltic trade after Tilsit made temendous demands upon the fleet sent there in 1808, but it facilitated a continuing economic life for the Baltic states and Napoleon's decision to invade Russia in 1812 can be traced directly to his exasperation with his feeble ally Tsar Alexander, whose subjects continued trading with Great Britain and thus defied the embargo he had agreed at Tilsit.

Aboard *Victory* (1), usually anchored in Vinga Sound, Vice-Admiral Saumarez was therefore preoccupied by two different, if inextricably inter-linked problems. The first was the diplomatic and strategic task of maintaining an alliance with Sweden whilst containing the Russians without unduly antagonising them. The second was the war with Denmark which was defensive, occupying his cruisers with the incessant demands of convoy protection. The enormous numbers of the merchantmen involved in Baltic convoys were uninsurable without naval escort. Saumarez was beset by demands made on his ships, not least from the Admiralty, which was constantly being pressed by the City and Lloyd's, where interested parties were investing sums in excess of £150,000 on 'speculations' of exports in expectation of shipping home naval stores.

The extension of Saumarez's cruisers covering this vital trade is typified by three convoys of 1810: in late May, 362 outward vessels were escorted by the *Princess Carolina*, 74, the former Danish *Prindsesse Carolina*; in late July 332 ships had only the escort of the frigate *Hussar*; the homeward convoy passing the Great Belt at the same time was of 220 ships, escorted by the frigate *Fisgard* and the brig sloop *Renard*.

While Danish attack was a constant danger, so was the weather. The passage of a convoy and the withdrawal of part of Saumarez's fleet in the winter of 1811 proved disastrous. In November a homeward convoy sheltered from severe weather at anchor off Nysted in the entrance to the Great Belt. Of the 72-ship convoy, 30 parted their cables and were wrecked on shore. One merchantmen fouled *St George*, 98, flagship of Rear-Admiral Reynolds, and severed her cable. *St George* drove aground and her masts were cut away to save her, but she was afterwards fitted with a jury rudder and made Vinga. Saumarez ordered her home with *Defence* and *Cressy*. Clearing the Skagerrak, they were struck by hurricane force winds and a heavy sea (2). Unable to stand offshore, the jury-rigged *St George* fell to leeward. *Defence* kept her company while *Cressy* wore and stood southward. Both *Defence* and

1. 'The Victory 1st Rate', aquatint and etching by Robert Dodd after his own original, published by the artist, 1807. *NMM ref PAG9421*

2. 'H M Ship St George in the Hurricane of 1805 in the West Indies, Commanded by Honble Micl De Courcy', watercolour by George Heriot, no date. The ship survived this storm only to be lost in a North Sea gale in 1811. *NMM ref PAD8634*

3. 'The Implacable, Captn T B Martin, Engaging the Sewolad Augt 26th 1808', aquatint engraved by Bailey after an original by Thomas Whitcombe, no date. *NMM ref PAD5773*

2

St George struck the Jutland coast, their masts falling and their guns breaking loose. Aboard *Defence* the sheet anchor was 'hove in upon the forecastle and killed a great many men . . . the next sea washed the boats overboard'. Both ships were destroyed and only six of the 850 aboard *St George*, and a dozen of the 530 from *Defence* survived. Further south another convoy of 120 sail was dispersed, its escort of *Hero*, 74, and the sloop *Grasshopper* being lost.

The delicacy of Baltic politics confined the heavy ships of Saumarez to the Damoclean role of a fleet in being. Coercion or intimidation were powerful levers, but infrequent producers of action. Saumarez had entered the Baltic originally to escort Sir John Moore's abortively dispatched army, with a fleet consisting of his flagship, *Victory*, 100, nine 74-gun Third Rates, two 64s, five frigates and a numerous and changing quantity of sloops, bomb vessels and gunbrigs, supported by subordinate rear-admirals. Moore's army having been sent home, by August 1808 Saumarez had deployed his ships in the Great Belt, off Langeland and Nyborg, and in The Sound near Copenhagen. *Goliath*, 74, was later sent on to reconnoitre Hangö where she discovered a powerful Russian squadron of nine lines of battle ships, two 50-gun ships, eight frigates and corvettes, two brigs and two cutters under Vice-Admiral Hanikov. A weak and poorly fitted out Swedish fleet of seven sail of the line and some frigates, almost a third of whose crews were suffering from scurvy, lay off Oro nearby and Saumarez dispatched Rear-Admiral Sir Samuel Hood in *Centaur*, with *Implacable* to reinforce them. These ships joined Rear-Admiral Nauckhoff's squadron on 20 August and on the

3

4

evening of the following day the Russian squadron was seen offshore, but made no attempt to attack. On the 22nd more Swedish ships joined Nauckhoff, bringing his line of battle to ten.

Hanikov's squadron reappeared in the afternoon of the 23rd, making a bold approach inshore with a west-southwesterly wind, but tacked and withdrew to the south. Early on the 25th the Anglo-Swedish squadron finally weighed in pursuit, sighting their quarry at 0900 off Hangö Udd, the southwestern extremity of Russian-occupied Finland. By around noon the two copper-bottomed British ships were drawing ahead of their allies and by 0400 on the 26th, *Implacable* was two miles ahead of *Centaur*, with the Swedes a dozen miles astern. Captain Byam Martin, observing that the Russians, under a press of sail in their determination to avoid battle, were widely scattered, pressed on. Shortly afterwards the leeward-most Russian, *Sevolod*, 74, crossed *Implacable*'s bow on the starboard tack and Martin immediately tacked in pursuit. Two hours later *Sevolod* put about again and opened the engagement. *Implacable*'s guns returned fire, then tacked in *Sevolod*'s wake and began to overtake on her on the lee side. By 0730 the two ships were lying board to board at 'pistol-shot'; *Implacable*'s cannonade shot away *Sevolod*'s colours, shortly afterwards the Russian guns ceased to fire and within half-an-hour Captain Rudnov had struck his pendant (3).

Coming up fast, Sir Samuel Hood had seen the two ships engage but also observed that Hanikov had worn his squadron and was running down to the support of *Sevolod*; he therefore ordered the recall flown from *Centaur*, obliging Martin to withdraw, abandoning *Sevolod*.

A Russian frigate took her in tow, while the two British ships fell back towards Nauckhoff some ten miles to leeward. During this lull, Martin repaired his rigging and signalling this to Hood, the rear-admiral hauled his wind and went after the Russians again. Although the Swedish admiral was still some distance away, *Tapperheten*, 66, and the Swedish frigates were closer. Hanikov again declined action and, taking advantage of a shift of wind to the northeast, headed for Ragersvik (near modern Tallin). Approaching her refuge, *Sevolod* grounded on a shoal and after the Russian squadron had anchored, Hanikov sent boats out to bring her in. By great exertion *Sevolod* was refloated clear of the shoal and that evening had been taken in tow by the boats. At this point Hood arrived and ran *Centaur* directly alongside *Sevolod*, fouling the Russian's bowsprit. As the two ships ground together and dragged past each other, *Centaur*'s guns fired into the Russian at point-blank until, foul of *Centaur*'s mizzen rigging, *Sevolod*'s bowsprit was lashed by *Centaur*'s officers under a hail of musketry. A furious hand-to-hand combat ensued in which each company tried to storm the opposing ship as *Sevolod*'s anchor was let go, bringing the two ships up in only six fathoms of water.

Implacable now ranged up and anchored a cable away, finally compelling the Russians to strike. However, shortly afterwards both *Centaur* and *Sevolod* were aground again and Hanikov ordered two of his ships to assist in the hope of once again liberating *Sevolod* and, if possible, taking *Centaur*. Both British ships' companies succeeded in refloating *Centaur*, heaving her into deep water; cheated, the Russian ships reanchored. Equally frustrated in being unable to get their prize off, the British removed all on board, set fire to *Sevolod* and withdrew (4).

Arriving off Ragersvik on the 30th to join Nauckhoff and Hood, Saumarez in *Victory*, with *Mars, Goliath* and *Africa*, found Hanikov had moored his ships to the shore and fortified his anchorage with chain booms and guns on East Raga Island (5). These defences were discovered by Captain Bathurst of *Salsette* and Captain Trolle of the Swedish frigate *Camilla*, but not before fireships had been prepared for an assault on the Russians. In the event Saumarez blockaded Ragersvik until October, when he and Nauckhoff retired to Karlscrona. Although Hanikov escaped to Kronstadt (6,7) before the onset of winter, there were to be no further fleet actions in the Baltic.

Nevertheless, the cruising ground off Hangö produced an occasional flurry. On 19 June 1809 the boats of *Bellerophon*, 74 cut out three small coasters and overran a shore battery of four guns. In July her boats were again in action, along with those of *Implacable*, 74, *Melpomone*, 38 and *Prometheus*, 18. *Melpomone* was in a poor condition after her brush with Danish gunboats off Nyborg in the previous May (see page 133 following) and the present affair

was to offer similar odds (8). Byam Martin in *Implacable* was detached to harry the Russian trade inside the Finnish archipelago and knew of gun-vessels and coasters being within the islands of Barö Sound. On 7 July 1809 the boats of the squadron approached their intended victims under a furious fire, captured six gun-vessels and sank a seventh, while the eighth escaped. Some twelve of the coasters were taken and although the raid cost the Russians 120 men in casualties and afterwards discouraged them from moving stores and matériel by sea, the losses of 17 killed and 37 wounded of the 270 British sent away was considered too high a price to pay. The following year the Admiralty were constrained to issue an order expressing their concern at the losses occurring in boat actions and instructing officers to consider carefully the true value of such attacks.

A few weeks later, on 25 July a similar attack was made on shipping in Frederickshamn at the head of the Gulf of Finland by the boats of *Princess Caroline*, 74, *Minotaur*, 74, *Cerberus*, 32 and *Prometheus*. Again the fighting was severe and heavy losses were sustained, though four vessels were taken, including Russian gunboats formerly of the Swedish oared flotilla.

Napoleon's rigorous tightening of the Continental System was given greater strength prior to the invasion of Russia and the occupation of the Baltic littoral by increasing numbers of French troops. It became much more difficult for British and so-called 'neutral' ships to operate from the ports of Prussia and Mecklenburg and while those carrying neutral papers were merely delayed for examination, overtly British vessels were quickly seized. One such was the *Uriana*, described as a 'large merchant ship' caught in the East Prussian port of Pillau on the eastern end of the Gulf of Dantzig at the end of June 1812. Pillau had been a place of importance both for the entry of British colonial produce and manufactures, and for the loading of important commodities such as oak, deals, flax and hemp. Word had reached Commander Ross in *Briseis*, a 10-gun brig cruising offshore, that *Uriana* had been seized, a circumstance confirmed when he approached the *Uriana* on 28th, to find her full of troops. Ross tacked offshore and awaited the night, intending to send in a boat. Being midsummer the approaching pinnace was seen and met with a fire from the *Uriana*'s small broadside and swivels, but the boarding party drove the troops into their own boats and successfully cut out the merchantman.

At this time Byam Martin was operating in the Gulf of

4. 'Burning of the Sewolod, Aug 27 1808', anonymous watercolour of the nineteenth-century British school, after Thomas Whitcombe, no date. *NMM ref PAD8660*

5. 'A View of the Russian Fleet moored in Rogerswick [Ragersvik] Bay in the Gulph of Finland on the 3rd of Sept 1808 taken from His Majesty's Ship 'Mars' the Advanced Ship of the English and Swedish Fleets', watercolour by L Gordon. *Mystic Seaport Museum, Mystic CT ref 54.1327*

6. 'Cronstadt in Russia', engraved by Hall after an original by F Gibson, published by Joyce Gold, 31 December 1807 (Plate CCXLVI from the *Naval Chronicle*, Vol XVIII). *NMM neg D9266*

Riga stiffening Russian resolve to defend the place against the advances of the extreme left of the Grand Army under Marshal Macdonald, but active sea warfare in the Baltic was now rapidly modified by events on land. Napoleon's retreat from Moscow turned into a rout, the Prussians rose in revolt and Macdonald was soon treating for terms. Though Saumarez came home for personal reasons, his tenure of command had seen the British cause triumphant and the Fourth Coalition was to endure until, in 1814, Napoleon abdicated.

The Danish mosquito war

WHILE the expedition against Copenhagen deprived Napoleon of ships, it brought a horde of mosquitoes about the heads of the British in what the Danes call 'The English War'. The nature of the Danish archipelago and its frequent calms, along with the Danish ability to conscript numerous seafaring men, lent itself to waterborne guerrilla warfare, and in the following summer of 1808 serious interdiction of the Baltic trade began. Nor did the Danes scruple to engage superior forces, though the employment of small escorts assigned to vast convoys, surrendered the initiative to the heavily armed and manned Danish gunboats.

In the wake of Gambier's withdrawal, Keats had been left cruising among the islands and with the spring thaw he returned in an attempt to intimidate the Danes and keep open the Great Belt for the passage of trade. Here Keats withdrew a division of Spanish troops which, during the period of rapprochement of Spain with France, had been in Bernadotte's corps and after the occupation of Denmark, stationed on the island of Fünen. After the Spanish uprising of 2 May 1808, the Spanish commander, the Marques de la Romana, accepted a British offer of repatriation. On 9 August Romana occupied Nyborg with some 6000 men, and after suppressing the opposition of two small Danish cruisers, Keats came inshore in the bomb vessel *Hound* and commandeered fifty-odd small craft and withdrew Romana's division to Langeland two days later to await transports. A further 2000 men were embarked from various units scattered about Jutland, and although two regiments on Zealand and some units were left in Jutland, the bulk of Romana's men were successfully repatriated.

In order to dominate the region, British cruisers pursued Danish vessels and interfered with their coastal trade whenever opportunity served. A few Danish warships had been absent during the British descent on Copenhagen. These had mostly retired to operate from Norway, but the brig *Admiral Jawl* was caught off Scarborough on 2 March 1808 by *Sappho*, 18. After a chase this unusually powerful Danish brig of 28 guns was engaged and, after half an hour's fierce contest struck her colours (1). On the 22nd, *Prindts Christian Frederic*, 74, was sighted making for the Great Belt, by the British 64s, *Stately* and *Nassau*. The chase which ensued lasted for over seven hours and the Danish colours were struck as the *Prindts Christian Frederic* ran aground on the shallows off Zealand, where Danish horse artillery soon appeared and the British, unable to recover their prize, set fire to her (2). By the evening of 23rd, she had exploded.

Exactly a month later, the boats of the ship sloops

1

Daphne, 20, and *Tartarus*, 18, were towed by the 12-gun brig *Forward* and sent in to destroy a convoy lying under the guns of Fladstrand, Denmark. Despite a heavy fire from the shore, the merchantmen, laden with supplies for Norway, were cut out. The ship sloop *Falcon*, 16, also raided the Danish coast that spring, burning boats and chasing a man-of-war schooner. She also lay in wait for artillery destined for a newly fortified harbour on the island of Samsø at the entrance to the Great Belt. After several wasted nights of lying inshore, the barges approached and were attacked. One was driven ashore and destroyed; the other, carrying a 13-inch mortar and 400 shells, was captured.

Norwegian waters also had to be secured, and on 14 March 1808, off Midby, the 14-gun brig *Childers* had just

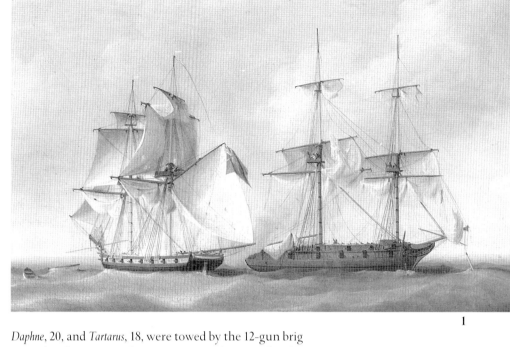

2

3

successfully cut a small vessel out from under the shore and was awaiting the return of her boats when the Danish brig-of-war *Lügum* hove in sight and bore down towards her. *Lügum* kept her distance, allowing *Childers* to secure her prize and recover the boats. She then went after *Lügum* as night fell, but, although aiming at the enemy's gunfire, *Lügum* was hidden against the mass of the land and *Childers* awaited moonrise before pressing an attack. She was an old ship armed with puny 12-pounder carronades and Danish shot passed right through the brig's ripe hull and she began to take on water. The action was intermittent as both vessel manoeuvred. Commander Dillon attempted to weather *Lügum* but the breeze shifted at the crucial moment and in the exchange of broadsides caused casualties on both sides, including Dillon (3). *Lügum*, however, drew off at about

4

0200 the following morning, leaving *Childers* in a sinking condition, though inexplicably in possession of her prize, the galliot *Christina*. In the succeeding hours *Childers* was saved and on the 18th anchored in Leith Roads. Dillon was promoted to post captain and later he became the recipient of a 100-guinea sword awarded by Lloyd's Patriotic Fund.

The *Lügum* meanwhile, continued to cruise off the Norwegian coast. She was next sighted on 19 June off Lindesnes, the Naze of Norway, by the brig sloop *Seagull* which attempted to draw close enough by sweeping to employ her 24-pounder carronades. But Commander Wulff kept his distance, using his long 18-pounders to good effect. When *Seagull* finally got within range, the sweeps were withdrawn and Commander Cathcart sent his men to the guns. At this juncture four gunboats, each mounting two long 24-pounders, approached from the shore under Lieutenant Fons, to trap *Seagull*. Repeatedly raked, hulled and taking in water, with eight killed including the second lieutenant and master, and 20 of the 94-strong crew wounded, Cathcart struck his colours. *Seagull* was towed and into Fosholm Bay, near Christiansand where she was saved and afterwards commissioned in the Danish navy.

The concealment offered by the fiords of Norway to commerce raiders were obvious and in May 1808, the frigate *Tartar*, 32, was searching for the Dutch frigate *Guelderland*, thought to be lying off Bergen (4). On the 15th, Captain Bettesworth entered Bergen Fiord, but found no sign of *Guelderland* (she was later taken off Ireland). Reprisals having been ordered against Danish shipping, he sent his boats to raid the vessels lying off Bergen, knowing this included three privateers. But the

5

harbour mouth was closed by a chain boom and defended by guns, so the boats retired to the becalmed *Tartar*. Immediately a Danish man-of-war schooner and five gunboats, each bearing a pair of long 24-pounders, swept into view. Bettesworth was killed almost immediately and the becalmed frigate was unable to bring the overwhelming fire of her broadside to bear until first Lieutenant Caiger swung her in a light, rising breeze, sank one of the gunboats and, as the wind strengthened, began to chase the other two vessels back towards Bergen.

But it was shipping destined for Britain which fared far worse, fatally compromised by weak escorts. One convoy of 70 merchantmen left Malmö in June 1808 'protected' by the bomb vessel *Thunder*, and the gunbrigs *Charger*, *Piercer* and *Turbulent*. Towards evening on the 9th, the convoy was becalmed off Saltholm, near Copenhagen. Here

twenty-five oared gunboats fell upon *Turbulent* which opened fire with her 18-pounder carronades, supported by shells and clusters of one-pound balls thrown from *Thunder*'s mortars. Within minutes *Turbulent* was damaged, boarded and overwhelmed. *Thunder* eventually drove them off after a fight lasting for four hours, but with the other two gunbrigs immobilised on the far side of the convoy, the Danes were able to triumphantly bear off a dozen merchantmen to Copenhagen.

Another victim that June was the gunbrig *Tickler*, patrolling the Great Belt and caught in a calm on the 14th. Attacked off Bougen-in-Bettet by four gunboats under Lieutenant C Wulff, a savage battle ensued during which, out of the *Tickler*'s crew of 50, 22 were killed and 22 wounded, including her commander. After four hours *Tickler* surrendered (5). The Great Belt proved a fatal cruising ground for British gunbrigs, armed as they were

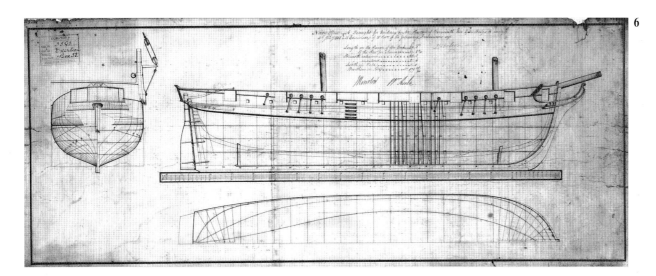

6

7

8

with short-range carronades, for on 1 July *Exertion* ran aground and was swiftly attacked by a schooner and two gunboats which badly damaged her (6). A month later *Tigress* was taken by sixteen gunboats.

On 11 June, the brig sloop *Cruizer* struck back. She had been in the Great Belt with *Euryalus*, 36, when a number of Danish vessels were sighted at anchor inshore, under cover of a battery and troops near the estuary of the River Nakson. Boats from both vessels attacked; a large Danish gunboat was seized and two troop transports set on fire. But when assailed off Vinga on 1 October by twenty armed cutters, luggers, gunboats and pulling craft, *Cruizer* only escaped by vigorous manoeuvring.

In fact Danish gunboats even attacked the convoy rendezvous at Malmo, taking the *Turbulent*, 12, on 10 June. Saumarez's reaction to these assaults on convoys was to augment the escort with a ship of the line, but this proved no solution. Early on the morning of 26 June 1808, *Dictator*, 64, was standing out of Kiøge Bay when she was attacked by six gunboats. After an action of over an hour *Dictator* prudently withdrew, leaving the Danes victorious (7). Nor was this incident isolated, for when *Thunder* and her gunbrigs mustered a convoy of 137 merchant vessels at Malmö on 20 October 1808, she was supported by the *Africa*, 64, which stood across the southern entrance to The Sound and anchored off Amager as a deterrent. Undaunted, the Danes sent out a flotilla of gunboats, whereupon Captain Barrett made sail in a dying wind. The Danish flotilla consisted of some 1600 men, manning twenty-five gun- and mortar boats, with seven armed launches estimated to have totalled about 80 heavy long guns. Barrett was now to regret his impetuosity, for in the calm the gunboats raked *Africa*, cannonading for almost four hours until darkness pressed (8). Twice *Africa*'s colours were shot away and twice the Danes thought themselves victorious, though in the end, having achieved a moral victory, they retired. *Africa*'s lower masts and rigging were badly damaged, she was hulled and her stern was shattered. She lost 9 killed and 50 wounded and was so reduced that she was obliged to put back to Karlscrona to refit. So dangerous had The Sound become, that the following year, 1809, all convoys were routed through the more tortuous and difficult navigation of the Great Belt.

9

Greater damage was caused to the frigate *Melpomene* in May 1809 when cruising with *Temeraire* and *Ardent*. Entering the Great Belt, *Ardent*'s people landed on the tiny island of Romsø to wash clothes and gather firewood overnight. Danish soldiers from Fünen surprised them, killing one man and taking prisoners. *Melpomene* was ordered to Nyborg with a flag of truce to treat for the captives. However, on the evening of 23 May 1809, returning empty-handed, *Melpomene* fell victim to a calm and anchored. Just before midnight she was beset by a score of gunboats which severely battered her though she was only five miles from *Temeraire* (9). In response to her blue lights *Temeraire* sent boats to assist, though while these were approaching, a light breeze allowed her to escape. Two months later *Melpomone* was obliged to return to Britain, too shattered to be of further use as a cruiser. Such events placed a severe strain on British resources and were a constant worry to Saumarez.

At some risk, the small cruisers left to the Danes carried the war farther afield. On 2 March 1809, the ship sloop *Egeria* took the Danish 6-gun cutter *Aalborg* (10), and in May off the Kurland coast of Latvia *Tartar* captured a Danish privateer, while *Cruizer* took the small 6-gun man-of-war *Christianborg* off Bornholm where she was lying in wait for British merchantmen. In August, *Lynx* and *Monkey* attacked three Danish luggers off Isehöved, driving them ashore where the departing Danes set charges to despoil the victors. The pursuing boats, however, reached their prizes before the charges blew and brought them off.

Off Norway on 12 May 1810, *Tribune*, 36, was attacked and damaged before driving off four brigs and their covering gunboats. However, these brigs, operating off Lindesnes, obtained a conclusive victory in July when they fell upon a homeward convoy of forty-two vessels bound to Orkney and Leith Road. The escorting gunbrig *Forward* was chased away and *all* of her charges fell to the enemy! On 10 September 1809 *Alaart*, 16, was captured by two of the brigs, and the *Minx*, 12, was lost to gunboats off the Skaw on 2 September, where she was acting as a lightvessel.

Danish enterprise continued to gain local superiority

10

1. 'HMS *Sappho* capturing the Danish brig *Admiral Jawl*, 2 March 1808: surrender of the brig', oil painting by Francis Sartorius (*c*1775-1831), no date.

2. 'Stately and Nassau (64s) burn Danish (74) Prinds Christian-Frederic near Sealand', black & watercolour pen and ink by T E Lonning, no date. *NMM neg A9288*

3. 'Battle between the Danes, under the command of First Lieutenant Wulff of the Lougen and the English, 14 March 1808', aquatint engraved by N Truslew after his own original, no date. *NMM ref PAF4768*

4. 'View near Bergen in Norway', engraved by Cook after an original by G T, published by Joyce Gold, 31 May 1808 (Plate CCLVII from the *Naval Chronicle*, Vol XIX). *NMM neg D9270*

5. 'The capture of HMS *Tickler*, 4 June 1808', anonymous oil painting of the nineteenth-century British school, no date. *NMM ref BHC0584*

6. Lines and profile draught of the gunbrig *Exertion*, 4 January 1805. *NMM neg DR6749*

7. 'Six Danish gunboats under J J Svenson engage the Dictator, 26 June 1808', coloured lithograph engraved by N Truslew after his own original, no date. *NMM ref PAF4769*

8. 'The Africa attacked by Danish gunboats', watercolour by George Schaar, 1808. *NMM ref PAF4776*

and achieve tactical victories in 1810. On 24 May the cutter *Alban*, 10, was taken by gunboats and on the calm evening of 31 July the cutter *Algerine*, 10, and brig *Brevdrageren*, 12, late of the Danish navy, fell in with a squadron of Danish men-of-war brigs off the Norwegian coast. This consisted of *Lollane*, 20, *Liiqum*, 18, and *Kiel*, 16, and the two British ships had to work hard to escape. Also off the same coast shortly after midnight on 2 September 1811, the British brigs *Manly*, 12, and *Chanticleer*, 10, fell in with a squadron of Danish brigs which immediately gave chase. The enemy were the *Lollane, Alsen* and *Sampso*, all of 18 guns, which separated the *Manly* from her consort, compelling her to strike.

These enemy brigs had been remarkably successful for too long (a further British 12-gun brig *Safeguard*, had also been captured in June), convoys were delayed and

Saumarez was under pressure to rid the Skaggerak of them. Moreover, the Danes had just commissioned *Nayaden*, a new 40-gun frigate, which had vanished from Copenhagen. Guessing she would join the brigs off the Naze of Norway, Saumarez sent *Dictator*, 64, the brig sloops *Calypso*,18, and *Podargus*, 14, and the gunbrig *Flamer*, 12, to cruise off Arendal, to the east of Lindesnes. Here *Nayaden* was found with *Lollane*, *Sampso* and *Kiel*, behind some rocky islets off Mardø on the evening of 6 July 1812. After *Podargus* and *Calypso* grounded temporarily, *Dictator* edged in, at times her yard arms within inches of the narrows, to where the Danish ships had anchored in Lyngoer harbour with supporting gunboats. Captain Stewart deliberately ran *Dictator*'s bows ashore, allowing his ship to swing, bringing her broadside to bear at dead short range on the *Nayaden* and the brigs. *Dictator* and *Calypso* now opened a heavy fire and 'literally battered to atoms' *Nayaden* and the three brigs which hauled down their colours as the gunboats were driven off and *Dictator* was refloated. *Podargus* and *Flamer* had also run aground, sustaining heavy damage from guns both ashore and in the *chaloupes*. It was about 0300 on the morning of 7 July when *Dictator* began working out with *Calypso* and two prizes, *Lollane* and *Kiel*. Their passage was inhibited by more gunboat attacks which succeeded in further wrecking the prizes and forcing them aground, to be abandoned out of consideration for the numerous Danish wounded remaining on board. Notwithstanding this, the destruction of the *Nayaden* was a worthy objective and British casualties were light compared with some 300 on the part of the Danes (11).

The following month the frigate *Horatio*, 38, destroyed a cutter and lugger off the Norwegian coast, but two weeks later, on 18 August 1812, in the Kattegat the gunbrigs *Attack* and *Wrangler*, though proceeding independently, were beset by gunboats during a near-calm night. *Wrangler* escaped, but *Attack* was overwhelmed and, after seventy minutes, a wreck, she struck in a sinking condition (12).

A useful base in the war against Denmark was the island of Helgoland, but the British occupation was an equal irritant to the French, as long as the island continued to negate the Continental System. In August 1811 a flotilla of gunboats was mustered in the shelter of the East Frisian island of Norderney with the intention of invading Helgoland, but word of this reached Captain Hawtayne, of *Quebec*, 32, the local commander. Ten boats and 117 seamen and marines were assembled from his squadron of three brigs and two cutters, under the command of Lieutenant Blyth of the *Quebec* to make a pre-emptive strike. Blyth's boats shoved off early on 1 August and crossed the mouth of the Jade on the 2nd, where they avoided a very superior force of enemy troops in boats. Passing through the tricky waters inside Wangeroog and Spiekeroog, piloted by James Muggridge the civilian mate of the *Princess Augusta*, to catch sight of the four heavily armed gunboats anchored off Norderney in the afternoon.

Each enemy *chaloupe* mounted a long 12-pounder and two long 6- or 8-pounders, were manned with soldiers besides their seamen and were ready to repel an attack. The British boats closed before the enemy could fire twice (13) and Blyth leapt aboard the leading gunboat, followed by Muggridge who shot one defender dead before being flung back into the sea by a bayonet thrust in the throat. Nevertheless the British seamen and marines gained the decks of their target and Blyth received the sword of the gunboat's commander, instantly turning its 12-pounder on her neighbour. Unable to find a match, the gunner of the *Quebec* touched off the gun with the spark off his own pistol, which in turn caused an explosion among loose cartridges. Blyth was flung into the sea, half his clothes burnt off him while a lieutenant of marines was severely scorched and seventeen others were killed or wounded. Though the enemy defended themselves, accounts of the action record they were largely driven below and secured as prisoners by the liberal application of fisticuffs, for they lost only a handful of men. Such murderous skirmishes characterised war in this quarter. There was little glory in them and much risk.

For the remaining two years of hostilities, the escorts provided by Saumarez deterred attack, for he had decided to move only large, well protected convoys. With the destruction of the brigs and *Nayaden* at Lyngoer, Danish resources were reduced to the point of impotence. A few

more British vessels were lost (*Magnet, Fama, Proselyte, Belette, Fly* and *Sentinel*) but not to the enemy, for the weather, navigational hazards, especially ice, were ever-present dangers.

In the Danish gunboats, the Royal Navy met its toughest opponents. Able to manoeuvre in the calms that immobilised their adversaries, they dashed out with their heavy guns and overwhelming manpower to attack the Royal Navy's usually under-manned sloops and gunbrigs. Armed predominantly with short-range carronades, they were quite inadequate and the Danes became adept at taking station out of their range, ahead and astern of their helpless enemy, firing directly into the hulls of the British ships. This tactic proved highly successful, combined as it was with small mortar fire, and quite capable of humiliating larger men-of-war. Although the large frigates of the new United States navy were to ring alarm bells in the British press, it was undoubtedly the Danes whose collective abilities as seamen most challenged the Royal Navy, and the Danes who, despite their abducted fleet, waged an incessant and telling war against British seapower.

Hostilities with Denmark ended on 14 January 1814 at Kiel. Denmark lost Helgoland to Britain and Norway to Sweden, along with half her remnant fleet. In compensation she was ceded Lauenburg. In the final analysis the Royal Navy was able to accept a degree of attrition and finally, by the organisation of huge convoys, enabled to thrust its way through the hostile archipelago, manifestly the superior seapower in the Baltic and its approaches.

9. 'HMS Melpomene engaged with twenty Danish gunboats, 23 May 1809', anonymous oil painting of the nineteenth-century British school, no date.
NMM ref BHC0590

10. 'H M Ship Egeria, Capt Lewis Hole, with the Aalborg, Danish Cutter, a prize, in tow, H M Brig Childers shewing her Nos March 2 1809', watercolour by 'W H', 1862.
NMM ref PAD9032

11. 'Plate 1st His Majesty's Ship's Dictator, Podargus, Calypso & Flamer entering the Passage of Mardoc on the Coast of Norway, at the time the Podargus which was leading, ran aground, July 6th 1812 . . . by George Andrews', coloured aquatint and etching published by George Andrews, 21 July 1813.
NMM ref PAH8104

12. 'Attack and Wrangler taken by Danish gunboats near Fortress 18 August 1812', anonymous gouache, no date.
NMM ref PAH4320

13. 'Boarding by a Man of War's Boats the Row boats of the Quebec, Raven, Exertion, Redbreast, brigs Alert & Princess Augusta . . . at Mid-day on the 3rd August 1811 off the Isle of Nordney gallantly boarding Four French Gun Vessels . . . ', coloured aquatint engraved by I H Clark after his own original, published by Edward Orme, 1 January 1813.
NMM ref PAH8099

 13

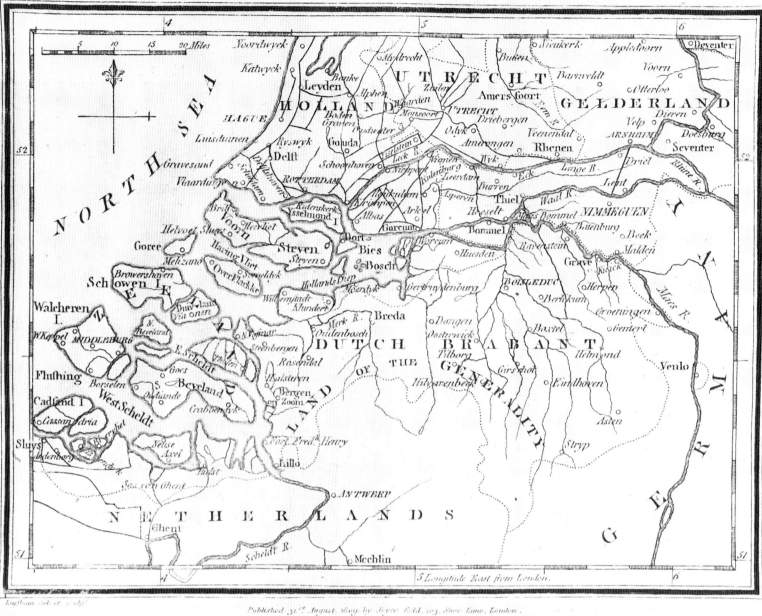

1

Walcheren, 1809 – the lost opportunity

1. Southern part of United Provinces engraved by Luffman published by Joyce Gold, 31 October 1809 (Plate CCXCI from the *Naval Chronicle*, Vol XXII).
NMM neg D9268

2. 'Pictural Plan of the grand Expedition, in the West Scheldt, Augt 1809; shewing the difficulty of approach to Antwerp', coloured aquatint engraved by Clark after an original by Captain Cockburn, published by Edward Orme, 12 October 1809.
NMM ref PAF4777

'NATURE,' the historian Archibald Alison wrote, 'has formed the Scheldt [sic] to be the rival of the Thames,' and the city of Antwerp, was 'a pistol held at the head of London'. Throughout the eighteenth century, threat of occupation of the Low Countries by France was sufficient cause for war and by 1809 there was an added complication. Since the failure of his earlier proposed invasion, Napoleon had transferred his efforts to the Schelde from Boulogne. Dutch shipyards had already produced ten new 74s which were in commission under Rear-Admiral Missiessy; four further 74-gun ships were on the stocks at Antwerp and six 80-gun vessels likewise at Flushing. Moreover, Antwerp's wet docks had

been enlarged and made capable of containing forty two-deckers supported by a great naval arsenal at a cost of 66 million francs; the Schelde's notorious channels had been dredged and cleared of blockships. Napoleon's intention to make Antwerp his principal naval base were furthered by coercing his brother Louis, King of Holland, to cede Flushing to France, for its deeper water provided capacity for a further twenty First and Second Rates.

For London, Antwerp had become a second Carthage: it had to be destroyed. By 1809, major strategic decisions were pressing. Despite Moore's withdrawal from Coruña, the British Government determined to renew the contest in the Iberian Peninsula, but to abandon a planned attempt to co-operate with the Swedes in North Germany. However, the imminence of war between France and Austria was accompanied by pleas from Vienna to relieve pressure on the forces of Austria against which the Grand Army was moving. The obvious target for such a diversion was therefore Antwerp. The city's defences were in such a poor state that 'there was a fair prospect of carrying the town at once by escalade, almost before the intelligence of its danger could reach the government at Paris'. With insurrection in Spain and Prussia, capture of Antwerp would also have a powerful moral effect on the disaffected inhabitants of occupied Europe. In short the meditated attack on the Schelde would yield much to the alliance against Napoleonic hegemony and it was not inconceivable that it could become a major offensive.

In hope of support, the Austrian armies had clashed with the French at Eckmühl and achieved success at Aspern-Essling, long before the end of May when the British cabinet, having fretted in the wake of Coruña, finally set in motion their grand design. Given the proximity of the objective and British experience of combined operations, what followed was a disastrous scandal.

Prevarications by the Government and the War Office provided the enemy with ample warning 'principally by the aid of the English journals'. The Admiralty had the bulk of the shipping ready by the end of June which might not have proved too late despite the French victory at Wagram on 5/6 July 1809, but assembly of the troops was delayed by fears of increasing social unrest in the country. It was not until dawn on 28 July that 29,715 infantry, 8219 cavalry and 5434 artillery, with two battering trains and a massive quantity of stores, ammunition and *matériel* sailed in an immense concentration of force consisting of 37 ships of the line (the majority of which had had their lower deck guns removed and their holds fitted out for the stabling of cavalry horses), five smaller two-deckers, 24 frigates, 31 sloops, 5 bomb vessels, 23 gunbrigs and a further 120 sail of smaller craft. To this total of 245 vessels were added about 400 transports. The naval commander, Rear-Admiral Sir Richard Strachan was instructed to capture or destroy all the enemy's ships on the Schelde, demolish the dockyards and arsenals at Flushing, Terneuzen and Antwerp, and render the river itself impassable for men-of-war. To carry out these orders the army were to occupy the southern bank of the river at Cadzand, and the islands of Walcheren and Zuid-Beveland forming the northern shore (1). To second him Strachan had three able men, Rear-Admirals Keats, Otway and Alan Hyde, Lord Gardner, as well as amphibious warfare experts like Sir Home Riggs Popham, commanding the 74-gun *Venerable*.

Strachan had a good reputation, but the army com-

mander, Lieutenant-General the Earl of Chatham owed his appointment more to faction than reputation. Well known for indolence, his appointment boded ill. Worse, Strachan and Chatham disliked each other and the combination, or total lack of it, was to prove fatal not just to the enterprise, but to the lives of thousands of British seamen and soldiers.

The two entrances of the Schelde are complex and encumbered by sandbanks. The islands of Walcheren, Zuid and Nord Beveland bisect the estuary of the Schelde. The Wester Schelde runs between Walcheren, and Cadzand Island to the south of the river. Passing on eastwards between Zuid Beveland and Terneuzen opposite, it then narrows at Lillo and swings south for the final approach to Antwerp. North of Walcheren and Nord Beveland runs the Ooster Schelde, enclosing both

2

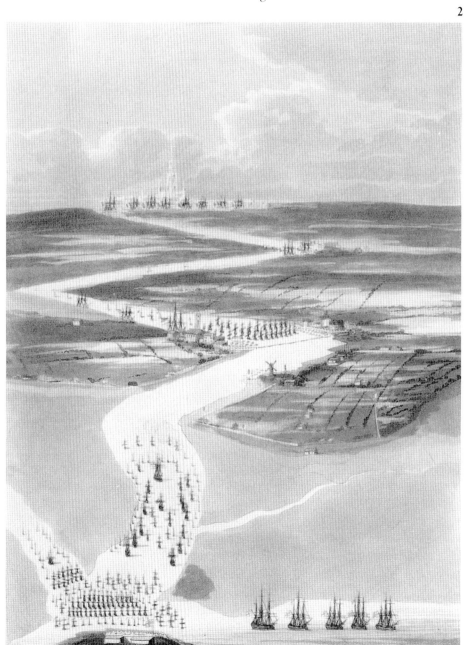

3

3. 'De Aankomst der Engelsche in Ter Veere, in Oogstmaand 1809', aquatint engraved by J Dietrich, published by J Groenewoud en Zoon, no date. *NMM ref PAD5783*

4. 'De Intreede der Engelsche in Middleburg, in Oogstmaand 1809', aquatint engraved by J Dietrich, published by J Groenewoud en Zoon, no date. *NMM ref PAD5782*

5. 'Forcing the Mouth of the Scheldt 14 August 1809', anonymous pen & ink, *c*1809. *NMM ref PAD8529*

6. 'Panoramic view of Bombardment of Flushing during Walcheren Expedition', anonymous watercolour, no date. *NMM ref PAG9649*

Bevelands to join the Wester Schelde just as it turns south towards the great Flemish city. The far northern shore of the Ooster Schelde is bounded by Schouwen, Duiveland and Tholen. On north Walcheren, at the entrance to the gatway between Nord and Zuid Beveland stands Veere, with Middelburg lying between it and Flushing (2).

Off the seaward coast of Walcheren lies an anchorage off West Kapelle and here, on the evening of 28 July, Popham's *Venerable* anchored with Strachan and Chatham on board. The seaward channel, the Roompot, had been marked with boats anchored off the shoals by *Fisgard*, 38, and during the night Popham's officers continued surveying. The following day a huge flotilla of transports bearing Sir John Hope's division, escorted by Keats, passed through the Roompot and anchored off Zierikzee between Nord Beveland and Schouwen. Sir Eyre Coote's 17,000 seasick men arrived later under convoy of Otway, but a landing on Walcheren was frustrated by weather until the 30th.

Bomb vessels and gunboats entered the Veere Gat on 31 July and began to pound the town (3). Meanwhile Coote's men overran Middelburg and invested Veere, assisted by a naval brigade of men from the *Caesar* and sloop *Harpy*. Veere surrendered on 1 August (4), followed by Fort Rammekens on the 3rd. Thereafter Flushing was

besieged but, a witness observed, 'it is said our army are slow in their operations, and that the enemy got a reinforcement thrown into Flushing.' Beyond the Veere Gat, Keats had landed Hope's division unopposed on Zuid Beveland and Hope had occupied Bathz. Keats's lighter vessels pushed southwards through the gatways and creeks towards Missiessy, whose powerful squadron fell back towards Antwerp, securing his ships behind the boom at Lillo.

In all the movements of the ships, difficulty was constantly experienced in the shallow water. Grounding was commonplace and great efforts were expended by the naval crews in lightening their ships, kedging and working their vessels over the banks, for the tides in the Schelde are strong with a large range. In addition to this labour, naval guns were landed to assist the military, while others were put into the now empty transports which, by virtue of their lighter draughts, could be employed as auxiliaries on the flanks of the army in the creeks surrounding the archipelago.

The entrance to the Wester Schelde was forced on the afternoon of the 11 August by ten frigates (5), and on the 13th the British 'began to fire on the town of Flushing, and a tremendous roar (such as has seldom been in battle) was kept up with shot, shells, rockets and musketry, enough to tear the place in pieces'. Bomb vessels and

gunboats in the Wester Schelde added to the bombardment, being joined next day by *San Domingo* (Strachan's flagship) and six other ships of the line (6,7,8).

On 15 August, after 31 hours of bombardment, General Mounet agreed to capitulate on the insistence of the inhabitants. Some 4000 troops and civilians had been killed and 4379 prisoners of mixed nationality were quartered aboard the fleet. When Schouwen and Duiveland surrendered peaceably on the 17th, the high water mark of the expedition had been reached. As Chatham advanced his headquarters to Goes, the principal town in Zuid Beveland, he left too large a garrison in Walcheren to achieve anything against Antwerp. From this point Chatham dithered fatally, beset by stories of French reinforcements, augmentation of the defences of Antwerp and the removal of the lightened French ships even further upstream, while his army was remorselessly eroded by sickness.

The British men-of-war did their limited best. Upon the fall of Flushing, the remaining British two-deckers left off Veere made the difficult passage past West Kapelle to Flushing. The smaller vessels were constantly employed and *Imperieuse* fired shrapnel shells into Terneuzen from her carronades. In early September, Strachan's squadron finally pushed up the Schelde, but could not pass the boom at Lillo, enfiladaded as it was by guns, Missiessy's squadron was thus unmolested. The delay in not penetrating the Wester Schelde immediately, now proved fatal. The delays along the canals between Veere, Middelburg and Flushing had widely infected both soldiers and seamen with mosquito-borne malaria and the numbers succumbing to 'Walcheren fever' increased daily.

Ruminating on his misfortune, Chatham threw in his hand and on the 14th sailed for home in *Venerable*, deserting his troops in a cool display of aristocratic indifference. By this time the army had 9851 men sick, and a week later Strachan left to report to London leaving Otway in command. The stalemate ashore condemned the ships to lying at anchor in the fierce tides of the Wester

7

7. 'Flushing during the Siege taken
from the Knole House Dyke',
coloured aquatint engraved by
Williams after an original by Henry
Aston Barker, published by T Patser, 6
February 1810.
NMM ref PAH8078

8. 'Het Bombardement der Stad
Vlissingen door de Engelschen, in
Oogstmaand 1809', aquatint engraved
by J Dietrich, published by J
Groenewoud en Zoon, no date.
NMM ref PAD5784

8

Schelde, where they were now hit by severe north-westerly gales.

Having landed Chatham, *Venerable* returned to the fleet, missed the channel marks in darkness and ran so heavily aground that her hold flooded and she lost two masts. She required immediate docking, but the fortunate Popham evaded responsibility, a court-martial dismissing her master for incompetence.

Meanwhile the contents of Flushing dockyard were being systematically looted. The frames of the *Royal Hollander* were removed for completion at Woolwich as the 74-gun *Chatham*, while the frigate *Fidèle* was added to the Royal Navy and a new-built brig was launched as *Voiture*. The Government sent General Don out to inspect the situation and with the Earl of Dalhousie, Coote and Rear-Admiral Otway, the decision was taken to abandon Walcheren. Rumours were circulating that Napoleon himself was advancing on Antwerp; more certain was

the repossession of Zuid Beveland by the enemy. As November drew to a close the seamen of the fleet were employed ashore wrecking the defences of Flushing, dismantling the dockyard facilities and recovering any usable Dutch guns.

Other transports were employed removing the numerous sick across the North Sea to Harwich, where a military hospital was set up. Less infected patients were sent on to Colchester, Ipswich, Deal, Portsmouth and Plymouth, while the dead were buried in limepits at Weeley. During this period of retreat the lesser craft and the boats of the fleet were constantly skirmishing along the river banks with French troops who were advancing towards Flushing. Held up by adverse weather, the evacuation fleet finally put to sea on 23 December, few of those on board considering the expedition anything but a complete fiasco.

The financial cost of this disaster was £835,000 and the spoilation of a considerable military resource. About 4000 men died on Walcheren, 106 of whom were killed in action. About 11,500 personnel were hospitalised, roughly a third of those who returned home, many of whom afterwards died. Of those who survived, most suffered from the pernicious and recurrent effects of the fever which for many became quotidian.

Whilst the small craft and seamen of the fleet on detached duty aided the military with great energy, the battleships were almost as under-employed as they had been at the Basque Road. The early forcing of the Wester Schelde would have provided the opportunity of attacking Missiessy before he could escape. As it was, the failure to mount a descent upon Missiessy's squadron was one of the greatest lost opportunities of the war. Nevertheless, the professionalism of the naval personnel whether in action ashore, surveying, or in the logistical duties they were called upon to perform, was of a high standard.

The Straits of Messina, 1806

THE defeats of Austria at Austerlitz and Prussia at Jena, enabled Napoleon to add the possessions of Venice to his Kingdom of Italy and to attempt its further extension by sending an army under Marshal Massena south to invade the Kingdom of the Two Sicilies. In contravention of a treaty of neutrality, King Ferdinand had permitted British and Russian troops to land in the Bay of Naples and this provided sufficient pretext. However, on the advance of superior French forces, the Russians embarked for Corfu and the British, with Ferdinand aboard the 74-gun *Excellent*, withdrew to Palermo in Sicily (1), abandoning the mainland portion of the Kingdom of the Two Sicilies, with the exception of two fortresses, one of which was Gaeta, situated on the Calabrian coast. At the end of March, Napoleon's older brother Joseph was proclaimed King of Naples.

Collingwood, the long-suffering Commander-in-Chief of the Mediterranean whose responsibilities extended from Cadiz to Constantinople, had sent a squadron under Rear-Admiral Sir William Sidney Smith with discretionary orders to support Ferdinand. Flying his flag in *Pompee*, Smith assumed command of the ships at Messina on 21 April. They consisted of the *Excellent*, 74, *Athenien* and *Intrepid*, 64s, *Juno*, 32 with the Neapolitan frigate *Minerva* and some gunboats. Smith, a dynamic but opinionated officer, immediately proceeded to Gaeta and in defiance of the besiegers, sent supplies of ammunition and four of *Excellent*'s guns in to assist the defend-

1

ers under the Prince of Hessen-Philippsthal, whereupon Smith left the *Minerva* and *Juno* to annoy the French.

The fortress had already received some naval relief in April when the frigate *Sirius*, 36, which was cruising off Civita Vecchia, learned of a flotilla of French naval craft moving south to attack the Sicilian frigate *Minerva* off Gaeta. The enemy flotilla consisted of the ship corvette *Bergère*, 18, a large brig *Abeille*, 18, two smaller 12-gun brigs *Légère*, and *Janus*, the bomb vessel *Victoire*, the gun-ketches *Jalouse, Gentille* and *Provençale*, and a cutter. The flotilla was well armed, the corvettes and gun-ketches also mounting 36-pounder carronades. On seeing *Sirius* bearing down, Commandant Chaunay-Duclos lay-to in

2

1. 'Cumberland – Mount Pelegrino; the Mole; Palace of Prince Belmonte – from the anchorage off Port Felice, Palermo Bay', watercolour by Lt William Innes Pocock, no date. *NMM ref PAF0030*

2. The *Sirius* Capt Prowse engaing a French Squadron off the mouth of the Tiber, April 17 1806, from a painting by Whitcombe, in the possession of Capt Prowse', watercolour by Thomas Whitcombe, no date. *NMM ref PAD8626*

3. 'View of the Island of Capri', engraved by Bennet after his own original published by Joyce Gold, 31 May 1811 (Plate CCCXXXVII from the *Naval Chronicle*, Vol XXV) *NMM ref PA12901*

4. 'Sir John Stuart of Maida', stipple engraving by Antoine Cardon after an original by T Wood, no date. *NMM ref PAD8292*

5. Plan of the Battle of Maida, engraved plate from Lt-Gen Sir Henry Bunbury, *A Narrative of Military Transactions in the Mediterranean, 1805-1810*, London 1851. *Chatham collection*

6. 'View of the Rock and Tower of Scylla,', engraved by Hall after an original by Pocock, published by Joyce Gold, 31 March 1812 (Plate CCCLIX from the *Naval Chronicle*, Vol XXVII). *NMM neg D9271*

3

4

close order for mutual defence not far from the Tiber and a shoal dangerous to *Sirius*, bringing almost 100 guns to bear on the British frigate.

Captain Prowse approached as the sun set in a light wind, conferring an advantage of manoeuvre on the flotilla, but, running between *Arbeille* and *Bergère*, Prowse employed both broadsides in a furious engagement which lasted for two hours before Chaunay-Duclos hailed that he surrendered (2). By this time the remainder of the flotilla had run inshore behind the shoals at the entrance to the Tiber and thus escaped in the darkness. *Sirius* lost 9 men killed and 20 wounded, half seriously. Although the *Bergère* was the only prize taken, Prowse's interruption of Chaunay-Duclos's endeavour was complete. Unmolested, *Minerva* was to act with Sir Sidney's Smith's squadron off Messina.

Smith next proceeded to the Bay of Naples with his main force, now augmented by the 74-gun *Eagle*, which on 11 May 1806, supported by Neapolitan gunboats, stood in for the Isle of Capri (3) and opened fire upon the defences from very short range. After an hour's cannonade, the boats of the squadron then landed a mixed force of seamen and marines which stormed the island with such fury that the garrison commander, Captain Chervet of 101st Regiment of the Line, was killed by Lieutenant Stannus of the Royal Marines and the defence petered out. Having lodged a British garrison on Capri, Smith sent a detachment of Neapolitans to destroy some barges and cannon at Maffa, and on the 19th the *Pompee*'s boats cut out a merchant vessel from Scalvitra. Then, on the 23rd, *Pompee* closed the beach at Scalea where the French had two heavy guns loaded into barges and, having warned the inhabitants of the town, 'a few of the *Pompee*'s lower-deck guns cleared the town and neighbouring hills', as Smith reported to

Collingwood. The marines and seamen of the flagship then landed and brought off the two 32-pounders and a quantity of powder, whereupon Smith retired to Palermo.

Smith had an audience with Ferdinand, who was much influenced by his wife, and between Queen Maria-Carolina, King Ferdinand, their British adviser Sir John Acton and Sir Sidney Smith, a project was hatched to further annoy the occupying forces in Calabria. Smith in turn persuaded the commander of the British troops which had been withdrawn to Sicily that they could be boldly employed against the French on the far side of the Strait of Messina. Due to the sickness of General Sir James Craig, command of the army had fallen on General Sir John Stuart, an ambitious yet not over-capable officer who embraced the project enthusiastically (4), refusing Smith a small force for annoying the French, but volunteering a larger under his own command which were embarked aboard the transports still lying at Messina.

Smith meanwhile was paying court to and being flattered by the Queen, who invested him with enormous powers, inflating a conceited officer still further. Smith therefore dawdled, rather than co-operate directly with Stuart, meditating grander designs, leaving Stuart to cross the Strait and land in the Gulf of Euphemia some fifty miles north of Reggio. A few days later, on 6 July, ten miles inland at Maida, Stuart's small force met a larger French corps force under General Reynier. Stuart's men deployed in line and inflicted a stinging defeat on Reynier's advancing columns by withering musketry and the bayonet (5). Stuart, whose absence of orders during the battle was remarked on with some astonishment by his Chief-of-Staff, then retired to his transports. Here he found Smith anchored offshore in *Pompee*. In an

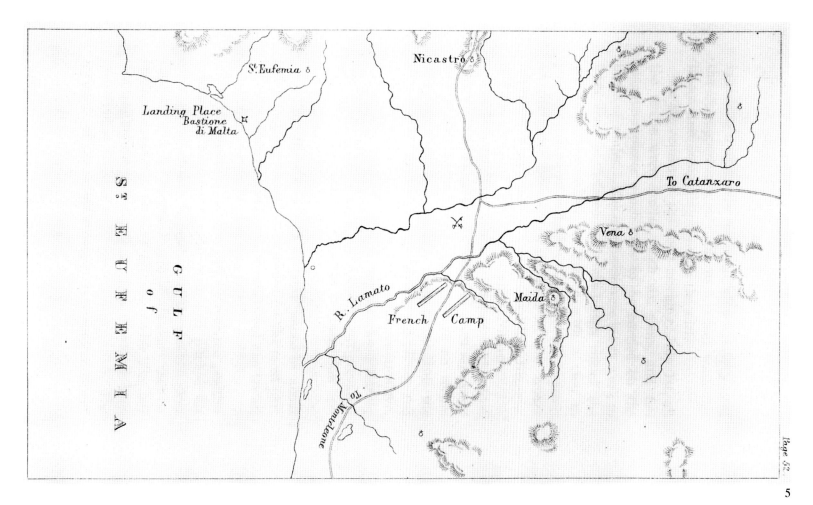

evening of self-congratulation and mutual admiration, the two commanders threw away the strategic gain Maida might have purchased. Stuart's main force returned to Sicily, abandoning Gaeta, which surrendered on 18 July. The Prince of Hessen-Philippsthal had been in daily expectation of succour from Smith, whose conduct ultimately earned him the censure of the government.

A garrison remained in the toe of Italy at Scylla (6) and a detachment of the 78th Foot was sent to encourage insurrection on the part of the native inhabitants. It was supported by the frigate *Amphion*, 32, commanded by the young William Hoste, and some Neapolitan gunboats. On 30 July, the Highlanders under Lieutenant-Colonel M'Leod, took the fortress of Cotrone, with 600 prisoners and stores.

The small successes at Maida and Cotrone were the direct fruits of seapower, and produced a brief evacuation of Calabria which lasted only until the French had completed the possession of Gaeta. Stuart's general ineptitude and Smith's indiscipline failed to grasp the significance of what their forces had achieved. However, and almost by default, the efforts of Smith and Stuart had reduced Massena's resources and encouraged the desultory partisan war of the *massi*, preserved one of the

Kingdoms of the two Sicilies, and made of the other a burden to the French Empire.

Sir Sidney left the Strait of Messina inordinately pleased with himself, invested as he was with a further order of knighthood. He had received instructions to join Sir John Duckworth's fleet which was under orders to proceed to the Dardanelles.

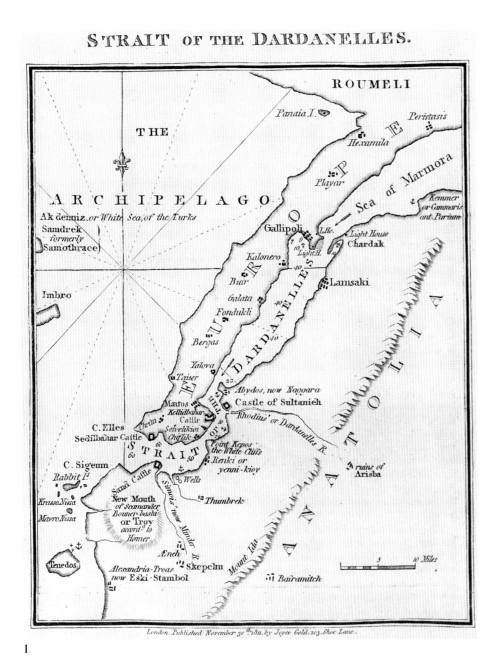

War with Turkey

TOWARDS the end of 1806 Napoleon's efforts to seduce Sultan Selim III from his alliance with Great Britain and Russia, and to close the Dardanelles to the passage of Russian ships were bearing fruit. In November a Russian army had invaded Moldavia, defeated a Turkish army at Groda and occupied Bucharest. This, and the news of the French destruction of the Prussians at Jena persuaded Selim to favour the French, whose emissary at the Sublime Porte was General Sebastiani.

Collingwood, the Mediterranean commander, had left the blockade of Cadiz to Duckworth and was at Malta, having already sent Rear-Admiral Louis eastwards in *Canopus*, 80, with *Thunderer*, 74, *Standard*, 64, *Active*,

38, and *Nautilus*, 18. At the end of the year Louis was on hand at Constantinople to withdraw the British ambassador, Mr Arbuthnot, the Russian minister and the entire colony of British merchants resident in the city, all fearful of being taken as hostages. Louis then dropped down to Tenedos, clear of the Dardanelles.

Collingwood had resumed his station off Cadiz where, on 12 January 1807, he received orders to demand the surrender of the Turkish fleet 'together with a supply of naval stores . . . sufficient for its complete equipment'. There was to be absolutely no chance of any augmentation of the French fleet by that of any new ally. Collingwood was directed to remain off Cadiz and send Duckworth on this task, 'to leave much to the discretion of that able officer' because it would call for 'ability and firmness'. Collingwood enjoined Duckworth not to negotiate 'for more than half an hour' and 'in the event of an absolute refusal, you are either to cannonade the town, or attack the fleet . . .' Duckworth joined Louis off Tenedos on the 10 February, having collected Sidney Smith's squadron at Malta. The combination of the three admirals resulted in a squadron of eight line of battleships (including *Royal George*, 100, and *Windsor Castle*, 98), two frigates and two bomb vessels.

The long strait of the Dardanelles possesses two constrictions before opening by way of the Hellespont into the Sea of Marmora (1). The entrance itself was guarded by the Outer Castles of Europe and Asia. The Inner Castles cover the first of the narrows. Between this and Abydos at Point Pesquies, lies the anchorage of Azire Bay and beyond the Point the strait widens for about twenty miles when from the western bank the Gallipoli peninsula again constricts the navigable channel. Several batteries supplemented the castles, and these were being strengthened with the help of French engineers. A Turkish squadron of one 64-gun vessel, four frigates, four corvettes, two brigs and some gunboats lay under Point Pesquies.

Duckworth got off to a false start on 11 February when the wind turned foul. He then wasted several days writing to Collingwood about the difficulties of his task, and lost one of his ships when on the 14th *Ajax* caught fire and blew up, only 380 of her company of 633 escaping (2).

On the morning of the 19th a favourable southsouthwesterly wind allowed Duckworth to move north. Guns were fired from the outer pair of castles, but on the advice of Arbuthnot, a general cannonade was forbidden and only the bomb vessels threw a few shells, though the 13-inch mortar of *Meteor* promptly burst. By the time the inner castles were reached, a change of heart resulted in the ships returning fire as they passed by (3).

Duckworth's ships now approached the Turks lying off Abydos, and Smith's rear division of *Pompee, Standard,*

Thunderer and the frigates were directed to attack. 'The Turks', Smith reported, 'fought desperately . . . as long as they could; but the superiority of our fire, within musket shot, obliged them to run on shore on Point Pesquies . . .' Partly abandoning their ships, many of the Turks followed their Pasha and joined 'a considerable body of Asiatic troops' on shore where an incomplete redoubt was situated. Smith dispersed the Turkish janissaries and set about the destruction of the enemy's ships. He landed all the remaining Turkish seamen, while his squadron's boats set fire to the beached vessels. By evening the redoubt had been wrecked by a force of seamen and marines. The zeal and activity of Smith's sideshow was to be the last evidence of these qualities in this sorry affair (4).

Having been rejoined by Smith, Duckworth weighed and under shortened sail, ambled north during the night. Passing Gallipoli and the Hellespont he decided to anchor again in the Sea of Marmora for the night of 20/21 February. To general incredulity Duckworth gave no orders to weigh next morning when a favourable south-easterly breeze sprang up. Instead Arbuthnot left for Constantinople in *Endymion* to open negotiations. Far from demanding an immediate response to the British government's ultimatum, Arbuthnot required a reply to his overtures by sunset the following day, though Duckworth's demand for the surrender of the fleet was to be replied to within thirty minutes of its translation. However, Arbuthnot was not allowed to land, so his papers were gleefully read by Sebastiani, and Selim was consequently prevailed upon to remain obdurate. No notice whatsoever was taken of Duckworth's demand.

Duckworth made the preparatory signal to weigh on the 22nd, but despite a favourable wind, it was never executed. By afternoon a calm prevailed, Arbuthnot fell ill and the whole diplomatic burden fell upon Duckworth's large, but inadequate shoulders. He wrote a blustering letter to the Sultan, stating that 'if the Sublime Porte really wishes to save its capital from the dreadful calamities which are ready to burst upon it' which were 'shocking to our feelings of humanity', representations should 'be here early tomorrow morning with full powers with me to conclude the work of peace. I now declare to you for the last time, that no consideration whatever shall induce me to remain at a distance . . . a single moment beyond the period I have now assigned . . . we are less disposed to threaten than to execute. But understand me well. Our object is peace and amity: this depends on you.'

There followed a prolonged to-ing and fro-ing which produced nothing except amusement and contempt in the Topkapi, some excellent copy for *Le Moniteur* forwarded by Sebastiani, and a great baiting of Sir John Duckworth. Sir Sidney Smith, himself one of the

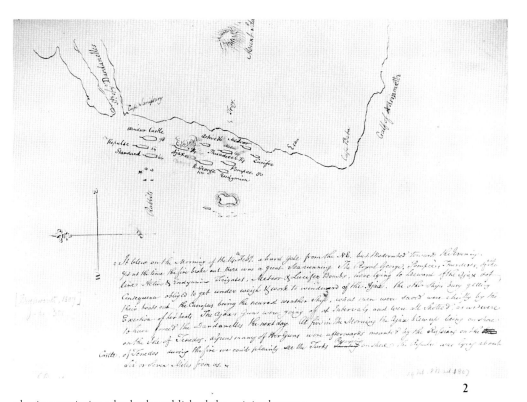

2

plenipotentiaries who had established the original treaty with the Porte some eight years earlier, was denied a hand in these negotiations. Meanwhile matters descended to farce: a midshipman and his boat's crew, blithely going to the neighbouring Isle of Prota for provisions, were captured, and the Turks fortified the island which was within range of the anchored ships. Irritated by this humiliation, Duckworth ordered boats from the fleet to land and to clear the place, though 'no risk whatever must be run'! The affair was bungled in the face of spirited defence directed by Sebastiani in person. Next morning, the Turks had cleared out of their own accord.

3

4

By the end of February Turkish ships had been warped into positions defending Constantinople (5) but Duckworth remained inactive until, on 1 March in a north-easterly breeze, the fleet weighed and spent the day beating pretentiously on and off Constantinople, as if challenging the inferior Turkish force to quit the protection of the city's guns and come out for a trial of strength. After dark, however, he squared away and carried the favourable breeze southwestwards, anchoring off Point Pesquies at sunset on the 2nd. The wind persist-

5

6

ed on 3 March and under topsails the fleet approached the narrows (6). Duckworth now ordered the formality of a thirteen-gun salute, which 'servile politeness' produced a barrage of heavy shot from the repaired battery on Point Pesquies and both castles. Thereafter every gun which bore upon the British fleet was fired. Some threw marble shot weighing up to one-third of a ton and, in an extreme case which hit *Active*, of six-feet diameter. Casualties were mercifully light, but several of the ships were damaged, an explosion occurring aboard *Standard*, while *Meteor*'s remaining 10-inch mortar burst. By noon the fleet was again anchored off Tenedos.

Here Duckworth was joined by a Russian squadron under Vice-Admiral Seniavin, who suggested the fleets combine and return to Constantinople. Duckworth declined. 'Where a British squadron had failed, no other was likely to succeed.' This piece of conceit was to backfire. Duckworth had achieved nothing beyond losing 138 men killed and 235 wounded and leaving a midshipman and four boys as prisoners aboard the Ottoman flagship. Despite the shambles, Duckworth was never called to account. The Government's fall a month later in April obscured matters, while the British public were misled by glittering accounts of Smith's achievements off Point Pesquies and awed by reports of huge cannon-balls the height of a man. Duckworth's greatest achievement is the masterpiece of self-exculpation in which he explains his conduct. In his dispatch to Collingwood, Sir John revealed his incapacity, saying he had left 'the territories of a people so ignorant and foolhardy, that no rhetoric could persuade, no threats intimidate them.'

Seniavin was of different mettle. He maintained a blockade of the Dardanelles from the south, while at the northern end of the Bosphorus a second Russian squadron under Rear-Admiral Poustouchkine sealed off Constantinople. This effectively eliminated the power of the Ottoman fleet and caused widespread distress in the capital, and the deposition of Selim III followed as a result of a mutiny of janissaries. After a series of movements designed to lure the Turks out, made complex by contrary winds, Seniavin fell upon them at Lemnos on 19 June 1807 and virtually destroyed their fleet. Aboard the 120-gun *Mesudiye* the Russians discovered Midshipman Harwell and his boat's crew. They were sent back to Duckworth aboard HMS *Kent*, a mute admonishment of what might have been achieved.

During Duckworth's vain manoeuvres in the Dardanelles, the British Government had optimistically decided to attack the Ottoman city of Alexandria (7). Embarking about 5000 of the troops still in Sicily under Major-General Fraser in thirty-three transports, Captain Hallowell in the *Tigre*, 74, with the *Apollo*, 38 and *Wizard*, 18, escorted the expeditionary force to Egypt. The

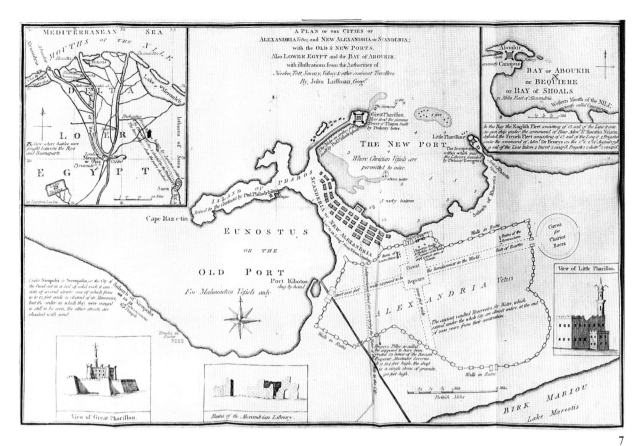

1. 'Strait of the Dardanelles', published by Joyce Gold, 30 November 1811 (Plate CCCL from the *Naval Chronicle*, Vol XXVI). *NMM neg D9272*

2. 'Duckworth's action in the Dardanelles, sketch plan showing the position of the ships 14 Feb, 1807 with descriptive notes by Pocock', watercolour by Nicholas Pocock, 1807. *NMM ref PAD8817*

3. 'Sir John Thomas Duckworth's passage of the Dardanelles, 17 February 1807', oil painting by Thomas Whitcombe, no date. *NMM ref BHC0575*

4. 'Destruction of the Turkish Fleet, Feby 19th 1807', coloured aquatint engraved by Thomas Sutherland after an original by Thomas Whitcombe, no date. *NMM ref PAD5770*

5. 'Vue generale du Port de Constantinople prise des hauteurs d'Eyoub', engraving and etching by Pillement Fils and Nee after an original by Melling, no date. *NMM ref PA10169*

6. 'Vue des Dardanelles', engraving and etching by Schroeder after an original by Melling, no date. *NMM ref PA10167*

7. 'A Plan of the Cities of Alexandria *Vetus*, and New Alexandria or Scanderia; with the Old and New Ports', engraved and published by John Luffman, 5 November 1798. *NMM ref PA13022*

8. 'City of Rosetta', coloured aquatint engraved by Thomas Milton after an original by I. Mayer, no date. *NMM ref PAH2856*

city was summoned on 16 March and the governor declared he would defend the place. On the 17th and 18th, about 1000 soldiers and a few seamen, with five guns, were put ashore near Lake Mareotis. The fort at Aboukir was captured and on the 21st Alexandria surrendered.

On 22 March Sir John Duckworth arrived. This baleful event persuaded Fraser to attack Rosetta (8) and in a bloody action in which 400 men were wounded or, like Fraser himself, killed, the British force was repulsed by Albanians in the Turkish service and thereafter occupation of Alexandria proved another disaster. The force was ill-supplied and inadequate to the task. Duckworth left the command on the coast to Louis who died aboard the *Canopus* on 17 May; unfortunately Smith had already gone home. By September the occupying force was in a sorry state, apprehensive of attack by the ferocious Albanians. A convention was concluded and the British withdrew.

British operations in the Levant had been little short of disastrous. By mid-April poor Collingwood aboard *Ocean* off Cadiz was suspecting the worst. 'Constantinople,' he wrote to his wife, 'appears to be more difficult to attack than has generally been supposed'. By August, Collingwood was off the Dardanelles himself with Seniavin's squadron, engaged in negotiations with the Turks, but by the end of the month Seniavin had handed his late ally 'a civil letter' telling him of the accord

reached by the Tsar and Napoleon at Tilsit. The two now hostile squadrons separated amicably. Collingwood lingered only until 16 September, leaving the *Kent* to attend the British ambassador, Sir Arthur Paget, as negotiations dragged on. In writing to Sir Alexander Ball, the governor of Malta, Collingwood drew the curtain down. 'How this Turkish war has embarrassed all our affairs, without a possibility of its having one good consequence from the beginning! It was undertaken in defence of Russian injustice; and behold how we are rewarded for it!' At the time the *Ocean* lay off Cape Matapan drawing yet another noose in the blockade, round the now hostile Russian ships which lay at their base of Corfu.

Seahorse v *Badere-I-Zaffer*

ALTHOUGH technically neutral after Tilsit, the Ottoman Empire was in the throes of a power-struggle and relations with the Turks remained strained. Attacks on Turkish men-of-war were infrequent: generally there was a desire not to press the Turks as relentlessly as other French allies, though the boats of the *Glatton* and *Hirondelle* had cut out a Turkish ship loaded with specie from the harbour of Sigri on Mytilene (modern Lesbos) on 1 March 1807. The only formality which had been concluded was 'an understanding' that no Turkish men-of-war would cruise in the Aegean or seek to exact tribute from the Greeks, and on that basis Collingwood had left Captain Stewart in *Seahorse*, 38, to ensure compliance with this. However, the Turks wished to extirpate a nest of Epirot rebels engaged in piracy and, knowing that only a lone British frigate was in the area, sent a squadron into the Gulf of Salonica.

Anchored off Skíros on 1 July, Stewart learned that Turkish warships were off Chiliodhromìa in the Northern Sporades and he weighed in search of them. By late afternoon of the 5th, *Seahorse* discovered the Turkish squadron of a big frigate, corvette and galley (1).

Clearing *Seahorse* for action, Stewart began to work up onto the windward quarter of the larger Ottoman ship, aware that she would be better manned than his own vessel which, in addition to suffering the under-manning then chronic in the Royal Navy, had men absent in prizes. By 2130, *Seahorse* was coming close to the starboard beam of the 52-gun *Badere-I-Zaffer*, whose consort, *Alis Fezzan*, 26, was to leeward of the larger frigate. All three ships had swung to the west in the darkness, with the light breeze on their starboard quarters, with *Seahorse* looming very close to *Badere-I-Zaffer*. At this juncture Stewart called upon his pilot, a Gibraltarian who, having been a slave of the Ottomans, spoke Turkish, to hail the *Badere-I-Zaffer* and demand she surrender.

This summons was ignored by Captain Scandril Kichuc-Ali, whereupon Stewart fired a double-shotted broadside into the Ottoman ship. Scandril responded immediately and a sharp action began, with Scandril edging away to allow the *Alis Fezzan* to engage while Stewart pressed him hard. As soon as Captain Duragardi-Ali's guns could play across *Badere-I-Zaffer*'s stern and hit *Seahorse*, Scandril swung to starboard intending to run alongside *Seahorse* and board her. Perceiving this, Stewart had his frigate's helm put hard over, hauled his yards round and luffed up sharp into the wind, continuing the manoeuvre until he had worked smartly round onto the port tack and exposed his starboard battery to the enemy.

Frustrated in his intentions, Scandril wore and both vessels now ran east-northeast some distance apart but converging. Seeing this Duragardi-Ali also paid off before the wind and, at about 2200, found *Seahorse* coming up fast on his port quarter, taking the wind from his sails and rapidly overtaking *Alis Fezzan*. Surging up, Stewart fired his starboard broadside into the Ottoman corvette and in fifteen minutes wrought havoc and caused an explosion

on board (2). Duragardi-Ali luffed under the stern of *Seahorse* and broke off the engagement, following the galley which had taken no part in the battle. Stewart stood on after *Badere-I-Zaffer*, closing her with such rapidity that at 2235 he clewed up *Seahorse*'s topgallants and re-engaged. Both vessels squared their yards before the now northerly breeze. For some minutes *Seahorse*'s starboard guns fired at *Badere-I-Zaffer*'s port battery until Scandril again attempted to close and board, but in doing so, *Seahorse* scraped ahead of *Badere-I-Zaffer* clearing a crowd of boarders mustered on her forecastle with grape from her stern chase guns.

Both ships suffered minor damage in this brush, and Stewart allowed Scandril to catch up, reopening fire as he did so but with his port guns exchanging fire with *Badere-I-Zaffer*'s starboard cannon, soon after which the latter's mizzen topmast fell. It was now approaching midnight and the guns of the Ottoman were falling silent. Stewart summoned *Badere-I-Zaffer* repeatedly, but no reply was forthcoming. Seeing the fall of her two remaining topmasts, Stewart crossed her stern and ranged up close on his opponent's port quarter to repeat his summons. Scandril replied with the discharge of some quarter guns whereupon *Seahorse* 'instantly discharged her starboard broadside'. It was now about 0115 on 6 July. Both antagonists hove-to, heading west, their exhausted crews falling asleep at their stations, though the British fired the occasional gun 'to keep the Turks awake'.

At daylight *Badere-I-Zaffer* was seen under way, her shattered courses squared before the wind and her ensign still aloft. *Seahorse* made sail after her, crossed her stern and raked her with her starboard broadside (3). Captain Scandril remained sitting on his quarterdeck, refusing to surrender to the infidels despite the decimation and wreckage all about him. However, a few of his officers seized him and hauled down the Ottoman colours. Brought aboard *Seahorse*, Scandril was reluctant to surrender his fine Damascus sword; meanwhile the British prize crew under Lieutenant Downie, who was

3

afterwards promoted, took possession of a shattered *Badere-I-Zaffer*. Wrecked aloft, hulled and leaking, she had lost about 170 killed and 200 wounded, many mortally, out of a total complement of 543, manifest evidence of the desperate courage of her company. The British frigate's sea-time and experience told against her enemy, Stewart's shiphandling was superb, particularly in a night action. *Seahorse* had suffered the minor loss of her mizzen topmast, though her sails were much perforated. As for casualties, she had only 5 men killed and 10 wounded out of a company of 251 men and boys.

Taking her prize in tow (4), *Seahorse* arrived at Miconi despite an attempt by Scandril, who had been returned to his former ship, to blow her up. It took three days to make *Badere-I-Zaffer* seaworthy while Stewart returned her crew to Constantinople in Greek vessels. *Badere-I-Zaffer* was towed to Malta and sold to Maltese traders who loaded her with a cargo of Egyptian cotton for London, after which she made a return voyage to Brazil before being broken up at Deptford.

After the action *Seahorse* took a British diplomat to Constantionople where she passed *Alis Fezzan* in a dismantled state. The diplomatic initiative resulted in a peace treaty being signed with the new sultan, Mahmud II, on 5 January 1809.

1. 'No 1 Sunset. H.M. Ship Seahorse Captain John Stewart. At 6.30pm 5th July 1808 standing to attack a Turkish Frigate, a Corvette and a Galley', watercolour by Lt Thomas Bennett, no date.
NMM ref PAF4770

2. 'No 2 Moonlight. H.M. Ship Seahorse, Captain John Stewart. At 10.30pm 5th July 1808, engaging the Turkish Frigate and Corvette. The Galley making off, and the Corvette blowing up forward', watercolour by Lt Thomas Bennett, no date.
NMM ref PAF4771

3. 'No 3. H.M. Ship Seahorse Captain John Stewart. At daylight on the 6th July 1808 making the Turkish Frigate strike; the Corvette not to be seen, her fate unknown . . .', watercolour by Lt Thomas Bennett, no date.
NMM ref PAF4772

4. 'H.M. Ship Seahorse Captain John Stewart, with the Baddere Zaffer in tow, on her passage to Malta', watercolour by Lt Thomas Bennett, no date.
NMM ref PAF4773

4

1

Boat actions

IT was incumbent upon the commander of a British cruiser sent 'on a cruise' to 'annoy' the enemy whenever possible. As more and more frigates commissioned, the cumulative effect of these annoyances was considerable. Local economic life often depended upon regular coastal trade while the occupying troops of France and her allies also relied upon moving military stores and supplies by sea. This was necessary either because of poor roads or a hostile population only too ready to plunder French supplies. Where both coincided, as in Spain after 1808, or the wilds of Dalmatia and Albania, sea transport was the only expedient open to French military authorities responsible for maintaining remote garrisons. Moreover, despite the proliferation of British cruisers, it was usually successful, convoy routes being chosen for their protected anchorages.

2

The interdiction of military communications was clearly therefore a desirable objective for the Royal Navy as part of its strategy of striking back, and while it might take the form of destroying a military convoy, or even cannonading troops on a coastal road, raids were often made on small, garrisoned ports with the storming and temporary capture of a place in order to disable its protective batteries, wreck its shipping and generally confound the enemy whilst encouraging the population to regard the occupying forces as the authors of their misfortune.

Such raids and attacks were generally made by a cruiser's boats, of which a frigate had several, from her cutters, usually in quarter or stern davits, to her much larger launch. Carronades had long been mounted as boat-guns by Admiralty order, and the seamen were trained in the use of small arms with the ship's marines providing the disciplined firepower and cold steel necessary to make an effective storming force. Boat actions were numerous and varied in character. Often requiring long passages under oars, often in chase, particularly of privateers, they might culminate in a murderous hand-to-hand engagement, the storming of a defended position, or setting fire to a score of coasters under fire. A number of attacks were made by the boats of an entire squadron, such as that on a fifty-ship convoy lying in the Gironde made by Hood's ships on 15 July 1806, and although many of these raids were successful, some were not and the mounting manpower crisis led the Admiralty to issue a cautionary instruction in 1810, discouraging them. Unfortunately, the thirst for glory and reputation prevalent among many young commanding officers frequently led them to make attacks whose tactical value was limited and strategic impact insignificant. However, they were the dividend of seapower, and the exploitation thereby was a constant reminder to the French and their allies that they ventured out even into their own coastal waters at some peril.

Boat attacks abounded in almost every theatre. Typical were the exploits of the 12-pounder, 32-gun frigate *Minerva*, commanded by Captain George Collier and cruising on the Galician coast of northwest Spain in June 1806. Collier had heard of enemy armed luggers being about and sent off his boats to search for them on the calm evening of the 22nd. The boats were commanded by Collier's first lieutenant, William Mulcaster, who was supported by Lieutenant Moore and the marine officer, Lieutenant Menzies. It was necessary to look into several bays before locating the luggers at anchor under the guns of a moated fort situated above a small town. Although alerted, the fort 'was carried in a very neat and masterly manner . . .' Retiring, Mulcaster 'took quiet possession' of five wine-laden luggers bound for Coruña and Ferrol. Despite the fire of a two-gun battery in the town, these were brought out to *Minerva*, which had worked up into Finisterre Bay (1). Mulcaster's men suffered nothing more than fatigue, something the contents of their prizes doubtless compensated them for.

A few days later, on 9 July, *Minerva* was anchored off Oporto. The local trade was suffering from attacks by Spanish privateers and pulling boats which lay in wait in the creeks and inlets north of the Portuguese port. Collier therefore sent Mulcaster off in the barge and after a long pull of over forty miles, the first lieutenant came upon the Spanish lugger *Buena Dicha*. The privateer mounted a single 8-pounder 'besides blunderbusses and musketry' and was manned by twenty-six 'desperadoes'. Braving the discharge of the bow-gun, the barge was pulled in with such dash, that the impetuosity of the assault quickly carried the privateer with no loss to the storming party, though one of the desperadoes was killed, the commander badly and two officers and two seamen less seriously wounded (2).

Minerva had returned to Galicia in October and lay at anchor off Oro island, near Vigo. Six Spanish gunboats were known to be based at Carril and Collier determined to try and find them. Menzies went with him in charge of 'a select party of marines' embarked in the cutter and barge. The seamen plied their oars for seven weary hours until they came across a Spanish gunboat, *No 2*, supported by a smaller gun-launch, anchored close to the shore. Once again, *Minerva*'s boats attacked directly, boarding *Gunboat No 2* on the quarter and took both Spanish craft without loss (3).

Until the Spanish rose against the French in May 1808, British cruisers aggressively harried their coasts. Late on the evening of 6 August 1807, for instance, the 38-gun frigate *Hydra* chased three armed polaccas into the

3

Catalan port of Bagur. Next morning *Hydra* stood inshore while Captain Mundy assessed the situation. Bagur was a narrow ria, surrounded by high ground, powerfully protected by towers and batteries, but Mundy 'having great faith in the firmness and resources of his people . . . resolved to attempt cutting out the vessels'.

Bringing *Hydra* to an anchor at the entrance and then clapping a spring upon the cable, her guns opened fire on the defences at about one in the afternoon (4). Mundy ordered fifty seamen and marines under Second Lieutenant Drury and the marine officer, John Hayes, to land and storm the main battery, which was achieved despite withering discharges of langridge from the ships inside the breakwater and musketry from every rocky vantage point. Leaving Hayes and some marines to pick off enemy snipers and clear the decks of the polaccas from which a galling fire still came, Drury advanced into

4

the town, quickly clearing it of opposition and reaching the beach. Here the party commandeered some boats and quickly captured the polaccas.

Mundy now sent in the rest of his boats under Lieutenant Little to help Drury warp out the three prizes, which emerged from the harbour entrance about four o'clock. Hayes then withdrew in good order under a harassing fire and brought off the first division of boats. The landing party suffered four wounded, while on board *Hydra*, one seaman was killed and two were wounded, the ship having been slightly damaged. Drury was promoted to commander on 9 October, though he had to wait ten years before being made post.

But such raids were not always successful, that at Palamos on 13 December 1810 being disastrous. The harrying of supplies to the French forces occupying Catalonia was a cornerstone of the retaliatory strategy of the Mediterranean fleet and the presence at Palamos of a Barcelona-bound convoy of eight laden merchantmen escorted by two small xebecs of 3 guns each and a 14-gun ketch attracted British attention.

The port, set on a rocky promontory, had been taken by the French the previous year after a siege (5). It was occupied by a detachment of about 250 French troops with two 24-pounder guns and a mortar. Against these defences, a considerable force was deployed under Captain Rogers of the *Kent*, 74, having under his orders *Ajax*, 74, *Cambrian*, 40, and two sloops. The boats of the squadron were mustered and, with 350 seamen, 250 marines and two of the small field pieces it had become customary to embark for such operations, Captain Fane of the *Cambrian* led the attack. The boats swept into the port covered by the two sloops and it was with the loss of only five men that the convoy was almost totally destroyed, all but two of the vessels being either captured or burnt.

Having so easily triumphed, the British fell back in relaxed order, descending through the town rather than proceeding directly to the beach. Here they were suddenly subjected to a deadly fire from the reinforced French, decimating the British who crowded into the boats in disorder. Neither *Sparrowhawk* nor *Minstrel* could offer covering fire, since the massacre was obscured by the masonry. In the confusion 33 men were killed, 89 were wounded; 86 men were captured including Captain Fane. These losses amounted to a third of the landing force and represent a considerable defeat, British complacency having got the better of British caution.

5

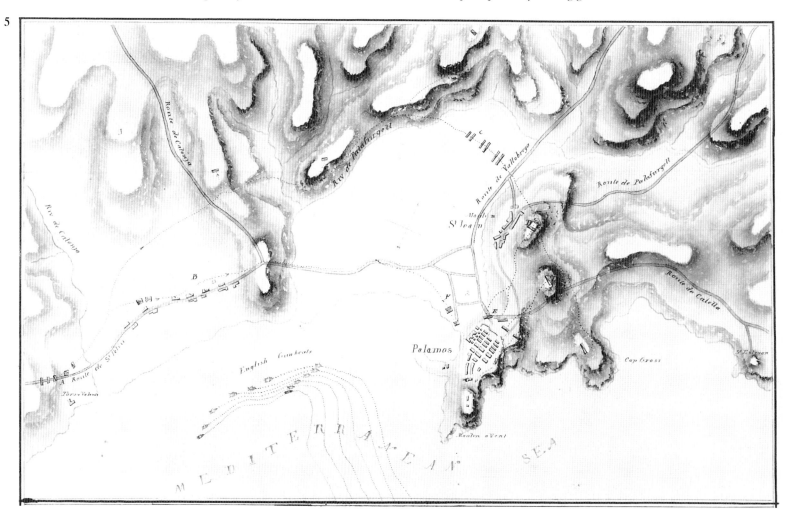

Adriatic and Ionian coasts, 1806-1810

THE long coastline of the Mediterranean is indented by vast gulfs, possesses islands of strategic importance and archipelagoes capable of adorning an adjacent territory, or of providing bases from which the civil authority of that territory might be attacked by sea. One such gulf or lesser sea, with its due proportion of islands, is the Adriatic. Flanked on one side by the Napoleonic vassal Kingdom of Italy, possessed of a fleet of some eighty vessels, with its French controlled arsenals at Venice and Ancona. On the eastern side lay the mountainous provinces of Dalmatia, Illyria and Albania (1). The French had occupied Dalmatia since Austerlitz in 1805 and steadily pushed down the coast, edging all the while toward Turkish territory. At the mouth of the Adriatic lay the seven Ionian Islands, the principal of which was Corfu (2). A Greek archipelago, the islands had passed from Venetian control to the French, from whom it was seized in 1799 by a Russo-Turkish squadron. Paying tribute to Constantinople, the Republic of the Seven Islands, or Septinsular Republic, was recognised in 1800 by Turkey, Russia and Britain. But one of the consequences of the rapprochement of Tilsit was the transfer of sovereignty from Russia to France, and the islands were garrisoned by a Franco-Neapolitan force under General Berthier at Corfu. Here too, for a while, lay Admiral Seniavin's squadron, fresh from its success at Lemnos. Despite a minor intervention by the sloop *Weazel* the garrison of Corfu was soon expanded to 7400 men, but it quickly became the central object of British attention and further reinforcements of 300 soldiers were captured by *Glatton*, 50, at the end of November 1807.

The proximity of Corfu to the heel of Italy at Cape Otranto made it increasingly important that the Royal Navy cruised in the Adriatic, to retain access to that sea, to annoy the French and their allies, and to keep alive the notion that submission to French hegemony was not inevitable. Dalmatia might have been a province after which a French marshal took his title, but its littoral, along with the whole of Illyria and the coasts of Italy from Venice to Brindisi were kept under intermittent observation by elements of Collingwood's far-flung fleet. A busy coastal trade crept along both sides of the Adriatic, to be harried whenever possible. The attentions

1

of the Royal Navy were thus chiefly focused upon blockading Corfu and annoying the commercial traffic of the Kingdom of Italy, adopting a less aggressive attitude to the populations of Illyria and Dalmatia upon whose coasts the British frigates relied for wood and water, attacking only military targets. The Dalmatian island of Lissa was 'occupied' by a tiny British garrison who established a lookout and signal station at Port St George, an anchorage used as a rendezvous and temporary base.

The work was begun in the autumn of 1807, by sloops, but by the following spring the first frigate was assigned to the Adriatic. This was the *Unité*, Captain Campbell, whose impressive exploits included the capture of four Italian brig corvettes, three in one action.

By this time, the blockade of Corfu was strengthening, but from time to time the French sought to maintain communications, the major effort by Ganteaume in 1808 actually only resulting in the arrival of the *Var*. However, in March of 1809, the 40-gun French frigates *Danaé* and *Flore*, employed as heavily armed storeships,

1. 'Sketches on the coast of Albania', grey pen and wash by Lt William Innes Pocock, no date. *NMM ref PAF0040*

2. 'Panoramic View of Corfu', anonymous watercolour, no date. *NMM ref PAI7714*

3. 'The Sanita at Santa Maura', coloured aquatint engraved by H Havell & Son after an original by Joseph Cartwright, c1820. *NMM ref PAI0151*

4. 'The Town and Harbour of Argostoli (Zante)', coloured aquatint engraved by H Havell & Son after an original by Joseph Cartwright, c1820. *NMM ref PAI0155*

5. 'View of the Town and Harbour of Vathi, in Ithaca', coloured aquatint engraved by H Havell & Son after an original by Joseph Cartwright, c1820. *NMM ref PAI0152*

6. Plan of citadel, Santa Maura engraved by Luffman and published by Joyce Gold, 1810 (Plate CCCXVIII from the *Naval Chronicle*, Vol XXIV). *NMM neg D9265*

2

fought their way past *Topaze*, 36, and the 18-gun *Kingfisher*. *Var* was captured in the Albanian port of Valona by the *Belle Poule*, Captain Charles Brisbane, on 15 February 1809.

Also arriving in the Adriatic in 1809, was an officer whose reputation was to be made there, William Hoste, of *Amphion*, 32. In company with *Redwing*, 18, Hoste's boats cut out an armed brig and a coaster from the Dalmatian harbour of Melada, taking three guns from a small bat-

tery ashore on 8 February. On 23 April, Hoste joined *Spartan* and *Mercury*, an ageing 28-gun ship recently reduced to a floating battery but refitted for service in the Adriatic.

On the evening of 1 April 1809 Captain the Hon Henry Duncan sent his boats into Rovigno under fire to seize the French gunboat *Léda*. On the 23rd *Mercury, Amphion* and *Spartan* bombarded Pesaro, to the south of Rimini, drove out the garrison and destroyed every vessel in the port left afloat by the retiring enemy. Cesenatico was briefly invaded by *Mercury* and *Spartan* on 2 May, when twelve coasters were captured and on the 15th Duncan burned seven more in Rodi. Further south, among the Seven Islands on 31 May 1809, *Topaze* cut out nine French and Neapolitan vessels from the harbour of Santa Maura (3).

The interference with the coasting trade was as relentless as it was ubiquitous. On 28 July an attack was mounted on a large convoy sheltering near Trieste. The boats of *Excellent*, 74, *Acorn*, 18, and *Bustard*, 16, landed marines and seamen, the former to take post on the high ground surrounding the port of Duino, while the seamen cut out six gunboats and ten coasters. Another landing was made on 27 August 1809 by the boats of *Amphion* to attack a Venetian battery situated on the estuary of the Piave at Cortellazzo. The guns were turned on six gunboats lying in the river which contested the approach of the appropriately named Lieutenant Slaughter, who boarded them and cut them out along with seven coasters. On 7 September 1809, the boats of *Mercury* cut out the 7-gun Neapolitan schooner *Pugliese* from the port of Barletta on the Gulf of Manfredonia.

As a result of intrigues between the British and the Albanians and Greeks during 1807 and 1808, it was decided to dispossess the French of the southern Ionian Islands, to reduce sources of supplies to the French garrisons of Albania and Dalmatia and to reduce the bases of privateers which preyed upon British and Sicilian ships sailing without convoy. Moreover, French moves against the Porte would be frustrated, particularly as the Ottoman government was in disarray and some encouragement might be given to Greek independence. Accordingly, Collingwod sent Captain Spranger in *Warrior*, 74, with the sloop *Philomel*, to escort 1900 infantry under Brigadier-General Oswald from Sicily. Off Cephalonia on 1 October, *Spartan* joined, and on the appearance of the force, the largely Neapolitan garrison of that island surrendered. Zante (4) and Ithaca (5) next capitulated and *Spartan* went on to take Cerigo.

Oswald wished to invade Corfu, but London demurred; the Government wanted troop reductions in the Mediterranean. Meanwhile Oswald raised a regiment of Greek infantry and, during the interregnum follow-

5

ing Collingwood's death in March 1810, Rear-Admiral Martin sent a squadron to assist in the reduction of Santa Maura (Levkás). The frigate *Leonidas*, 38, had been blockading the island and was joined by the 74s *Magnificent* and *Montagu*, the frigate *Belle Poule* and sloop *Imogene*. These arrived with troops from Zante in transports accompanied by gunboats under Oswald. Early on the morning of 22 March a landing was effected under the cover of *Imogene* and the gunboats, and on 8 April 1810 fire was opened on the fortress which capitulated eight days later (6). The display of the Greek national flag and incorporation of Richard Church's Greek light infantry had ensured the desertion of the local levies, depriving General Camus of almost half his force. Corfu itself remained garrisoned by the French until 1814; but it also remained blockaded by the British navy.

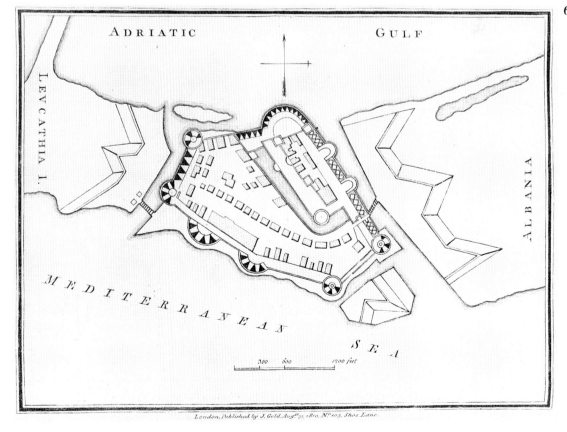

6

London, Published by J. Gold, Aug.st 31, 1810. N.o 103, Shoe Lane.

1

The predicament of Portugal

ONE of the secret clauses in the accord between Tsar Alexander I and Napoleon at Tilsit on 25 June 1807, intended the augmentation of their combined navies by the seizure of the Portuguese fleet. Napoleon had been engaged in intimidating Portugal for some time. In the autumn of 1806, Earl St Vincent had entered the Tagus with a view to stiffening the Portuguese government's resolve and in support of the considerable British commercial interests in the country. This had worked for some months, but after Friedland, Napoleon reapplied pressure with a demand that Portugal close her ports to British ships, sequestrate British property and detain all British subjects within her borders. To enforce this, Napoleon sent a large army into Portugal under General Junot and, yielding to this *force majeure*, the Prince Regent Dom João acquiesced on 29 October 1807. Immediately, a squadron under Sir Sidney's Smith's command was ordered to sail from Portsmouth and Plymouth for the Tagus. Smith, who had enjoyed a short furlough after his employment with Duckworth at Constantinople, flew his flag in the 120-gun *Hibernia* and had with him the *London*, 98, the *Foudroyant*, 80, and the 74s *Elizabeth, Conqueror, Marlborough, Monarch, Plantagenet* and *Bedford*.

On his arrival off the Tagus, Smith was met by the British minister, Lord Strangford, on 17 November. A few Britons and their property had been seized and Smith enforced a strict blockade of the estuary. On the 27th, Strangford boarded the sloop *Confiance* and returned to Lisbon under a flag of truce with the demand that the Portuguese fleet should either be surrendered to Great Britain or transferred to Brazil if the House of Braganza wished to preserve itself from the usurpation of the house of Bonaparte. With the exception of the *Vasco da Gama*, 74, the Portuguese fleet was ready for sea and Dom João needed little time to consider. On the 29th the Regent, with his insane mother, Queen Maria II, other members of his family and a considerable retinue, embarked in the men-of-war (1). Dropping downstream with a score of armed merchantmen, they were met by Smith's powerful squadron, which gave a 21-gun salute and escorted the Portuguese vessels to the south and west before Smith detached. *Marlborough, London, Monarch* and *Bedford* continued to accompany the Regent to Bahia, where the Portuguese court landed on 6 December.

The day following the departure, Junot entered Lisbon and during Smith's absence, Admiral Seniavin arrived. His squadron had become an enemy as a conse-

2

quence of Tsar Alexander's hostile declaration against Britain. Having separated from Duckworth off Tenedos and made first for Corfu where he had left Rear-Admiral Grieg, Seniavin was now attempting to get home to the Baltic. News of the preponderant force of British ships in the offing persuaded him to slip into the Tagus where Smith now blockaded him. Investing the Tagus in *Hibernia* and *Elizabeth*, Smith retained the *Foudroyant, Conqueror* and *Plantagenet* which were bound for the Cadiz squadron until they were relieved by the 74s *Ganges, Defence* and *Alfred*, and the 64s *Ruby* and *Agamemnon*. These ships had left Portsmouth on 6 December as a consequence of the hostile declaration of Tsar Alexander made at the end of October being known of in London on the 3rd.

On 7 December 1807, the day after the reinforcements for Smith left Portsmouth, a squadron under Sir Samuel Hood sailed from Cork in southern Ireland (2). Hood flew his flag in the *Centaur*, 74 and had with him *York*, 74, *Captain*, 74, *Intrepid*, 64 and the frigates *Africaine, Alceste, Shannon* and *Success*. The men-of-war had on board a body of troops under Major-General Beresford bound for Madeira (3). Aware of the exile of their government, the Portuguese authorities surrendered the island on 26 December, two days after the unopposed landing of the British, thus denying it to the French and making of it an Île de France in the Atlantic.

Early revelations of the secret clauses between the two emperors had enabled Britain to use her seapower to neutralise their intentions and frustrate their grand design against her oldest ally. Insignificant though they might appear, combined with the descent upon Copenhagen, they demonstrated not merely the resolution of the British government, but its ability by means of its maritime strength, to strike counter-blows of overwhelming power, offsetting the disasters in the eastern Mediterranean.

3

1

The Transport Service

THE commencement of the Peninsular War vastly increased the commitment of the Transport Board to provide for 'the hiring and appropriating of ship's and vessels for the conveyance of troops and baggage, victualling, ordnance, barrack, commissariat, naval and military stores of all kinds'. By 1810 the tonnage employed on this service amounted to about 980 vessels amounting to 250,000 tons burthen, about a tenth of the British merchant marine (1).

Based in London, the Transport Board was composed of six commissioners holding the rank of post captain, with resident agents (usually elderly lieutenants), at Deptford, Deal, Portsmouth, Plymouth, Cork, Dublin, Liverpool, Dublin and Leith. At Deptford on the Thames, and at Portsmouth the resident agents were captains and the transports were generally surveyed and hired at these two places, coppered vessels being most favoured.

Other officers served as 'agents afloat', acting as commodores in charge of groups of transports. Vessels of 350-500 tons chartered as transports were often specially fitted with horse-stalls (2) or cabins (four soldiers to each), with an infantry battalion of 600 men requiring three ships, a statistic giving proportion to the immense size of many expeditionary forces and troop convoys.

Naval storeships, of which there were between 40 and 50 during the period, were employed solely to convey naval stores to overseas bases, but it was support of the army in the Peninsula that most preoccupied the Transport Service. In 1810, 320 vessels plied directly to Portugal and Spain, with a further 120 to Gibraltar and the Mediterranean. Of the remainder, only 15 were required to maintain detachments in Helgoland and the Baltic and 19 for other locations such as the Cape of Good Hope, Canada, South America and the West Indies.

2

Troops sent to India were conveyed in the Company's vessels. On the home coast and Irish Sea services another 54 transports were in use. At this time the rate of hire was 25 shillings per ton on a coppered hull, 21 shillings for a wood-sheathed hull and 20 shillings for a plain, payed hull.

Most transports were commanded by their civilian masters and manned at the rate of five men and a boy for every 100 tons. However, naval manned and 'armed transports', usually commanded by superannuated lieutenants, were either used as escorts to groups of ordinary transports, or sailed independently. These vessels were either merchantmen hired without a crew, or frigates or small two-deckers armed *en flûte* with a much reduced armament to make room for their human cargo.

Most unusual of the commissioners was James Bowen (3). Born in Ilfracombe, Devon, he followed his father into merchant ships, rising to command by 1776. On the outbreak of the War of American Independence, he served as master in the frigates *Artois* and *Druid*, and *Cumberland*, 74. After commanding the revenue cruiser *Wasp*, he was appointed Inspecting Agent of Transports on the Thames in 1789 and on the outbreak of war in 1793, Earl Howe requested him as master of *Queen Charlotte*. Bowen distinguished himself during the Glorious First of June and the officers of the fleet appointed him their prize agent as a mark of their esteem. When Howe said Bowen could have anything which lay within his personal gift, Bowen replied he wanted a lieutenant's commission. Howe remonstrated that he would become the Royal Navy's most junior lieutenant, but Bowen, conscious he was otherwise debarred from further advancement, insisted. Within a year Bowen was first lieutenant of *Queen Charlotte*, being promoted commander for his part in Bridport's action off Lorient on 23 June 1795. Thereafter Bowen quickly reached post rank, commanding *Prince George*, 98, *Thunderer*, 74, and then *Argo*, 44, in which ship he was sent

to Algiers on a successful mission to free Christian slaves. He was in command of naval forces on the African coast at the Peace of Amiens.

Shortly after the renewal of hostilities in 1803, Bowen was appointed a Commissioner of the Transport Board. In 1809, as agent afloat he commanded the fleet of Transports which extricated Moore's shattered army from the clutches of Marshal Soult at Coruña, a feat which earned him the thanks of both Houses of Parliament. In 1816 he became a Commissioner of the Navy, sitting as befitted a man of his diverse and active experience, on the Navy Board. He retired in 1825 as a superannuated rear-, or 'yellow', admiral and died shortly afterwards.

3

1. 'Ship Harriett James Baillie commander (inscribed 660)', watercolour by Nicholas Cammillieri, 1815. Transports were numbered, carrying their identifier painted on the bow or quarter; the number also appeared against the ship's entry in Lloyd's *Register*.
NMM ref PAH8448

2. 'Embarking troops and horses at Margate, ca. 1800', watercolour by John Augustus Atkinson, no date.
NMM ref PAH3977

3. 'Captain James Bowen (1751-1835), anonymous oil painting of the nineteenth-century British school, no date.
NMM ref BHC2566

1

The Navy and the Peninsular War

THE uneasy alliance between Spain and France was undermined by the actions of Napoleon which culminated in his abduction of the Spanish royal family to Bayonne. Compelling Ferdinand to abdicate, Napoleon imposed his elder brother as king, 'transferring' Joseph from Naples to Madrid and filling the Neapolitan 'vacancy' with his brother-in-law, Marshal Murat. The consequential riot of 2 May 1808, suppressed by Murat himself who was then in Madrid, rapidly escalated into a patriotic, national uprising. Thus it was Napoleon himself who opened the Spanish ulcer.

Ironically, the event had an immediate effect on the naval war, reversing Napoleon's policy of increasing his fleet, for Rosily's squadron at Cadiz was lost, as was control of the Spanish fleet. The Royal Navy was relieved of the task of blockading Ferrol, Vigo, Cadiz and Cartagena, Spanish privateers ceased preying on the Portuguese coast and cruiser operations could be relaxed. Economically the opening of Spanish South America raised British exports by 10 millions and relieved the social distress in the manufacturing towns of England.

But it was the military effects of what was to become the Peninsular War which was to have such a determinative effect upon Napoleonic imperialism, not least because it eventually tied down over 500,000 troops in a vain attempt to hold a country which, until the Emperor's fatal intervention, posed no threat to France. In this the actions of the British were crucial. Her Royal Navy swung from a strategy of energetic blockade to an even more active offence, supporting the Spanish patriots, harrying and raiding French ports and, in due course, mustering the huge resource of the merchant marine to support the army landed in the Peninsula.

Matters got off to a good start. The half-hearted Spanish siege of Gibraltar was raised, the investors marching on Madrid. General Junot lost half his army in Portugal as most of its large Spanish component abandoned him. He compelled 5000 to stay, asking Seniavin to detain them. The Russian declined, the Tsar not being at war with Spain. Junot was left isolated, trying to hold down a hostile country with Seniavin demanding Junot supply him with victuals for 6000 sailors. An anglophile, the Russian admiral was in contact with Admiral Cotton, then blockading the Tagus. On 3 September 1808 Seniavin agreed to transfer his nine of the line and a frigate to Britain until after a peace with Russia was concluded. The Russian crews were repatriated by British ships.

2

3

Meanwhile the British Government had declared their support for the Spaniards who, in turn were initially unwilling to accept help. A British expeditionary force was therefore sent to Portugal to dislodge Junot. On 1 August 1808, 13,500 men were put ashore at Mondego Bay, near Coimbra (1). With them landed the future Lord Wellington, Lieutenant-General Wellesley, an officer whose experience in India was disparaged in the War Office and who was accompanied by Generals Burrard and Dalrymple who remained offshore. Nevertheless, the 'Sepoy General' defeated Junot at Vimeiro, north of Lisbon on the 21st, whereupon Burrard and Dalrymple landed, forbade Wellesley to pursue, and concluded the Convention of Cintra next day in which they agreed to repatriate Junot and his army (2). Having thus wrested defeat from the jaws of victory, they courteously returned Junot to his master. Only Wellesley survived the subsequent inquiry.

Shortly before Vimeiro, General Dupont had been defeated at Baylen by the Spanish and, by December 1808 Napoleon marched with reinforcements into Spain. By now Romana's Corps, repatriated from Denmark, had been landed at Santander (see page 129) and the British were ready to commit 40,000 men under General Moore (3) in support of the now willing Spaniards. Napoleon's columns marched through a hostile Spain and in January 1809 threatened Moore at Salamanca. Greatly outnumbered, Moore began a harrowing retreat through the precipitous Cordillera Cantabria towards Coruña, in Galicia, sending word to London that he

4

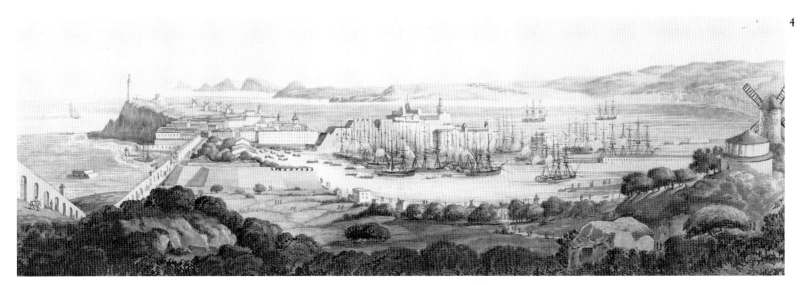

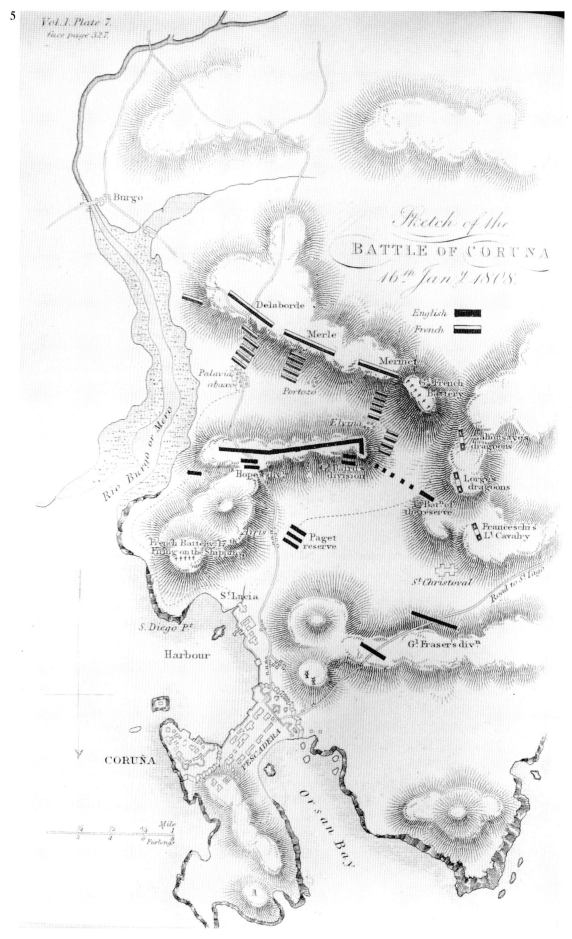

1. 'The Landing of the British Army at Mondego
Bay', engraving by J Vendramini after an original by
H L'Eveque, published by Colnagi & Co, 2 April 1812.
NMM ref PAG9049

2. 'Embarkation of General Junot after the
Convention of Cintra', engraving and etching by
Francesco Bartelozzi after an original by H L'Eveque,
published by Colnaghi & Co, 1 January 1813.
NMM ref PAI5079

3. 'Lieut. Genl. Sir John Moore, K. B. Engraved for
Gifford's History of the War from an original
Picture', stipple engraving by H R Cook, published
by William Lewis & Co, 1 June 1816.
NMM ref PAD8268

4. 'South view of Corunna from the Heights near the
Convent of St Margaret', coloured aquatint engraved
by H Merke after an original by Rev Francis Lee (?)
and published by Edward Orme, 1 May 1809.
NMM ref PAI0007

5. Plan of the Battle of Corunna, from Maj-Gen Sir
W F P Napier, *History of the War in the Peninsula . . .* , Vol I,
London 1832.
Chatham collection

6. 'Wellington Landing in 1809 at Lisbon to take
command in the Peninsular War', anonymous
coloured aquatint and etching, no date.
NMM ref PAH8076

7. 'Wellington Landing in 1809 at Lisbon to take
command in the Peninsular War', anonymous
coloured aquatint and etching, no date.
NMM ref PAH8077

8. 'Comet, Andromache and Sparrow-Hawk from a
drawing by Capt Tobin RN', watercolour by Captain
George Tobin and W M Kelly, no date.
NMM ref PAD8533

9. 'Destruction of the Filibustier Octr 13th 1813.
From a sketch by Captn Scriven', coloured aquatint
engraved by W Bailey after an original by Thomas
Whitcombe, no date.
NMM ref PAD5844

wished for transports to meet him there or at Vigo. Napoleon threw up the chase himself, returning to France and leaving the pursuit to Soult.

With only its rearguard earning Moore's approval, his otherwise indisciplined, disorganised and exhausted army reached Coruña on 11 January 1809, seeing the masts of 140 ships 'with indescribable feelings' (4). These however, turned out to be hospital and store ships, Commissioner Bowen's transports (See page 159, *The Transport Service*) being wind-bound at Vigo, where it had been supposed Moore would go and whither he had sent Craufurd's Light Brigade. Fortunately Soult was delayed in bringing up his guns and Moore prepared to wait, embarking his sick and filling the storeships. These yielded an issue of new firelocks and fresh powder, an advantage conferred by seapower and denied the French with their attenuated communications. On the 13th the British rearguard were dislodged from their position and fell back on the town: the battle of Coruña had begun.

The following evening 110 transports, escorted by *Ville de Paris, Victory, Barfleur*, seven two-deckers and two frigates, stood into the bay. Moore retained a handful of guns and began the embarkation at once with Soult now forcing the pace (5). The cavalry were obliged to shoot their horses and Moore was mortally wounded at the head of the Black Watch, but by the 17th, with the defence left to the townspeople who, 'unmindful of themselves . . . braved a superior enemy to assist a friend,' provided sufficient delay to allow the withdrawal of the last of the wounded and the rearguard. Before Soult could close the bay, the ships slipped out and were driven home by a southwesterly gale. So tightly packed were many of the transports, ships of no more than 200 tons, that in one an officer was posted with a drawn sword to prevent the packed men from moving about as the ship heaved in the heavy weather. Some of the exhausted infantry were still asleep when Bowen arrived at Portsmouth and their condition shook the public, but seapower had extricated a force of 28,000 men.

The setback limited British involvement to a garrison in Lisbon, but by the spring of 1809 Wellesley was back in Portugal, forming a regular Anglo-Portuguese army (6,7). In June he sallied into Spain to defeat Marshal Jourdan and King Joseph at Talavera. He then fell back on Lisbon, drawing after him Massena's counter-attack, confronting the able marshal with a series of defensive lines at Torres Vedras. As the French approached, naval gunboats in the Tagus added to the integrated defensive system and the enemy attack ground to a halt. Massena's besieging force starved before the lines throughout 1810, Wellesley having denuded the country, while the Anglo-Portuguese were well supplied by sea.

Wellington began offensive operations in the spring of

6

1811. Massena was defeated at Fuentes de Oñoro and Beresford gained a bloody victory at Albuera. Then in 1812, Wellington took the border fortresses of Cuidad Rodrigo and Badajoz, beat Marmont at Salamanca in July and entered Madrid. Though frustrated at Burgos and falling back on Portugal for the winter, the following June Wellington again thrashed Jourdan and Joseph at Vittoria and advanced to the Pyrennes, crossing the Bidassoa into France on 7 October 1813. Until Wellington moved out of Portugal, an incessant stream of convoys landed military stores at Lisbon, but as he advanced, arrangements had to be made to supply his front more directly and he came to rely upon Santander. As Wellington candidly admitted, the success of the Anglo-Portuguese army in the Peninsula depended upon its self-sufficiency, which in turn relied upon the Royal

7

8

Navy and the mercantile marine. The Royal Navy also materially assisted the Spanish patriots in all theatres.

The regular Spanish army enjoyed some success, but was no real match for the French; the Spanish guerrillas were quite another matter. They constantly compromised the long lines of communications, demoralising their enemy, and they received the Royal Navy's support. In the summer of 1811 the successive landing and re-embarkation of Ballasteros on the Andalusian coast tied down disproportionate enemy forces. Commodore Codrington had been detailed with three of the line to assist the Spaniards at Tarragona, but was unable to prevent its fall to Suchet, though he assisted with landing supplies and removing the wounded to Valencia.

But it was on the north coast that most was achieved and which Napoleon considered vulnerable, for he had ordered the fortification of every coastal church, convent and strong-point between San Sebastian and Santander. Here, the combination of the Royal Navy and the Spanish *partidas* tied down Caffarelli's 120,000 strong 'Army of the North'. From mid-1812 this war was most

actively prosecuted by Home Popham in *Venerable*, 74, supported by *Magnificent* and the frigate *Surveillante*. Popham had with him a huge quantity of small arms and extra marines for co-operating with the guerillas. Their most important combined achievement was the capture of Santander on 2 August , an all-important safe haven for supplying the army.

Wellington, held up at Burgos by a lack of siege artillery, finally agreed to his staff's suggestion to obtain 24-pounders from Popham's ships at Santander. Two were landed and reached Reynosa, 50 miles away on the 18th, before an impatient Wellington abandoned the siege and withdrew to Cuidad Rodrigo, leaving the French a respite to deal with the guerrillas. A meditated attack on Santoña was given up as *Venerable* was ordered home, where Popham arrived on 30 December; to his chagrin, he never returned. It was left to Collier to render material assistance to the guerrillas and on 5 April 1813, with guns landed by Collier, they took Tafalla to the south of Pamplona. Collier went on to play a major part in the fall of St Sebastian in September, the frigate *Andromache* (8) being detailed to escort the surrendered garrison to Britain.

By now Wellington was advancing from Portugal for the last time and Popham's legacy of Santander came into its own as a supply-base. The French held out in Santoña, and an attempt to restock the garrison was made in October. The 14-gun brig corvette *Filibustier* lay at St Jean-de-Luz, awaiting a favourable wind, but the approach of Wellington's army made the place increasingly untenable and at daylight on the 13th she anchored off the bar of the Adour. Here she was within sight of the British gunbrig *Constant*, brig sloop *Challenger* and schooner *Telegraph* which began to work up to her as she lay anchored. Shortly before 1900, Lieutenant Scriven placed *Telegraph* athwart the hawse of *Filibustier* and raked with his 12-pounder carronades (9). The crew of *Filibustier* set her on fire, then pulled away in their boat. The abandoned corvette exploded within sight of the bivouac fires of the contending armies on the banks of the Adour.

The contribution of Wellington's Anglo-Portuguese army in the Peninsula to the overall Allied effort lay in the fact that his small army of some 50,000 men occupied the attention of a large number of Napoleonic troops. This enabled the Spaniards everywhere to maintain a guerrilla war of extreme ferocity tying down even greater numbers. Without the Royal Navy and merchant marine to support him, Wellington could not have maintained his army, while the direct action of Popham's squadron in particular contributed to the worries of Napoleon's commanders. For all his faults, the 'damned cunning fellow' demonstrated what Sir Charles Oman called 'the beauty of naval operations'.

9

Italy and the Central Mediterranean, 1808-1814

AS in the Adriatic and the east, so in the western basin of the Mediterranean; the coasts of the kingdoms of Naples and Italy, the south coasts of France and Spain were subject to the depredations of British cruisers. While Collingwood and his successors Cotton and Pellew maintained the blockade of Toulon, the relentless business of intimidation went on. Cruisers were also used to supplement the blockade by maintaining a watch upon the coasts and smaller ports, to discover the movement of not merely merchantmen, but men-of-war making their way towards the arsenal of Toulon from their building yards at Spezia or Livorno, or creeping back from Corfu.

The great exponent of the art of coastal raiding was Lord Cochrane. In 1808 he commanded *Imperieuse*, 38, in whose company was the young midshipman and later novelist, Frederick Marryat. Cochrane's exploited his discretionary orders to the full in attacking coastal shipping, landing and destroying signal towers, and bombarding military installations and even a strategic road along the Catalan coast. He was later ably seconded by Brenton's *Spartan*, which took up the baton when Cochrane returned home in 1809.

Brenton was employed along the Italian coast, with orders that included defending the Neapolitan islands of Procida and Ischia in the Gulf of Naples, taken by the

British in June 1809. Late on the afternoon of 1 May 1810, Brenton caught sight of a squadron of Neapolitan men-of-war. These turned out to be the *Cerere*, 40 and *Fama*, 30, which had been action with British sloops the previous year, together with the *Sparviero* and *Achille*, each of 8 guns. On the approach of the British frigates, Captain Ramatuelle of *Cerere* withdrew his force into Naples and Brenton determined to offer the Neapolitan better odds, and sent away Ayscough in the *Success* to a rendezvous off Capri. Ramatuelle, meanwhile, embarked 400 Swiss troops in his two frigates and, supplemented by half a

1

1. 'The Spartan engaging a French Squadron in the Bay of Naples, 3rd May 1810', watercolour by Thomas Whitcombe, no date. *NMM ref PAH8082*

2. 'To Captain Jahleel Brenton . . . This Plate of His Majesty's Ship Spartan having defeated the French Squadron, takes possession of the captured brig Sparviere 3 May 1810', aquatint engraved by J Baily after an original by Thomas Whitcombe, published by George Andrews, April 1812. *NMM ref PAH8083*

2

weather gauge and as *Cerere* drew up on *Spartan*'s port, and lee, bow, the action commenced. Brenton held his fire until the two ships were abreast on reciprocal courses and then opened fire with a triple shotted broadside. Due to the lightness of the wind and the slow transit of the ships, *Spartan* had time to repeat this process with all the Neapolitan ships as they ghosted past in succession (1). The *Achille* with the gunboats coming up astern, turned to the southeast to escape the approaching British frigate. Brenton stood on towards them, brought *Spartan* into the wind and as she swung, fired her port broadside into them, reserving the starboard for the heavier ships she had just left. Ramatuelle did not follow round after Brenton, but wore his ship and stood inshore, heading for the cover of the batteries at Baia. Brenton continued his swing to starboard, and wore after *Cerere*, intending to bring her to close action.

The breeze was now failing as the sun rose and *Spartan* found herself with the *Cerere* lying across her bow, *Fama* and *Sparviero* on her port bow and *Achille* and the gunboats sweeping back towards her from astern. *Spartan* was now the centre of a ring of fire. Brenton was wounded and handed over command to his first lieutenant, Willes, and *Spartan*'s situation might have been dire had not the wind strengthened again, allowing *Spartan* to draw ahead and come up upon *Cerere*'s starboard quarter and *Fama*'s star-

3

dozen heavily armed gunboats, made his own preparations. Early on 3 May 1810, with a light southeasterly breeze, Brenton stood into Naples Bay, only to find Ramatuelle coming out to meet him with *Fama* and *Sparviero* in line ahead, astern of *Cerere*. Brenton held the

4

board bow. *Spartan*'s gunners then poured a terrible fire into their targets, so that the gunnery of *Sparviero, Active* and the gunboats was more of an annoyance. *Cerere* dropped out of the action to windward as she closed the support of the guns of Baia. *Fama*, having been badly raked, was taken in tow by the gunboats, while *Spartan*'s port broadside forced Commander de Cosa to surrender *Sparviero* (2). The loss to *Spartan* was 10 killed and 22 wounded including Willes, who was afterwards promoted, and Brenton who was unfit for further service and was made a baronet two years later. Ramatuelle's ships lost at least 130 men.

British dominance of the western basin made it very difficult for the French to fulfill long-term strategic aims like the expansion of their blockaded battlefleet, since important supplies were continually interrupted. To give one example, two armed storeships and a merchantman,

laden with shipbuilding timber for Toulon, were attacked while taking shelter in the Corsican port of Sagone by the frigates *Pomone* and *Unité*, and the sloop *Scout* on 1 May 1811. The port was too heavily defended to risk a boat action, and the wind was too light to sail in, so the British ships were towed into range by their boats. After two hours firing the French set fire to the storeships, and burning brands from the subsequent explosions also destroyed the other ship and even the defensive gun-tower (3).

One of the flotilla that escaped *Sirius* off the Tiber was seen from the *Alacrity*, 18, off Corsica at dawn on 26 May 1811. The French brig *Abeille*, 20, was a converted American brig and under Lieutenant de Mackau lay-to and awaited the British sloop. De Mackau very ably raked *Alacrity* repeatedly, pouring a destructive fire not at her top-hamper, but at her decks. Wounded early in the action, Commander Palmer went below to have a cut

hand dressed and failed to reappear on deck. His only lieutenant, Rees, fought the ship until he was killed. The master and master's mate were wounded and command devolved upon the boatswain, James Flaxman, who fought the ship hard until Palmer sent up word that the colours should be struck. Flaxman threatened to shoot the first man who touched the ensign halliards, but the gunner insisted, and *Alacrity* submitted (4). Palmer contracted tetanus poisoning from his trivial wound and was accordingly allowed the dignity of having 'died of his wounds'. De Mackau distinguished himself, was promoted and became a Baron of the Empire. Such set-backs were rare exceptions, though they made excellent copy for *Le Moniteur*.

The Honourable Henry Duncan had taken over Cochrane's famous *Imperieuse* in September 1810, keeping up the ship's reputation as a highly effective raider. On 11 October 1811, celebrating the anniversary of his father's

8

Palinuro revealed the presence of ten Neapolitan gunboats and a body of laden merchantmen. Duncan sent Captain Napier to Sicily and *Thames* returned with 250 men of the 62nd Foot. On the evening of 1 November, Napier landed at the head of a body of seamen, infantry and marines and by dawn the raiding party was in possession of some high ground. However, it was clear little could be achieved, so Duncan recalled Napier and both frigates closed the gunboats and opened a heavy fire (6). Two sank and the rest struck, whereupon the ships silenced the fort and the marines went in to wreck it. During the 2nd and 3rd, the troops and marines destroyed two more gunboats, six were brought out along with twenty-two feluccas and some valuable spars, and the works were mined. Remarkably only 5 men were killed and 11 wounded.

Increasingly two-deckers were detached as cruisers, *Leviathan* and *America*, 74s, being very active during 1812 in the Gulf of Lyons and in the Ligurian Sea. The usual target was the coastal convoy system, a typical example occurring in June. On the 27th a French convoy was caught at its assembly ports of Laiguelia and Alessio on the Gulf of Genoa by *Leviathan*'s squadron. This now consisted of *Imperieuse, Curaçoa* and *Eclair*. It was almost calm, but *Eclair* worked inshore to cover the boats carrying the combined marine detachments, who cleared the beach between the two towns of a larger detachment of enemy infantry. The French retired into the two towns, occupying buildings overlooking the harbours, with the

great victory at Camperdown, Duncan stood into the Gulf of Salerno and anchored within short range of the fort at Positano under the guns of which lay three gunboats. Duncan cannonaded the fort, then sent in his boats to destroy the artillery, blow up its magazine and take the gunboats (5). A few days later *Imperieuse* was joined by *Thames* and their boats captured ten oil-laden polaccas which had been put in a defensive posture in the charge of soldiers. On the 21st, a reconnaissance of

9

marines following and taking two batteries, spiking the guns and smashing the carriages. The marines were then brought off to the ships which, with the exception of *Eclair*, had anchored close inshore. Now becalmed, *Eclair* manoeuvred with her sweeps in support of the boats which attempted to enter the harbours. The boat carronades failed to clear the French, whose musketry prevented the attack being pressed. The eighteen lateen and square-rigged vessels had been securely moored, their sails sent down and their rudders unshipped. Pinned down and unable to easily extricate any prizes, the British seamen withdrew and the squadron's guns shattered the assembled coasters (7).

By this stage of the naval war the superiority of the Royal Navy was so well established that even weak forces were rarely challenged. When in August 1812 the *Imperieuse* and sloop *Cephalus* were sent into Naples Bay on a reconnaissance mission, a large squadron led by a 74-gun ship and comprising a frigate, corvette and twenty-two gunboats got underway to chase them away. However, when the British ships showed no inclination to retreat, the collective nerve of the Neapolitans failed; a long range cannonade was followed by the whole enemy force retiring (8).

In February 1813 ,Vice-Admiral Pellew sent Captain Charles Napier in the *Thames*, 32, accompanied by Mounsey's *Furieuse*, 38, to take the Neapolitan island of Ponza in the Gulf of Gaeta. The two frigates embarked the 2nd battalion of the 10th Foot under Lieut-Col Coffin and approached the island, suddenly altering course and anchoring in the entrance to the port where they opened a smart fire, whereupon the astonished governor called for a truce and then capitulated (9). By May Napier had transferred into *Euryalus* and had interdicted the coastal trade on the Côte d'Azur. On the 16th, having been joined by *Berwick*, 74, the boats of both ships were sent in to Cavalaire Road, where numerous coasters were sheltering. The protecting batteries were stormed, the 10-gun xebec *Fortune* was captured with a large number of merchantmen, and the remainder were sunk or burnt.

That month a second attack was made on the Kingdom of Naples. A defended military camp had been built on the Calabrian coast at Pietra Nera, and a large convoy with gunboats and stores for Naples lay offshore. Captain Hall, in command of the Sicilian gunboats at Messina, embarked four companies of the 75th Foot from the British garrison and by dawn on the 14th landed his mixed Anglo-Sicilian force (10). The soldiers carried the heights, but the gunboat fire was disappointing and the troops and seamen had to carry the batteries with cold steel. Several of the enemy craft were captured, the majority of the rest being burnt.

10

11

By November 1813, the coastal trade along the Italian and French coasts was under constant threat and the Mediterranean had become a British lake. In January 1814 King Joachim Murat of Naples, signed a secret treaty with the British, effectively ending the war in the southern half of the Italian peninsula, but in the north attacks on coastal shipping continued. In April 1814, for example, Brisbane in the *Pembroke*, 74, assisted by the frigates *Aigle* and *Alcmene* chased a twenty-ship convoy into Port Maurice in the Gulf of Genoa; four were cut out and others destroyed (11). Concluding operations in this area, in March and April a squadron under Captain Rowley in *America* took La Spezia and Genoa. Here the 74-gun *Brilliant* was found on the stocks ready for launching and was added to the Royal Navy as *Genoa*, a second was found half-built, and four corvettes, *Coureur, Renard, Endymion* and *Sphinx*, were also captured.

Before the year was out Napoleon had abdicated, but the cunning Talleyrand had preserved France intact, and with her, her fleets still safe in their great ports of refuge. Ironically it was left for the Royal Navy to attend the deposed Emperor.

8. 'The Imperieuse & Cephalus engaging an enemy's squadron in sight of the town of Naples. Augst 17th 1812. From a drawing by Mr Hood', coloured aquatint engraved by Thomas Sutherland after an original by Midshipman Hood and Thomas Whitcombe, no date. *NMM ref PAD5819*

9. 'Capture of Ponza February 26th 1813 by the Thames & Furieuse frigates Commanded by Captains Charles Napier and Mounsey, and a Body of Troops under Leunt Col Pine Coffin', watercolour by Joseph Cartwright, 1814. *NMM ref PAH3988*

10. 'View of Murat's Camp & Flotilla in Calabria with a division of British Gun Boats standing across to Attack', anonymous coloured aquatint published by John Harding, 1815. *NMM ref PAH6291*

11. 'The Squadron under the command of Sir J Brisbane attacking Fort Maurigio', coloured aquatint engravedby Thomas Sutherland after an original by Sir J Brisbane and Thomas Whitcombe, no date. *NMM ref PAD5848*

1

The foundations of seapower: the maritime infrastructure

B Y 1806, although the port of London still presented a picture of congestion and confusion, 'often so
crowded between the Tower and Limehouse that
a Wherry sometimes is scarce able to pass with Safety
between the Tiers, much less a vessel', new excavations
had greatly increased the capacity of wet docks. These
now existed at Blackwall and Rotherhithe (1), the West
India Docks could accommodate 600 vessels and in 1805
the 'London' docks at Wapping were also opened for the
unloading of vessels carrying spirits and tobacco.
Alongside this new complex stood a warehouse which
covered no less than five acres. The East India Company
had long had its own bonded warehouses in the City
(whence the cargoes of the East Indiamen were taken in
armoured carts with an armed guard from the

2

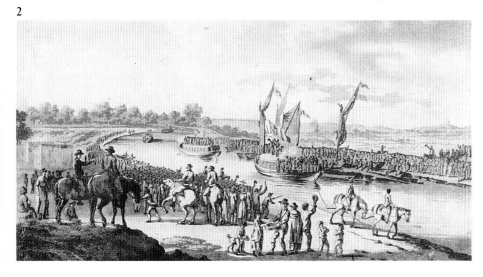

Brunswick Dock at Blackwall), and had enjoyed the
additional privilege of not paying import duty until the
imported goods were actually sold. This was now
extended to all dutiable goods landed into bond, improving the flow of money and acting as an added induce-
ment to owners not to accept percentage losses. The East
India Company also improved its facilities, retaining its
City warehouses, but the Brunswick Dock was circum-
vallated and deepened so that the largest class of East
Indiamen of some 1000 tons could berth within a tideless
dock and no longer had to ride in the stream of the river.
This development was completed in 1806 and a further
extension of the system, used for imports of timber and
grain, was completed a year later on the opposite bank of
the Thames with the opening of the Surrey Commercial
Docks.

These measures went some way to reduce the formidable amount of theft that had hitherto taken place
from shipping in the open tiers of the river. The increase
of trade, however, did little to reduce congestion, but
contrary to experience in later wars, this did not have an
effect on the efficiency of the convoy system, for commodities were rarely required immediately on arrival.
The consumer of the day was less voracious in his
appetites and delay was an accepted part of life. In fact
the timing of convoys was well-regulated and their size
often huge.

Although London was the premier port of the kingdom, Liverpool had long had wet docks and, after suffering a disastrous fire in 1802 when £300,000 worth of sugar,

coffee, cotton, spices, hemp and grain in the Goeree warehouse was destroyed, enlarged and improved warehouses were built on the banks of the Mersey. One-fifth of the 600-odd ships owned in Liverpool were 'Guineamen' employed in the slave trade which enriched the capitalists of Manchester and Birmingham as well as those of Liverpool itself. The abolition of the trade in May 1807 compelled many slavers to fit out as privateers, a tradition of which had long existed in Liverpool. Liverpool's trade was chiefly with North America, Norway and the Baltic, with whaling and the fisheries providing additional scope for local investment. Extensive shipbuilding was carried out on the banks of the Mersey along with allied industries such as ropemaking, while large quantities of tar, hemp, iron, turpentine and timber were maintained in store. Although affected by the war with America which broke out in 1812, at the termination of hostilities with the United States two years later the revival was quick. By this time trade with India and China had begun, following the abolition of the East India Company's monopoly. The first Liverpool ship to sail for the Far East, in 1814, was the *Kingsmill* of 516 tons, owned by John Gladstone, father of the statesman. For its defence, Liverpool raised its own militia, armed with artillery and which, at the height of the invasion scare in 1804, numbered 4000 men, for merchant seamen, particularly those from a port noted for its privateers, were conversant with the principles of gunnery and handling small-arms.

Across the country these great ports were linked by the canal system (2), which reached its apogee during this period, with the expanding centres of manufacturing such as Manchester, Sheffield and Birmingham. New roads were also being built, facilitating the mails and linking smaller ports, while engineering works threw up innumerable breakwaters, improving small, traditional fishing and coastal ports all around the shores of England, Ireland, Wales and Scotland.

Merchant shipbuilding was carried out in a myriad of locations wherever tidal waters and timber supplies were available either from local sources or, more common by this time, abroad. Yards such as Bayley's on the River Orwell at Ipswich even built East Indiamen occasionally (3). Private yards built to order, on speculation or on Government contract. Small yards built fishing craft and coasters, revenue cruisers and smuggling craft. Alongside building went repair and refitting, with thousands of men employed in the ancillary trades. Numbers of craftsmen, from sailmakers to shipwrights increased, that of the latter doubling in Liverpool alone. Underwater work was carried out either by careening or in a graving dock (4). Whilst coppering was now widespread as a means of saving the underwater hull from the ship-

3

worm, methods of construction underwent no great change, though the shortage of oak and compass timber were a cause of anxiety, in particular to naval constructors. However, some innovations were creeping in. East Indiamen were increasingly characterised by their gradual adoption of the flush deck, their early use of iron knees and their abandonment of tumblehome. Cargo capacity and strength were thus improved, the decks were kept drier and a better spread was given to the standing rigging. However, designers shackled by the archaic tonnage rules, failed to appreciate the superior stability conferred by beam and occasionally built deep and crank ships. It was not until after the war that, faced with increased competition from superior American-built vessels, revision of the rules released ship design from their constraints.

3. 'A Portrait of the East Indiaman, built at Mr Bayley's Ship-Yard, Ipswich. Launched 17th August, 1817', lithograph engraved by Jesse W Ward, 1884.
NMM ref PAD6398

4. '*Sandown* in the floating dock', watercolour illustration from the title page of the manuscript log of the slaver *Sandown*, 1793.
NMM ref LOG/M/21

4

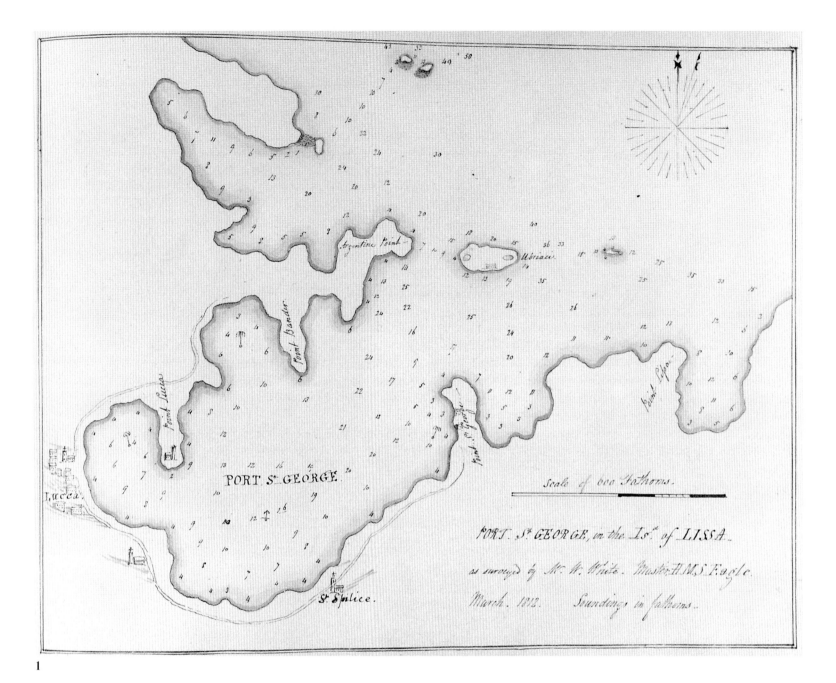

1

'Remember Nelson' – Hoste at Lissa

THE British frigate squadron harassing the north-ern Adriatic in the summer of 1810, which used an anchorage on the Dalmatian island of Lissa named Port St George as a base (1), was commanded by Captain Hoste of the *Amphion*, 32, and included the *Active*, 38, and *Cerberus*, 32. That autumn he learned that a French squadron had arrived to reinforce the Venetians and seize command of the Adriatic from the British. This was by no means impossible, given the geography of the region and would secure trade on the Italian, Dalmatian and Illyrian coasts from the disruption of British cruis-ers. On 29 September, the Franco-Venetian squadron joined forces at Chioggia near Venice under Com-modore Dubourdieu in *Favourite*, 44.

In the autumn there was some skirmishing between the squadrons, including a daring raid by Dubourdieu on Port St George, which had taken possession of prizes anchored in the bay and driven into the hills the shore party left in charge of the signal station. Dubourdieu immediately retired to Ancona on Hoste's return and lay there until, on 11 March 1811, he had received reinforce-ments and had embarked some 500 soldiers. His squadron now consisted of the French frigates *Favourite*, *Flore*, and *Danae*, the Venetian frigates *Bellona*, *Carolina* and

Corona, and the lesser vessels *Principessa Augusta,* 18, *Principessa di Bologna,* 10, *Lodola,* 2, and *Eugenio,* 6; with these he intended to take Lissa.

Hoste's three frigates, with *Volage,* 22, fell in with Dubourdieu in the small hours of 13 March, off the north point of Lissa. There was a strong breeze from the north-northwest and Hoste threw out the night signal to chase which required the British to work to windward and intercept, but at daylight Dubourdieu bore down from the north in two divisions. *Favourite, Flore, Bellona* and *Principessa Augusta* formed the starboard or weather division, with *Danae, Corona, Carolina* and the others in the lee or port division. Hoste stood across the line of the enemy on the starboard tack with *Active, Volage* and *Cerberus* in *Amphion*'s wake, with the signal 'Remember Nelson' aloft (2, top).

It was Dubourdieu's intention to break the enemy line in two places, but the close formation of the British and the ferocity of their gunfire foiled this. Dubourdieu fell as the action began in mid-morning, *Favourite*'s decks being swept by hundreds of musket balls from a howitzer aboard *Amphion.* About forty minutes later, being close inshore, Hoste's squadron wore round onto an easterly heading and although *Cerberus*'s rudder was fouled by a shot, *Volage* turned inside her to take the lead on the port tack. Meanwhile *Favourite* ran aground (2, bottom) and out of action, to leave Captain Péridier's *Flore* leading the allied weather division. As Hoste stood away to clear the island, *Flore* ran across *Amphion*'s stern and hauled her yards onto the port tack, taking station on *Amphion*'s starboard and lee quarter. Following Péridier, Captain Duodo of *Bellona,* came up on Hoste's opposite quarter.

Meanwhile, leading the allied lee column, *Danae,* wore onto the port tack with the *Corona* and *Carolina* in her wake, to engage *Volage.* The sloop was close enough to damage the enemy with her 32-pound carronades, but Duodo hauled out of range, whereupon Hornby of *Volage* increased his charges until his carronades broke their breechings and split their slides, reducing *Volage*'s armament to her 6-pounder bow chasers. *Corona* meanwhile, had engaged the short-handed *Cerberus,* which endured a punishing fire from the Venetian frigate, a sharp contrast to her consort *Carolina,* which avoided action.

Having dodged *Active* in favour of attacking the weaker *Volage, Danae* was now caught by her as Captain Gordon pressed up to the assistance of those ahead. *Active*'s intervention saved the *Cerberus* and *Volage,* whose opponents now made sail to the eastward.

Captain Hoste, engaged with both *Flore* and *Bellona,* now boldly crossed close ahead of the *Flore* to pour shot

1. Map of Port St George in the Island of Lissa as surveyed by Mr W White, Master HMS Eagle, March 1812', watercolour by Lt William Innes Pocock, no date. *NMM ref PAF0043*

2. 'Different modes of painting line of battle ships. Two separate drawings of line of battle ships annotated with ships' names, one drawing showing gunfire', grey pen and wash by Lt William Innes Pocock, no date. Despite the caption, this shows two stages of the Battle of Lissa, as confirmed by the ship names under the drawing. Pocock was an eyewitness to the action. *NMM ref PAF0050*

3. 'To the Officers . . . of His Majesty's Ship's Amphion, Cerberus, Volage and Active, their situation and the Enemys Squadron at the time of the Blowing up of the French Commodore off the Island of Lissa in the Adriatic on the 13th March 1811', coloured aquatint engraved by H Merke after an original by Webster, no date. *NMM ref PAH8094*

4. 'The Islands of Lessina & Brazza — from Hostes Island. Entrance of Port St George, Lissa', watercolour by Lt William Innes Pocock, no date. *NMM ref PAF0041*

2

3

into her lee bow, until she struck her colours. But Duodo crossed astern of *Flore* and raked *Amphion,* whereupon Hoste coolly wore *Amphion* to approach *Bellona* on the opposite tack. *Amphion*'s broadsides caused *Bellona*'s Venetian colours to be struck at noon and a few shot at *Principessa Augusta* caused her to sheer away. Lowering a boat to take possession of his prizes, Hoste now hoisted the signal for a general chase, wore round again and stood after his other three vessels, only to see the *Flore* making sail. *Cerberus* and *Volage* were not able to pursue, so *Amphion* and *Active* went after the enemy, *Danae* having made sail to cover the escape of *Flore*. *Active* was now in pursuit of *Corona* and eventually engaged her from her lee beam, compelling *Corona* to strike after about three-quarters of an hour.

Carolina and *Danae* then joined the *Flore* and the smaller men-of-war seeking the shelter of the guns of Lessina, an island to the eastward. Hoste was stung by the escape of the *Flore*, whose officers took advantage of the fact that *Amphion* was unable to launch a boat at the time of their striking. Damage and casualties were heavy on both sides; the British suffered 45 killed and 145 wounded, with Hoste among the latter. In *Bellona* Duodo was among the 70-odd casualties and died of his wounds. Dubourdieu had been killed at the outset by *Amphion*'s howitzer fire and his flag captain, La Marre Le Meillerie was dead among the 150 casualties, while Péridier of *Flore* was badly wounded. *Favourite*'s crew set the grounded frigate on fire (3) before scrambling ashore to surrender to the two British midshipmen left on Lissa in charge of the signal station and the prizes (4).

Whilst the action was in progress, the Venetian schooner *Lodola* stood into St George's Bay and summoned the Sicilian privateer *Vincitoire*, which promptly surrendered. The midshipmen then put off in boats and drove off the *Lodola* to retake *Vincitoire. Danae* and *Flore* hid in Ragusa where the French sought to replenish them, but the brig corvette sent from Venice was spotted off the Istrian coast by Brisbane and Maxwell in *Belle Poule* and *Alceste*. Driven into Parenzo, the frigates coolly took the island of San Nicolo, placed three guns and two howitzers on the eminence, bombarded the port and sank the brig.

4

The foundations of seapower: the technological edge

THE Royal Navy has long been regarded as technologically conservative, and historians often represent prudent caution in the approach to unproved innovation as a hidebound lack of vision. The traditionally smaller and more economic warships of Britain are similarly described as inferior designs, yet they consistently outsailed and outfought their opponents. Much of the Royal Navy's superiority at sea can be put down to other factors – a bigger pool of seamen, more sea-time, better training, sounder finance, etc – but the service also enjoyed a technological edge in a number of minor but significant areas. Within parts of the administration there was also an openness to innovation and experiment that has largely slipped the notice of history. Britain, after all, was the first nation to go through the industrial revolution, and many of its benefits accrued to the Navy.

Ironfounding improvements gave the Navy what were probably the best cannon in the world. The guns introduced by Thomas Blomefield from the 1790s were not only a good design but underwent the most rigorous proofing before being allowed into service. This meant that they could cope with the increased power of the new gunpowder manufactured from cylinder charcoal that was widely issued after 1801. The British had also invented the carronade (1), a light but potent short-range weapon that gave the Navy's warships a high fire-power-to-tonnage ratio. The French response, a brass *obusier*, was a poor weapon by comparison and was eventually replaced by a copy of the British iron weapon. Experiments with guns – especially lighter long guns – were frequent, and novel mountings were also tested, although few would meet the necessarily robust standards for use in action.

British warships were traditionally strongly built, and as suitable timber became scarcer the Dockyards increasingly turned to the new iron technology to retain the rigidity of hulls while using lighter scantlings and fewer pieces of expensive naturally-grown 'compass' timber. Roberts' iron plate knees (2), developed by one of the Master Shipwrights, were among the most common systems, and were successfully used during the last decade of the war. Towards the end of the conflict, another highly important product of the iron industry was introduced in the form of water tanks (3). These had a number of subtle but important ramifications. Because so little space was lost compared with stowage in casks,

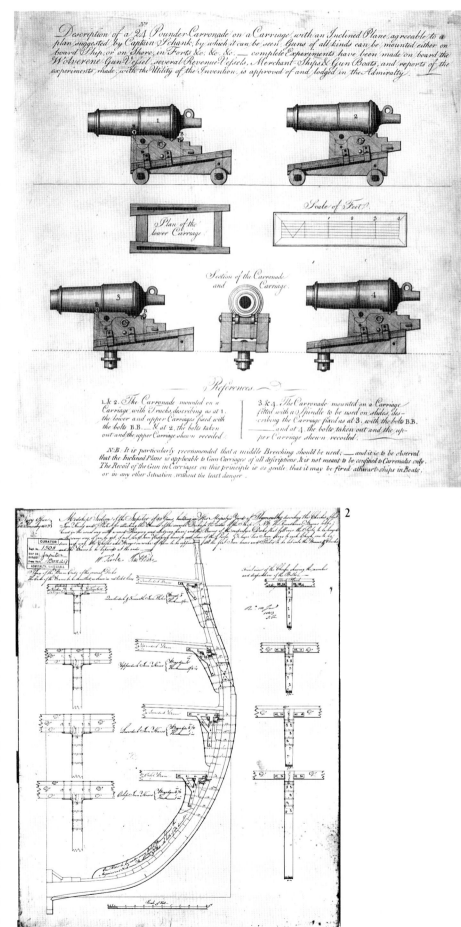

1

2

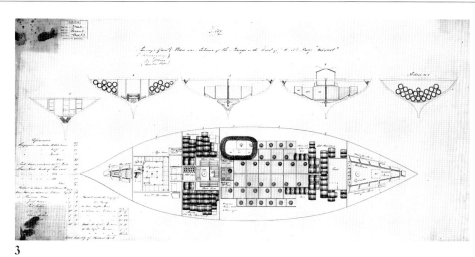

3

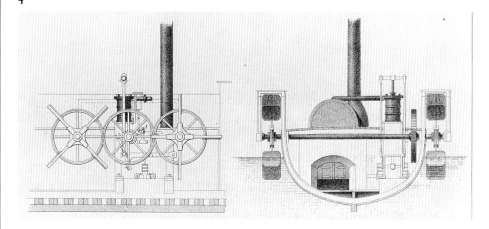

4

ships could either carry more or could sail at a lighter draught, making them faster; but with the weight lower in the hull, it also improved stability for a given lading. Furthermore, no shingle (a notorious source of pollution) was needed to bed down the casks, removing a potential source of disease. And the backbreaking work of watering ship was made far easier with the aid of pumps and hoses – the most common occupational disorder was rupture (29,712 trusses were issued in the period 1808-1815), often caused by hoisting casks, and thus at least one source of potential disability was removed. Another health improvement making a tentative appearance at the end of the war was canned meat. Although the solder was to cause a degree of lead poisoning (a problem which also arose with the earlier lead-lined water tanks), it proved the lesser of two evils when compared to the older method of casking in brine.

Besides iron, the other great engine of the industrial revolution was steam. The Admiralty's attitude to steam propulsion was not as dismissive as is often thought. By 1812 the *Comet* (4) was plying the Clyde and it was clear that steam had its uses, but fifteen years earlier the Admiralty had sunk some money into the Earl of Stanhope's attempt to produce a steam warship in the *Kent Ambinavigator* of 1793; ultimately, this was compromised by lack of a practical method of propulsion, its

'ducks' feet' being far less efficient than a paddle wheel. In most cases Their Lordships were content to let private speculators bear the burden of research. Richard Trevithick's steam fireship of 1805, intended for attacks on Boulogne, suffered from a boiler explosion, and the American entrepreneur Robert Fulton approached both Paris and London with various designs, before his wild and unsubstantiated claims and ambitious notions of reward quickly stifled official interest. Nevertheless, the British gave his towed 'torpedoes' extended and expensive trials in action off Boulogne in 1804-5, but with so little result that neither his ideas for submarines or steamers were followed up.

Steam as a power source for plant was another matter, and in the dockyards it became common. In 1795 the Admiralty had employed Samuel Bentham, who had served a shipwright's apprenticeship and afterwards reached the rank of general in the Russian army, with the new post of Inspector General of Naval Works. His wide-ranging brief included making technical improvements in both ships and the yards. By 1803 he had introduced steam powered bucket dredgers to the Royal Dockyards at Portsmouth and Woolwich and interested himself in matters as diverse as improvements of water supplies at Plymouth which, by 1809, not only supplied water to ships and workshops, but formed a fire-main. He completely reorganised Portsmouth dockyard, greatly improving the enclosed wet-dock and graving dock accommodation. Bentham designed the caissons which closed these off from the tidal harbour, using steam pumps for the draining the latter. Steam also powered a woodmill in which timber could be planed, rebated and to which timber could be hauled. By the period under consideration, this included Marc Brunel's blockmaking machinery (5) which mass-produced the wooden blocks essential for the rigging of sailing ships. Bentham also master-minded a steam traction engine which hauled loads about the dockyard and a rolling-mill in which old copper sheathing removed from ships in dock could be recycled. Steam was used in ropemaking, though not as extensively as it might have been, for Bentham's ideas often ran into opposition from the Navy Board whose considerations about expense and delay while improvements were implemented, often countered Bentham's enthusiasms.

By and large, Bentham's in-house production methods were designed to reduce contractors' profits and the associated embezzlement, ensure quality and quantity at a time of increasing demand. He was content to leave the detail to men like Brunel and Henry Maudsley, so that the blockmaking machine, for instance, was producing 150,000 blocks annually by 1808 and Maudsley's machine tools were in common use. During the last years of the

Napoleonic War, although Bentham fell from favour, the developments at Portsmouth were extended to the other Royal Dockyards at Sheerness, Woolwich, Deptford, Chatham and Plymouth.

Bentham also influenced ship design and construction. He was responsible for two highly original 'sloops', *Dart* and *Arrow*, and some schooners, but although they had some advantages, neither the hull form nor innovations like solid bulkheads were really appropriate for larger vessels (see *Nelson against Napoleon*, pages 102-4, in this series). Bentham's designs also featured sliding keels, another naval initiative of the 1790s and the brainchild of Captain Schank. These were adopted extensively for the gunboat programme, but longer experience proved that the casings could never be kept watertight and the large wooden centreboards were always jamming, so they were removed. This is often seen as a retrograde step, but in truth it was typical of the Navy Board's pragmatic attitude to innovation: if it had worked, it would have been retained.

Being a permanent bureaucracy, and keeper of the Navy's purse, the Navy Board tended to be more conservative than the politically appointed Admiralty, and most of the 'outside' influences in ship design owe their adoption to the patronage of the senior body. In terms of the amount of money spent, it might even be argued that the Admiralty was too open to new ideas. To give one example, an experimental vessel was built in 1802 to the design of Richard Gower, a former East India officer, who produced a slender-hulled, vee-sectioned vessel. Intended to be fast, sail close to the wind and require only a small complement, the four-masted *Transit* presaged the barquentine of later in the century (6). *Transit* was tried against the reputedly fast sloop *Osprey*, and the

Admiralty were persuaded to build a modified copy as a dispatch vessel in 1808. Although Gower later claimed that official interference spoiled his concept, trials proved that the naval *Transit* was indeed fast and weatherly, but like all extreme hull forms there were also drawbacks: she was very unhandy and a poor seaboat, and had to be shortened a year later.

The cumulative value of such improvements, of small cost savings and greater efficiency, of better quality provisions and of safer ships, is difficult to quantify but must have had an impact both on budgets and those unquantifiable abstract values, such as morale and confidence.

Second size Shaping machine. **5**

1. A 24pdr carronade on an experimental Schank's mounting, c1797. The 'inclined plane' was designed to dampen the recoil, a constant theme in carriage inventions of the period.
NMM neg P3837

2. Structural section of *Jupiter*, 1813 showing chocks and Roberts' iron plate knees.
NMM neg DR1508

3. Hold section showing iron water tanks in *Recruit*. This is a late example from 1847, but the layout is similar and much clearer than that of the early plans.
NMM neg DR3743

4. 'Engine and paddle wheels of Bell's *Comet* 1812', lithograph engraved by C F Cheffins after an original by H B Barlow, 1 July 1848.
NMM ref PAD6639

5. 'Large shaping machine', a pen drawing from Marc Brunel's own notebook, showing one of his blockmaking machines. *NMM ref SPB/11.*
NMM neg D9231

6. 'A representation of the Transit in two points of view (a vessel constructed by R H Gower Esqr)', aquatint and etching by J Jeakes after an original by Thomas Whitcombe, 10 November 1802.
NMM ref PAH8455

6

Adriatic and Ionian coasts, 1811-1814

AFTER the Battle of Lissa in March 1811, the French continued to dispute command of the Adriatic but their most important problem was supplying Corfu. The French frigate *Uranie*, 40, attempted to escort the *Corcyre* (a frigate reduced *en flûte*) to the island in November 1811. They were intercepted by *Eagle*, 74, which took the latter but so disabled her that in standing by, *Uranie* escaped. *Active*, 38, meanwhile, had destroyed a grain convoy bound for Ragusa (Dubrovnik) on 27 July and by autumn was at Lissa with *Alceste*, 38, *Unité*, 36, and

Acorn, 20. It was known that the French had not abandoned hope of dislodging the British from Port St George, while in addition to *Uranie*, several other enemy men-of-war had escaped Hoste's action in March. A report of approaching ships, therefore, compelled Captain Maxwell of the *Alceste* to take defensive measures. Disembarking all the marines and a party of seamen as garrison, and leaving Bligh in *Acorn* to command the anchorage, Maxwell left Lissa in *Alceste* with *Active* and *Unité*, and stood to sea. On the following morning, 29 November 1811, Maxwell came in sight of a French frigate squadron on passage from Corfu to Trieste, consisting of *Pauline* and *Pomone*, of 40 guns, and the 26-gun *Persanne*. Soon after sighting the British, Commodore Montfort bore away to the northwest before a strong east-southeasterly wind with the British in hot pursuit. *Persanne* fell behind, so Maxwell left her to *Unité*, pressing on after the heavier frigates.

Alceste was first in action in the early afternoon, had her main topmast shot away by *Pomone*, and dropped astern. *Active* soon afterwards brought *Pomone* to close action from leeward, whereupon *Pauline* tacked back to assist until the sloop *Kingfisher* made her appearance, whereupon Montfort made sail to the westwards and the dismasted *Pomone* was left to strike to *Active* and *Alceste*. However, neither frigate was in a condition to pursue and *Pauline* escaped (1). *Unité*, meanwhile, had engaged *Persanne* and after a four hour action, received her surrender. Light though British losses were, they were disproportionate in view of the under-manned condition of the frigates.

British intelligence in the Adriatic was excellent and news of the completion of the 74-gun *Rivoli* at Venice resulted in *Victorious*, 74, and the sloop *Weazel* arriving in the gulf by the middle of February 1812. *Rivoli* emerged under the cover of fog on the 21st, bound across the gulf for Pola (2) in company with the 18-gun brig corvettes *Jéna* and *Mercure, Mamelouck,* 10 and a pair of gunboats. As the fog cleared Talbot of *Victorious* began to chase and very early on the morning of the 22nd, he ordered *Weazel* to cut off the *Mercure* which had dropped astern of the French line. *Rivoli* had shortened sail a little and *Jéna* also dropped back, though she did not long engage *Weazel,* which brought *Mercure* to close action as *Victorious* succeeded in coming up with *Rivoli,* opening a running fight at about 0400. Talbot took a splinter in the face, adding to the confusion of darkness, fog and smoke, so much of the action was commanded by Lieutenant Peake. After about forty minutes *Mercure* blew up with the loss of all but three of her crew and *Weazel* rejoined *Victorious* (3). By this time *Rivoli* had become almost unmanoeuvrable and Commander Andrew placed *Weazel* athwart her hawse and raked. At about 0900 *Rivoli* struck, having lost about half the 860 men on board in killed and wounded. Taken to Lissa, the badly damaged *Rivoli* (4) was afterwards commissioned into the Royal Navy.

In August 1812, Captain Hoste, now commanding *Bacchante*, 38, and anchored off Rovigno, sent his boats to raid the Canale de Leme. The boats took nine merchantmen, two gunboats and a small xebec, *Tisiphone.* Next month Hoste was at the other end of the Adriatic and lay becalmed when in pursuit of eighteen escorted coasters. Sending his boats after them, the enemy ran their craft aground and fled inland. Also on the Apulian coast by now and under Commander Black, *Weazel* was raiding the coast in December and joined Hoste in January 1813.

Black was cruising in *Weazel* to the north of Lissa early on 22 April 1813 when he intercepted a convoy making for Spalato (Split). This divided, the majority covered by ten gunboats making for a defensible anchorage in Bassoglina Bay. *Weazel* approached and was received by a furious fire from the heavy guns in the gunboats and the brig sloop sustained considerable damage as Black anchored her with a spring on her cable, opening a terrific fire (5). This forced the coasters to work further up the bay where three field pieces and a detachment of infantry gave some covering fire. By mid-morning three gunboats had struck, two were aground and one was sunk, but four more arrived from the detached portion of the convoy and caught *Weazel* on her offshore side. Black was equal to the task and before long the newcomers had run inshore of him and worked round behind a spit of land which hid their hulls but allowed their guns to continue to play on the brig. With one

3

short break, gunfire continued until evening, by which time *Weazel* was reduced to a wreck, her pumps were disabled and she was filling with water. After dark, Black sent in his boats which destroyed the surrendered gunboats and some of the coasters (6). His men brought off some anchors which they now laid out, to warp the brig clear of the bay in which an onshore wind now threatened to trap her.

She was not clear by dawn when the gunboats renewed their assault with little response from *Weazel*

4

5

since most of her people were engaged in the business of warping, a fatiguing process that went on all that day and the following night. At noon on the 24th a battery opened fire from a headland and the gunboats pressed closer, to be deterred by a broadside. *Weazel* finally got clear and made sail with a loss of only 5 killed and 25 wounded, including Black.

Black was posted in late July, so was still in the repaired *Weazel* on the night of 4/5 August 1813, taking command of his own and the boats of the 74-gun *Milford* in a landing on the Dalmatian island of Rogoznica. At dawn the French garrison awoke to British cheers on the heights, soon after which they were driven from their works and their guns were disabled. Then, on the 24th, Black captured two gunboats, *Auguste* and *Tonnante*, off Cape Otranto.

By January 1813, the naval forces in the Adriatic were under the command of Rear-Admiral Fremantle who had begun mopping up the isolated garrisons of the Dalmatian islands, which were no longer possessions of Marshals Marmont or Soult but were victims of British seapower. He dispatched *Apollo*, accompanied by a privateer, *Esperanza*, with troops to take the islands of Lagosta and Curzola which lay to the southeast of Lissa. British cruisers were now familiar with the coast and in May Hoste took *Bacchante* after a convoy into the Carlopago Channel. Finding it empty, he destroyed newly erected defensive works on the island. From Brindisi to Trieste, the Adriatic lay under British domination. The cruisers were everywhere, *Apollo* and *Cerberus* dominating the Strait of Otranto in May, while the 74-gun *Eagle* attacked

the Croatian island of Cherso, landing her men after a cannonade, carrying the works at Farasina and destroying them. Joined by *Elizabeth*, the two Third Rates took the Istrian port of Umago on 8 June, while four days later on the Abruzzi coast, off Giulianova, *Bacchante*'s boats savaged a well armed convoy. *Elizabeth* continued her work on the Istrian coast, took Dignano and its garrison on 20 June, while the sloops *Saracen* and *Weazel* captured the Dalmatian islands of Giupppana and Mezzo in June and July.

On 3 June, Fremantle in *Milford*, with *Elizabeth, Eagle* (all 74s), *Bacchante*, 38, and *Haughty*, 12, appeared before Fiume, sending in the sloop and boats to attack, while the heavier ships bombarded the defences. A shift in the wind compelled a change of plan and the order was given to storm the town from all ships. The seamen and marines swarmed ashore. With trifling losses of one killed and six wounded the garrison were driven out, the guns disabled and ninety vessels taken, of which thirteen were sent with useful stores to Lissa, and the rest destroyed. Now the approach of the British meant the enemy either scuttled or abandoned their merchantmen. The former happened at Maltempo in July, the latter at Rovigno when only *Bacchante* and *Eagle* appeared offshore.

French hegemony, never very strong on the eastern coast of the Adriatic was fragmenting and Hoste, learning from the British garrison at Curzola of the instability south of Ragusa, arrived off Castelnuovo in 11 October 1813 in *Bacchante*, with the sloop *Saracen*. Boats were sent on south to Cattaro under Harper of *Saracen*, who roused the population, seized some gunboats and forced the

6

surrender of the French garrison on San Giorgio island. Operations came to fruition that month further north, with Fremantle arriving off Trieste as the Austrians invested it. Bombardment from the flagship *Milford*, followed by a landing of guns, seamen and marines to invest the principal fortress, contributed to its surrender on 29 October.

One of the most active in support of Austrain forces was the Hon George Cadogan of the frigate *Havannah*, which in the first six months of 1813 took, burned or destroyed 7 gunboats, 43 armed vessels and transports, and 8 merchantmen. Towards the end of the year, operating with the sloop *Weazel*, he contributed two 32-pounder carronades, eight 18-pounder and seven 12-pounder guns to the siege of Zara (Zadar), which capitulated on 6 December following thirteen days' bombardment (7).

In January 1814 Hoste and Harper reappeared off Cattaro and intermittently bombarded the place into submission ten days later. Ragusa fell to *Bacchante* and *Saracen*, with British and Austrian troops embarked, on the 28th, and Richard Church arrived off Paxo aboard *Apollo* and went ashore with his infantry. By 16 February Fremantle was able to inform Pellew, the C-in-C, that in co-operation with the Austrians, every French post had been reduced. Thus French power was utterly broken in the Adriatic; a steady augmentation of the British naval force having eroded it as surely as water will a stone.

7

1

The final frigate actions

TO the very end of the war, the French sent out their frigates in pairs on cruises against British trade. These ships benefited from being commanded by able officers and manned by prime seamen. They were also heavily armed, newly built, fitted and coppered. In short, despite all the constraints of the British blockade, French frigates were first-class cruisers in first-class condition. Their weakness lay in their lack of sea-time and their over-reliance on keeping in touch with the shore which engendered a lack of resolution. However, despite the overwhelming force of the Royal Navy, the final frigate actions were not always British victories.

Typical of these late sorties was that of *Aréthuse* and *Rubis*, both newly built and of 40 guns, which left Nantes on 25 November 1812, bound for Sierra Leone on the West African coast. They arrived off the Ilsas de los Idolos on 27 January 1813, surprising the British sloop *Daring*, whose commander burnt her, rather than allow her to be overwhelmed. The two French frigates then entered the river of Sierra Leone where both ran aground, *Rubis* fatally, being obliged to transfer her people into *Serra*, a Portuguese prize. *Aréthuse* was refloated and refitted her own rudder.

Daring's commander, Lieutenant Pascoe, carried word to Freetown where lay *Amelia*, 38, and the British frigate sailed in pursuit. Concerned about the state of his crew

2

who were weakened by sickness, Captain Irby avoided action until the evening of 7 February when he realised neither *Rubis* nor *Serra* were a threat, whereupon he closed *Aréthuse* to rake. The night was moonlit with a gentle breeze. Bouvet avoided Irby's first manoeuvre (1), but soon afterwards, having shot away *Amelia*'s main topsail braces, she collided with *Aréthuse*. A storm of musketry and hand grenades swept *Amelia*'s decks, but the parties mustering to board were deterred by the British marines and Bouvet, throwing all aback, made a stern-board clear of *Amelia*. Irby now tried to work across *Aréthuse*'s bow to rake, but crashed back alongside until the gun-muzzles of the ships almost touched. The guns' crews tore the sponges and rammers from each others' hands and slashed at each other with cutlasses in a vicious hand-to-hand encounter. Musketry from *Aréthuse* meanwhile decimated *Amelia*'s officers so that command devolved upon Mr De Mayne, the master.

It was now calm and the gun concussions slowly drove the two ships apart. Just before midnight they drifted out of range and the action ceased. Both ships, more-or-less equal in force, were badly shattered both alow and aloft, with heavy casualties. *Amelia*, already under orders for England, reached Spithead on 22 March. Bouvet, with *Rubis* wrecked, also went home, arriving at St Malo on 19 April, with a further fourteen prizes to his credit.

At the end of 1813 the new French frigates *Clorinde* and *Cérès* left Brest. Having parted company, *Cérès* was soon taken by *Niger* and *Tagus*, but *Clorinde* cruised successfully to the west of Ushant until 25 February 1814, when she was sighted from the new pine-built frigate *Eurotas*. The British frigate had been equipped with the experimental medium 24-pounders cast to Congreve's pattern in an attempt to fit her to meet the heavy American frigates operating in the Atlantic. Being lighter than the standard pattern, the Congreve guns were subject to violent recoil, though Captain Phillimore had demonstrated them to the squadron off Brest and expressed himself delighted with them.

Eurotas caught up with *Clorinde* late that afternoon and in a dying wind, raked her. But in luffing up alongside *Clorinde*'s port side, *Eurotas* had her mizzen mast shot down, though she in turn felled *Clorinde*'s fore topmast as the French frigate drew ahead and swung across *Eurotas*'s bow, intending to rake. Phillimore, however, passed under his opponent's stern and raked, whereupon the two vessels lay muzzle-to-muzzle causing mutual damage until *Clorinde* drew out of range. Phillimore was severely wounded and his ship was dismasted; *Clorinde* had lost her main and mizzen, but overnight the British raised a serviceable jury rig, while *Clorinde* failed to effect any repairs (2). Thus, upon the appearance of *Dryad*, 36,

3

and *Achates*, 18, at daylight, having neglected to escape, Captain Lagarde struck his colours.

The autumn of 1813 had also seen the sortie of two pairs of French frigates. Having seized several prizes, *Iphigénie* and *Alcméne* were captured in January 1814. The second pair, *Etoile* and *Sultane*, both of 40 guns, cruised in the Atlantic before making for the Cape Verde Islands and the comfort of an anchorage. Here they were found on 23 January by *Creole* and *Astraea*. Weighing, a fierce running fight ensued, culminating in the French beating off their pursuers and making for St Malo. Off Roscoff on 26 March in fog they almost ran down the sloop *Sparrow*, disabling her rigging. But the British 36-gun frigate *Hebrus* was close and engaged. Her gunfire attracted the 74-gun *Hannibal*, which made sail as the fog cleared. Shortly afterwards the wind changed, the French separated and *Hannibal* signalled *Hebrus* to pursue *Etoile* while she bore down and captured the jury-rigged *Sultane*.

By midnight the wind was dying in the Alderney race, and *Etoile* closed the coast at Jobourg, with *Hebrus* boldly working inshore of her as they doubled the Nez. Just after 0200 on the morning of 27th it was almost calm and both frigates were in shoal water. *Etoile* now slowly crossed ahead of *Hebrus* and her raking fire, aimed high, carried away the *Hebrus*'s head gear. At 0300 a light land breeze allowed Captain Palmer to edge athwart *Etoile* to rake her successively with such effect that she finally struck her colours (3).

1. 'Engagement between His Majesty's Ship Amelia . . . and L'Arethuse French Frigate . . . off the Isles of Loss, on the coast of Africa', coloured aquatint engraved by Thomas Sutherland after an original by John Christian Schetky and Thomas Whitcombe, published by J Jenkins, 1 April 1817.
NMM ref PAG7102

2. 'This View of His Majesty's Ship Eurotas under jury Masts, on the morning of the 26th Feby 1814 on the point of coming up with the Imperial French Frigate La Clorinde', coloured aquatint engraved by Robert Dodd after his own original, published by the artist, June 1814.
NMM ref PAG9083

3. 'The Hebrus and L'Etoile off Cape La Hogue, March 27th 1814', coloured aquatint engraved by Robert Havell after an original by Nicholas Pocock, published by Thomas Rickards, 19 October 1819.
NMM ref PAH8151

NAPOLEON DEPOSED

AT the beginning of 1814, with the vast allied armies of Russia, Prussia and Austria massing against him, Napoleon dismissed all compromises, insisting upon the retention of Antwerp as a condition of peace in an attempt to detach the continental allies from the British. The Tsar ended the discussions and despite Napoleon's brilliance at defeating the allies piecemeal during the campaign of France in the succeeding weeks, the allies' cumulative strength was overwhelming. Napoleon's last plea was to his father-in-law, Emperor Francis of Austria: 'since I can approach neither the English, whose policy centres on the destruction of my fleet, nor the Tsar, because he thinks only in terms of passion and revenge'. But with Chancellor Metternich behind him, the Kaiser recalled disparaging remarks made about his troops, left his daughter to the cynical seduction of Count Neipperg and abandoned his son-in-law. Britain further stiffened the alliance with a subsidy of five millions sterling; the Baltic was open again, there had been a good harvest and the year was to see exports soar.

More important, Wellington's army had crossed the Pyrenees and entered France. On 23 February, the Marquess decided to by-pass Soult at Bayonne by crossing the Adour at its estuary. Offshore was a squadron under Rear-Admiral Penrose, who lay off the river's ferocious bar in the sloop *Porcupine*. Several attempts were made to penetrate the surf and there was considerable loss of life before a few boats got over. Although 'the zeal and the science of the officers triumph[ed] over the difficulties of the navigation', their efforts had been largely futile. Wellington and his engineers had accomplished the crossing almost without naval help (1).

1

2

3

At the same time the outposts of the empire were falling. A revolt in the Netherlands had already thrown off French rule, and by 1814 the Kingdom of Italy was in its last days. Napoleon's viceroy, Eugène de Beauharnais, was unable to stem the Austrian advance, and on 9 March a British fleet conveying 10,000 troops arrived off Leghorn (2). Lord William Bentinck's proclamation exhorted Italians to assert their freedom, and the following month Eugène was forced to sign an armistice.

Defending Paris, Napoleon's exhausted troops faltered at Laon, 9-10 March, and at Arcis-sur-Aube ten days later. On the 25th, 17,000 men under Marshals Mortier and Marmont were smashed by 100,000 men at La Fère-Champenoise and the allies reached Montmartre. The end came when Marmont, Duke of Ragusa, capitulated and Paris was occupied on the 31st (3). The remaining marshals forced Napoleon to abdicate in favour of his son on 6 April, but this was unacceptable: the allies wanted the Bourbons restored.

Having avoided Bayonne, Wellington had detached Marshal Beresford to advance on Bordeaux, and Penrose entered the Gironde to co-operate in *Egmont*, 74, on 21 March. On 2

April *Porcupine* was ordered on to Pauillac and from here boats were sent higher in pursuit of a number of small men-of-war. These were attacked by seamen and marines, who hauled off a brig, six gunboats, one armed schooner, three *chasse-marées* and an imperial barge, four craft being burned. On the 6th *Centaur*, 74, arrived. It was Penrose's intention to take the French 74-gun *Régulus* and three brigs lying in the river, but the ships were burnt during the night. In the next few days, seamen and marines led by Captain Harris of *Belle Poule* destroyed the batteries lining the river.

At this time Wellington was pressing Marshal Soult at Toulouse. The allied army stormed the heights dominating the city, but Soult slipped away in the night. It no longer mattered, it was 11 April. At Fontainebleau Napoleon submitted to the allied terms in a preliminary treaty formalised on 13 April 1814. The definitive Peace of Paris was signed on 30 May.

By this time Louis XVIII and his suite had embarked at Dover aboard the Royal Yacht, *Royal Sovereign*. Escorted by Admiral, HRH The Duke of Clarence flying his flag in HMS *Impregnable*, 98, and accompanied by the British frigate *Jason*, the French frigate *Polonais*, two Russian frigates and two buoy-yachts of the Trinity House, he was landed at Calais on 24 April (see Frontispiece).

After a debate as to whether to incarcerate Napoleon at St Helena or to purchase an island in the Portuguese Azores, the late Emperor was assigned the miniature 'kingdom' of Elba, largest of the Tuscan islands. He was accordingly embarked aboard Captain Ussher's frigate *Undaunted* at Fréjus on 28 April 1814 (4) for passage to his new home, to be landed with due ceremony at Porto Ferrajo on 4 May. As a young man he had harangued The Directory: 'Either our Government must destroy the English monarchy, or must itself expect to be destroyed by the corruption and intrigue of those active islanders . . . Let us concentrate all our activity upon the navy, and destroy England. That done, Europe is at our feet.'

Fortunately, for the corrupt and intriguing islanders, and Europe itself, he had consistently failed to take his own advice.

1. 'View of Bayonne, Taken from the Sand Hills on the left of the Adour,when occupied by the British Forces on the 12 of March 1814', coloured aquatint engraved by Clark and Dubourg after an original by Lt George Brander Willis, published by Edward Orme, 24 June 1814. *NMM ref PAH9985*

2. 'A View of His Britannic Majesty's Squadron and 50 transports with Ten Thousand Troops, in the act of casting anchor in the Road of Leghorn the 9th March 1814', engraving and etching by Aliprandi after an original by D Scotti, published by J Wagner, no date. *NMM ref PAH8147*

3. 'The entry of the Allies into Paris by the Porte St Martin, March 31 1814', contemporary print. *Chatham Collection*

4. 'Embarkation of Napoleon Bonaparte from St Raphael for the Island of Elba 1814', aquatint engraved by J Baily after an original by Lt G S Smith, published by Joyce Gold, 29 June 1816. *NMM ref PAD5928*

4

Notes on Artists, Printmakers and their Techniques

These brief notes cover most of the artists and print-makers who appear in the volume, as well as the principal printing techniques. They are intended only to put the artists in context with the period and readers wanting further information on their art and lives should turn to the sources; in many cases there is little more to tell. This volume contains a number of sketches and paintings by the officers and men who served in the Royal Navy at the time, but details of their lives have been omitted if they did not pursue an artistic career, since little or nothing is known of their work.

Andrews, George Henry *(1816-1898)* English water-colourist of marine subjects who was trained as an engineer. He also did drawings for a number of journals such as the *Illustrated London News* and the *Graphic*.

Aquatint A variety of etching *(qv)* invented in France in the 1760s. It is a tone rather than a line process and is used principally to imitate the appearance of water-colour washes. The process involves the etching of a plate with acid through a porous ground of powdered resin. The acid bites small rings around each resin grain and gradations of tone are achieved by repetition of the biting process and the protection of areas of the plate with varnish.

Atkinson, John Augustus *(1775-1831)* English history painter and aquatint engraver who worked at the Court at St Petersburg before returning to London in 1801. He painted any number of Russian subjects, but is particularly remembered for his depiction of the battle of Waterloo to which he was an eye-witness.

Barker, Henry Ashton *(1774-1856)* British painter and engraver of panoramas and topographical scenes. His earliest dated work is his *Panoramic View of London* of 1792. In the early years of the nineteenth century he travelled widely through Europe visiting, amongst other countries, France, Italy and Turkey.

Bartelozzi, Francesco *(1727-1815)* Italian printmaker, draughtsman and painter of portraits, and decorative and historical subjects after his own designs as well as those of his contemporaries and old Masters. In 1776 he moved to London as engraver to the King, where he developed his distinctive style of stipple engraving. During the 1780s his output was dominated by an enormous range of portrait engravings after contemporary English portrait painters, and at one time his studio employed some fifty assistants.

Beechey, Sir William *(1753-1839)* English portrait painter who studied under Zoffany. He was made portrait painter to Queen Charlotte in 1793 and for the rest of his career produced a steady output of fashionable subjects. A contemporary portraitist, James Opie, said of his pictures that they 'were of that mediocre quality as to taste and fashion, that they seemed only fit for sea captains and merchants'.

Boydell, John *(1719-1804)* English engraver, publisher and print seller who was patron of most of the painters of his day whose works he engraved and supplied to every European market. This export market made him a considerable fortune and in 1790 he became Lord Mayor of London. The outbreak of war with France in 1793, however, destroyed his hopes of expanding his export market, and the last ten years of his life were fraught with financial worry.

Buttersworth, Thomas *(1768-1842)* English marine painter who served in the Royal Navy from 1795 until he was invalided out in 1800. His vivid watercolours of the battle of St Vincent and the blockade of Cadiz, painted while he was at sea, suggest first-hand experience. After leaving the Navy he devoted himself full-time to his painting and created a very considerable body of work.

Cardon, Antoine *(1772-1813)* Flemish engraver of portraits and decorative subjects after his own designs as well as military and sporting scenes after his contemporaries, such as *The Battle of Alexandria* after de Loutherbourg.

Canot, Pierre Charles *(1710-1777)* French line engraver of topographical views and marine subjects after his contemporaries. He moved to England in 1740 where he lived and worked for the rest of his life.

Cartwright, Joseph *(1789-1829)* English landscape and marine painter and member of the Society of British Artists who was also a naval paymaster. He was made marine painter to the Duke of Clarence and painted a number naval scenes particularly of actions in the Mediterranean including *The Battle of the Nile* and *The Euryalus Frigate Becalmed in the Channel of Corfu*.

Chambers, George *(1803-1840)* English marine painter, born in Whitby, whose early years were spent as crew onboard east coast merchantmen. An early desire to paint and draw led, in around 1820, to a move to London where he began to paint the ships and scenes of his boyhood. In time, from these, came naval commissions and it is for his naval compositions that he is now best remembered. Most of these were done in the 1830s and one of his most significant commissions was *Bombardment of Algiers*, painted for the Greenwich Hospital in 1836. He died young, of tuberculosis, thus ending a promising career.

Chavane, E English engraver active around the 1850s.

Chinnery, George *(1748-1847)* English portrait painter who exhibited regularly at the Royal Academy until 1796 when he moved to Dublin and continued a successful career. After the break-up of his marriage he sailed to India and though he continued as a portrait painter some of his best work can be seen in his more informal drawings and watercolours of local life. He moved on to Macao to escape his creditors in 1825 and there lived for the remainder of his life working both as a portraitist and landscape painter.

Clark, John *(fl late eighteenth and early nineteenth centuries)* English draughtsman and aquatint *(qv)* engraver of topographical views and marine subjects. Nothing at all is known of his life. Further confusion exists as engravings of plates of very similar style are signed both 'J' and 'T' Clark. Many of his engravings were done with Dubourg *(qv)* and Atkinson *(qv)*.

Cook, Henry R *(fl first half of the nineteenth century)* English engraver, mainly of portraits.

Craig, William Marshall *(fl late eighteenth and early nineteenth centuries)* English illustrator and watercolourist, miniaturist and engraver, amongst whose work were a number of military and naval scenes.

Cruikshank, Isaac *(1764-1811)* Scottish printmaker, draughtsman and caricaturist who moved to London around 1785. He had considerable success as a cartoonist working for, amongst others, Laurie & Whittle in Fleet Street. Father of the better known George Cruikshank, much of whose work was inspired by the Napoleonic Wars.

Daniell, William *(1769-1837)* English draughtsman, watercolourist and aquatint *(qv)* engraver of topographical, marine and architectural views. He was the nephew of Thomas Daniell with whom he travelled to India when he was sixteen. Apart from his *Oriental Scenery* he is probably best known for his plates for *A Voyage around Great Britain*.

Dodd, Robert *(1748-1815)* English marine and landscape painter and successful engraver and publisher, best known for his portrayals of the naval battles of the American Revolutionary and French wars. He is also known for his formal portraits of ships in which three views are included in a single image.

Drypoint Intaglio *(qv)* engraving *(qv)* technique in which the image is scratched into a copper plate with a steel needle which is held like a pen. Ridges – burr – are created around the lines which give drypoint its characteristic fuzzy effect. The burr is delicate and quickly wears away during the printing process so that print runs are short.

Dubourg, Matthew *(1775-1831)* English aquatint *(qv)* engraver of topographical views and military subjects after his contemporaries. He sometimes worked with John Clark *(qv)*.

Duncan, Edward *(1803-1882)* English landscape painter and engraver of marine and sporting subjects as well as topographical subjects after his contemporaries.

Durand-Brager, Jean-Baptiste-Henri *(1814-1879)* French marine painter and traveller. As well as official history paintings for the French Government of naval scenes, he also accepted commissions from the Tzar and the Austrian Emperor.

Elmes, William *(fl late eighteenth and early nineteenth centuries)* English draughtsman and engraver who made caricatures much in the manner of George Cruikshank, including two of Napoleon, published between 1811 and 1816.

Engraving The process of cutting an image into a block or metal plate which is used for printing by using a number of techniques such as aquatint *(qv)*, drypoint *(qv)*, etching *(qv)*, or mezzotint *(qv)*. An engraving is a print made from the engraved plate.

Etching An intaglio *(qv)* process by which the design is made by drawing into a wax ground applied over the metal plate. The plate is then submerged in acid which bites into it where it has been exposed through the wax. An etching is a print made from an etched plate.

Evans, William *(fl late eighteenth and early nineteenth centuries)* English draughtsman and engraver of portraits and some decorative subjects mainly after his contemporaries.

Faden, William *(1750-1836)* English cartographer and publisher, and the partner of Thomas Jeffereys whose business he ran in the Charing Cross Road after the latter's death in 1771. He is best known for his *North American Atlas*, published in 1777, *Battles of the American Revolution* and *Petit Neptune Français*, both of 1793.

Garneray, Ambroise-Louis *(1783-1857)* French marine painter whose early life was spent at sea in the French navy and ashore as a shipwright in Mauritius, before being taken prisoner by the British in 1806. Confined on a prison ship at Portsmouth he made an income painting portraits. Returning to France in 1814 he exhibited his first shipping scenes in 1815. He is probably best known for his work illustrating the ports of France which was published in *Vues des côtes de France dans l'océan et dans le Mediterranée* (1823).

Gauci, Paul *(fl mid nineteenth century)* English printmaker and lithographer who produced mainly topographical views after his contemporaries.

Gold, Joyce *(fl early nineteenth century)* English printer and publisher whose works included Rowe's *English Atlas* (1816). Also the publisher of the *Naval Chronicle*.

Greatbach, William *(born 1802)* English engraver of historical and more sentimental subjects such as *Alpine Mastiffs Reanimating a Traveller* after Landseer.

Gwyn, Edward *(fl late eighteenth century)* An unknown English draughtsman who produced at least one sketch book of ship portraits which is held by the National Maritime Museum.

Hamble, J R *(fl early nineteenth century)* English aquatint *(qv)* engraver of topographical views and naval subjects who often worked with John Clark *(qv)*.

Harraden, Richard *(1756-1838)* English engraver best known for his scenes of Paris, after Thomas Girtin.

Havell, Robert *(1769-1832)* English aquatint *(qv)* engraver of topographical views as well as transport and military subjects, after his contemporaries and his own designs. He was probably the uncle of Daniel Havell *(fl early nineteenth century)* and the father of Robert Havell (1793-1878), both also prominent engravers of topographical views and history subjects.

Heriot, George *(fl late eighteenth and early nineteenth centuries)* English marine painter of ships and seascapes.

Huggins, John William *(1781-1845)* English marine painter who spent his early years at sea with the East India Company until around 1814 when he established himself as a painter. He produced an enormous number of ship portraits, many of them engraved by his son-in-law, Edward Duncan, as well as a number of large-scale naval battles, in particular the battle of Trafalgar. In 1836 he was made marine painter to King William IV.

Hunt, Charles *(fl early to mid nineteenth century)* Eminent English aquatint *(qv)* engraver of topographical views and animal and transport subjects after his contemporaries and his own designs.

Intaglio printing The method of printing using metal plates which can be worked as aquatints *(qv)*, drypoints *(qv)*, engravings *(qv)*, etchings *(qv)*, or mezzotints *(qv)*. Once the lines have been made on the plate, by whatever method, printing is done by pressing damp paper hard enough against the plate so that the ink is lifted out of the incised lines. This explains why prints done by this method have slightly raised lines, a distinct characteristic of the process.

Jeakes, Joseph *(fl early nineteenth century)* English engraver of aquatints *(qv)*, notably of topographical scenes and naval engagements after his contemporaries, particularly Thomas Whitcombe *(qv)* and his own designs.

Joy, John Cantiloe *(1806-1866)* English marine painter and brother of William Joy *(qv)*.

Joy, William *(1803-1866)* English marine painter who worked mainly in collaboration with his brother John Cantiloe, and the two are often referred to as the 'brothers Joy'. As well as paintings of naval incidents they were commissioned by the Government in the 1830s to record and make drawings of fishing craft.

Laurie & Whittle *(fl late eighteenth and early nineteenth centuries)* English publishers and engravers who amalgamated with Imray, Norrie & Wilson. Robert Laurie developed a method for printing mezzotints (qv) in colour. Works included *American Atlas* (1794) and *East India Pilot* (1800).

Lithograph A print made by drawing a design on porous limestone with a greasy material. The stone is then wetted and ink applied to it which adheres only to the drawn surfaces. Paper is then pressed to the stone for the final print. Lithography was discovered only at the very end of the eighteenth century but quickly developed into a highly flexible medium.

Lönning, Terkel Eriksen *(1762-1823)* Danish marine watercolour painter who spent all his working life in Copenhagen and who specialised in naval subjects.

Luny, Thomas *(1759-1837)* One of the leading English marine painters of his generation. A pupil of Francis Holman, he served in the Royal Navy until around 1810 when he retired to Teignmouth. His remarkable output amounted to some 3000 paintings and many of these were engraved.

Melling, Antoine Ignace *(1763-1831)* French topographical painter who travelled to Egypt and the Near East. He illustrated and published between 1809 and 1819 the *Voyage pittoresque de Constantinople et des rives du Bosphore*.

Mezzotint A type of engraving *(qv)* in which the engraving plate is first roughened with a tool known as a rocker. The rough surface holds the ink and appears as a black background and the design is then burnished onto it by scraping away the rough burr to create lighter tones and by polishing the surface for highlights. Thus the artist works from dark to light, creating a tonal effect which was particularly suited to reproducing paintings and had its heyday in eighteenth-century England.

Milbourne, Henri (*fl early to mid nineteenth century*) French marine, landscape and animal painter, who exhibited at the Salon between 1833 and 1848. His depictions of twenty-one sea battles are held by the Musée de Dunkerque.

Milton, Thomas (*1743-1827*) English aquatint (*qv*) engraver of landscapes and portraits after his own designs and those of his contemporaries, and son of a marine painter.

Moses, Henry (*1782-1870*) English draughtsman, engraver and sometime painter. While he engraved mostly classical subjects after his contemporaries, he also made engravings of marine subjects after his own designs and published several booklets such as *The Marine Sketch Book* (1826) and *The Cruise of the Experimental Squadron* (1830)

Northcote, James (*1746-1831*) English portraitist and history painter. He was a pupil of Sir Joshua Reynolds and travelled to Italy before settling in London in 1781. A large number of his history paintings were engraved.

Payne, William (*c1760-1830*) English topographical painter and drawing master. His early work included five views of Plymouth which were exhibited at the Royal Academy in 1786. He moved to London in 1790 where he established himself as a successful drawing-master, teaching his fluent style of sketching with grey washes. A tint of grey is still referred to as 'Payne's grey'.

Pocock, Lt William Innes (*1783-1863*) English marine painter and a son of Nicholas Pocock (*qv*). Like his father he went to sea in the merchant service before spending ten years in the Royal Navy from 1805 to 1814, during which time he recorded incidents in sketch books, many of which are held by the National Maritime Museum. His oil paintings are very much in his father's style and suggest that he spent time as his pupil.

Pocock, Nicholas (*1740-1821*) Foremost English marine painter of his day. He was apprenticed in the shipbuilding yard of Richard Champion in Bristol before being appointed to command the barque *Lloyd*, setting sail to Charleston in 1768. This was the first of a number of voyages for which there are illustrated log books, some of which are at the National Maritime Museum. He was present at the West Indies campaign in 1778 or '79, and completed an oil painting in 1780, receiving helpful criticism from Sir Joshua Reynolds. Thereafter he devoted himself to his art and painted numerous depictions of the struggles with Revolutionary France.

Pringle, James (*fl late eighteenth and early nineteenth centuries*) English marine painter, mainly based in Deptford, who exhibited a number of naval works at the Royal Academy. The National Maritime Museum has a series of small drawings of warships which demonstrate skilled technical draughtsmanship.

Prout, Samuel (*1783-1852*) English watercolour painter of topographical scenes and architectural subjects, who came to be admired by John Ruskin for his fine draughtsmanship. Perhaps as a result of his boyhood years in Plymouth he was particularly attracted to coastal scenery and, even after the 1820s, when he focussed entirely on continental topographical subjects he continued to paint the occasional marine watercolour. Books such as *Illustrations of the Rhine* (1824) in which his illustrations were reproduced by lithography (*qv*) brought his work to the attention of a wide public.

Pugin, Augustus Charles (*1760-1832*) Architect, illustrator, designer and watercolourist, born in Paris, who settled in England during the French Revolution. He worked for John Nash and was one of the best architectural draughtsmen of his day as well as an expert on Gothic detail. His son, Augustus Welby Pugin, is now best known for his interiors of the Houses of Parliament.

Roux, Joseph Ange Antoine (*1765-1835*) French marine painter of naval battles, and ship portraitist.

Rowlandson, Thomas (*1756-1827*) English humorous draughtsman, caricaturist and engraver of scenes on urban and country life. He also did a number of topographical scenes. The images were characterised by much picaresque detail and were well suited to such contemporary novels as those by Lawrence Sterne which they illustrated.

Rugendas, Johann Lorenz (*1775-1826*) German painter and engraver whose subjects were mainly battle scenes and portraits. He spent his life in Augsbourg where he was head of the Academy.

Sartorius, Francis (*fl early nineteenth century*) English marine painter from a family of painters better known for their sporting scenes. No paintings are known after 1808 which suggests that he died thereabouts. As well as a number of naval scenes he executed a pair of paintings depicting the rescue of a crew from a wrecked ship using Captain Manby's rocket and line.

Sayer, Robert & Bennett, John (*fl mid-late eighteenth century*) London publishers, based in Fleet Street, of sporting subjects, topographical views and maps.

Schetky, John Christian (*1778-1874*) Scottish marine painter from a cultured background whose early interest in the sea led to his joining the frigate *Hind* in 1792. He soon returned to land and in 1801 embarked on a continental tour. He was drawing master at the Royal Military College, Great Marlow, and later Professor of Drawing at he Royal Naval College, Portsmouth, where he remained for 25 years. His painted subjects ranged from ship portraits to reconstructions of naval battles of the Nelsonic era. He continued to paint until his death at the age of 95.

Serres, John Thomas (*1759-1825*) English marine painter and elder son of Dominic Serres, the elder. Though he painted a number of dramatic naval battle scenes in the manner of de Loutherbourg whom he greatly admired, his main activity was drawing the coasts of England, France and Spain in his capacity as Marine Draughtsman to the Admiralty. A selection were subsequently published in *Serres Little Sea Torch* (1801). He died in debtors' prison as a result of the pretensions and wild extravagances of his wife, the self-styled 'Princess Olive of Cumberland'.

Solveyns, Franz Balthazar (*1760-1824*) Belgian marine painter who spent the early years of his working life in India where he made some 300 etchings, after his own designs, for two series on local craft: 'Pleasure Boats' and 'Boats of Lading'.

Stadler, Joseph Constantine (*fl late eighteenth and early nineteenth centuries*) A prolific aquatint (*qv*) engraver, of German extraction, who was based in London between 1780 and 1812. His subjects ranged from decorative designs to topographical views and military and naval scenes.

Sutherland, Thomas (*fl late eighteenth and early nineteenth centuries*) English aquatint (qv) engraver of sporting, naval and military subjects and portraits after his contemporaries.

Truslev, Niels (*1762-1826*) Danish engraver of naval battles and a portrait painter.

Wale, Samuel (*1762-1826*) Prolific English engraver and illustrator, and also an occasional painter of history subjects.

Walters, Lieutenant Samuel, RN (*1778-1834*) Royal Navy Lieutenant and accomplished amateur painter who trained as a shipwright before joining the Navy in 1796. He retired on half pay in 1815 and little is known of his life after that date. He is not to be confused with his nephew, the celebrated marine painter, Samuel Walters (1811-1882).

Webster, George (*fl late eighteenth and early nineteenth centuries*) English landscape and marine painter who also did battle scenes.

Whitcombe, Thomas (*born c1752*) English marine painter who, like Pocock (*qv*) and Luny (*qv*), was celebrated for his huge output of paintings depicting the French Revolutionary Wars. He contributed some fifty plates to Jenkins' *Naval Achievements of Great Britain* and also painted numerous works for engravings. There is no record of his death.

Wood, Thomas (*1800-1878*) English painter of land- and seascapes and architectural subjects. He also worked as an engraver and taught drawing at Harrow School.

INDEX